THE EMPIRE AND THE ARMY

THE EMPIRE AND THE ARMY

By
JOHN FORTESCUE
LL.D., D.Litt.

The Naval & Military Press Ltd

Published by

The Naval & Military Press Ltd
Unit 5 Riverside, Brambleside
Bellbrook Industrial Estate
Uckfield, East Sussex
TN22 1QQ England

Tel: +44 (0)1825 749494

www.naval-military-press.com
www.nmarchive.com

*In reprinting in facsimile from the original, any imperfections are inevitably reproduced
and the quality may fall short of modern type and cartographic standards.*

To

THE MEMORY OF

THE BRITISH EXPEDITIONARY FORCE

WHICH PERISHED GLORIOUSLY IN 1914

BEQUEATHING ITS SPIRIT

TO THE

SOLDIERS OF THE EMPIRE

PREFACE

THIS little book is written primarily for the British soldier. At the conclusion of a course of lectures delivered by me to an audience drawn from the London Command, a staff-officer asked me if I could not write a textbook for the candidates for the highest certificates of education in the ranks. This request led to conversation with my friend, Lord Ruthven, then commanding the London District, and this again, through his mediation, to further conversation with Major-General Knox, Director of Military Training; with the final result that this book was written, and that the Chief of the Imperial General Staff was good enough to think it worthy of the kind and, I fear, too flattering Foreword with which he introduces it to the Army. To him and to Major-General Knox my best thanks are due for their sympathetic encouragement, and to Major-General Knox further, for valuable hints and other help.

PREFACE

Whether the volume will commend itself to a wider public than the Army I cannot say; but I have endeavoured to make it, in some degree, a book of reference. I can claim nothing for it, except that it represents thirty years of hard work and research, both at home and abroad. But it is written, as I have said, for the soldier, who deserves the best that I can give. If he be satisfied, I shall be very well content.

J. W. F.

CONTENTS

	PAGE
CHRONOLOGICAL TABLE	xv
FOREWORD	xxix

CHAPTER I

THE BEGINNINGS

A Short Tour of the Empire	1
The British Soldier's Pedigree	5
The Infancy of the Army	7
Companies and Regiments	11
Uniform Clothing and Arms	13
The Germs of the Regular Army	14
The "New Model." The First Regular English Army	15
The "New Model" Cavalry	16
The "New Model" Infantry	18
The "New Model's" Work at Home	21
The "New Model's" Work Abroad	23

CHAPTER II

THE FOUNDATION OF THE STANDING ARMY

Growth of the Empire in the 17th Century	26
Additions to Empire and Army under Charles II	28

CHAPTER III

THE COMPOSITION AND NATURE OF THE STANDING ARMY	31

CONTENTS

CHAPTER IV

THE BEGINNING OF THE FIGHT FOR EMPIRE

	PAGE
King James II and the Army	39
The First War for Empire; New Regiments and the Mutiny Act	41
William III's Campaigns in the Low Countries. Campaign of 1692	43
Campaign of 1693. Landen	45
Colonial Wars, 1692–1697. The Peace of Ryswick	46

CHAPTER V

THE WAR OF THE SPANISH SUCCESSION

Marlborough, his Plans and his Difficulties	51
Campaigns of 1702 and 1703	52
Campaign of 1704, Blenheim	52
Campaigns of 1705 and 1706, Ramillies	54
Campaign of 1707	55
Campaign of 1708, Oudenarde	56
Campaign of 1709, Malplaquet	57
Campaign of 1710	58
Campaign of 1711	59
Peace of Utrecht, 1713. Additions to the Empire	61
Accession of the present Royal House; Death of Marlborough	62

CHAPTER VI

THE INTERVAL OF PEACE, 1714–1739, AND RENEWAL OF WAR FOR EMPIRE, 1740–1763

The War with Spain, 1739, Carthagena	71
The War of the Austrian Succession	74
Campaign of 1743, Dettingen	76
Campaigns of 1744–1745, Fontenoy	78

CONTENTS

	PAGE
Campaign of 1746, Roucoux	80
Campaign of 1747, Lauffeld	81
The Situation in America	84
The Situation in India	87
French Capture of Madras. Robert Clive	88
Fighting in India, 1751–1754	89
The Fighting in America	90
Braddock's Defeat near the Ohio	92
The Seven Years' War	94
The Campaign of 1758, Louisburg	95
The Year of Victory, 1759	97
The West Indies	97
Canada, Quebec	98
Ste. Foy and Montreal, 1760	99
India, 1756–1760, Plassey, Condore, Badara, Wandewash	101
Germany, 1759–1760, Minden, Warburg	102
Other Operations of the Seven Years' War	105

CHAPTER VII

THE BURDEN OF EMPIRE

India, 1760–1776	108
Undwa Nala and Baksar	109
Hyder Ali and the Mahrattas, 1767–1776	110
The Dispute with the American Colonies over Imperial Defence	112
Colonel Bouquet's Red Indian Campaigns, 1763–1764	113
The Breach with the Americans	114
Campaign of 1776	116
Campaign of 1777, Saratoga	117
The Americans Ally themselves with France	118
St. Lucia, 1778	120
Operations in America, 1778	122
Spain declares War; Danger at Home, 1779	123

CONTENTS

	PAGE
Operations in America, 1780	124
Operations in America, 1781, Yorktown	126
Minorca and Gibraltar	129
Operations in India, 1778–1782, Hyder Ali and Tipu Sahib	130
Reflections on the American War	132
Lessons learned in America	134
The Ten Years of Peace, 1783–1793	137
The War in Mysore. The First Capture of Seringapatam, 1792	138

CHAPTER VIII

THE WAR OF THE FRENCH REVOLUTION

The Younger Pitt's Military Policy	141
Operations in the Low Countries, 1793	142
Toulon, 1793	144
The West Indies, 1794	144
Corsica, 1794	145
The Low Countries, 1794	147
Operations in the West Indies, 1794–1798	149
Events in Europe, 1795–1797	151
Operations in the Mediterranean, 1798	153
The Expedition to North Holland, 1799	155
India. The Final Capture of Seringapatam	158
The Great Opportunities Lost in 1800	159
The First Rifle	161
The Campaign in Egypt, 1801	162
Peace of Amiens	165

CHAPTER IX

THE WAR OF THE FRENCH EMPIRE

The Mahratta War in India	166
The Campaign in Ceylon, 1803	170

CONTENTS

	PAGE
Operations in the West Indies	171
Operations in Europe, 1804–1805	172
The Cape and Buenos Ayres, 1806	174
Operations in the Mediterranean, 1806	175
Operations on the Rio de la Plata, 1806–1807	177
Operations in Egypt, 1807	179
The Treaty of Tilsit and the Berlin Decrees	180
Critical Situation of England	181
Castlereagh's Military Measures	182
Napoleon's Invasion of Spain	183
The Peninsular War. Wellesley's Campaign of 1808	184
Moore's Campaign of 1808–1809	185
The Walcheren Expedition, 1809	188
The Peninsular War. Wellington's Campaign of 1809	190
Wellington's Military Policy	194
Wellington's Campaign of 1810	196
Wellington's Campaign of 1811	197
Operations Outside the Peninsula, 1809–1811	201
Operations in the East. Capture of Mauritius	202
The Expedition to Java	203
The Peninsular War. Wellington's Campaign of 1812	204
Wellington's Campaign of 1813	208
Wellington's Campaign of 1814	211
The American War, 1812–1814	212
Operations in Italy and Holland, 1814	218
The Waterloo Campaign, 1815	219
Quatre Bras and Ligny	220
Waterloo	220

SURVEY OF THE EMPIRE AND ARMY, 1793–1815

The Duke of York's Reforms	222
Barracks	222
Recruiting	223
The Cavalry	225
The Artillery	225

CONTENTS

	PAGE
The Infantry	226
Transport and Supply	227
The Medical Department	227
The Chaplains' Department	228
Wellington's Tactics	229
Additions to the Empire	230

CHAPTER X

THE CONSOLIDATION OF THE EMPIRE

The Nipal War of 1814–1816	233
The Pindari War, 1817–1819	233
The Kandyan War, 1818	234
The Burmese War, 1824–1826	235
Siege of Bhurtpore	238
The First Ashanti War	238
The South African War, 1834	240
Improvements in the Treatment of the Soldier	241
The Australasian Colonies and Canada	242
The Percussion-Cap	243
The First Afghan War, 1839–1842	244
The Conquest of Sind, 1843	247
The First China War, 1841–1842	247
The Gwalior War of 1843	248
The First Sikh War, 1845–1846	250
The Second Sikh War, 1848–1849	252
The New Zealand War of 1845	254
The Second Burmese War, 1852	254
The South African War of 1850–1853	255
Neglect of the Army, 1815–1854	257
The Crimean War, 1854–1856	258
Alma, Balaclava, Inkerman	260
The Siege of Sebastopol	261
Reforms during the Crimean War	263
The Persian War of 1856–1857	264

CONTENTS

	PAGE
The Second China War, 1856–1857	264
The Indian Mutiny, 1857–1859	265
The Third China War, 1860	268
The Umbeyla Expedition, 1863	269
The Second New Zealand War, 1860–1869	270
The Abyssinian Expedition, 1868	271

CHAPTER XI

THE ARMY REFORMS OF 1870–1899

The Abolition of Purchase, 1871	274
Enlistment for Short Service, 1870	275
The Territorial System, 1881	276
The Army Service Corps, 1888	279
Training and Armament	279
Clothing	281
The Soldier's Comforts	282
Extension of the Empire in Africa	284

CHAPTER XII

CAMPAIGNS OF 1870–1901

The Second Ashanti War, 1873	286
The Second Afghan War, 1878–1880	286
The South African Wars, 1878–1881	290
The Boer War of 1880–1881	293
The Egyptian Campaign of 1882	294
The Sudan War, 1881–1885	296
The March Across the Desert	297
The Sudan Abandoned	298
The Third Burmese War, 1885–1891	299
Third Ashanti Expedition of 1896	300
Second Sudan War, 1896–1898	301
The Tirah Expedition, 1897–1898	302
The South African War, 1899–1902	304

CONTENTS

	PAGE
The Initial Failures	305
The Situation Restored	306
Last Period of the War	307
The Period 1902–1914	309

CHAPTER XIII

MR. HALDANE'S REORGANIZATION

The "Old Contemptibles" of 1914	312
The Empire Springs to Arms	313
A Review of the Past	315
The Present Army	322
INDEX	327

CHRONOLOGICAL TABLE

B.C.
55–54. Cæsar's two Invasions of Britain.
A.D.
401. The Roman Legions Evacuate Britain.
1017–1035. Reign of Canute—Professional Soldiers Reappear in England.
1066. *October 14th.*—Battle of Hastings.
1154–1189. Reign of Henry II, first of the Angevin Kings.
1181. The Assize of Arms, for Regulating the National Force.
1285. The Statute of Winchester, Re-enacting the Assize of Arms, and Establishing Long-bow-men by Statute.
1338. Beginning of Edward III's Wars in France.
1346. *August 26.*—Battle of Crécy.
1347. Capture of Calais.
1356. *September 19.*—Battle of Poitiers.
1415. *October 25.*—Battle of Agincourt.
1420. Henry V. Acknowledged Regent and Heir of France.
1453. All of France Lost to the English, Except Calais.
1485. Yeomen of the Guard formed by Henry VII.
1537. Honourable Artillery Company Founded.
1558. Final Loss of Calais.
1572. The First English Volunteers go to Holland.
1600. East India Company's First Charter Granted.
1606. Virginia Founded.

CHRONOLOGICAL TABLE

- 1609. Bermuda Settled.
- 1620. The Pilgrim Fathers Land in America; Beginning of the New England States.
- 1627. Barbados Settled.
- 1634. Maryland Founded.
- 1639. First British Troops Raised by the East India Company, in Madras.
- 1642. The Civil War Begins.
- 1645. The New Model Army Formed.
- 1649. Cromwell's Irish Campaign.
- 1650. Monck's Regiment (Coldstream Guards) Formed. *September* 3.—Battle of Dunbar.
- 1651. *September* 3.—Battle of Worcester.
- 1652. Naval War with the Dutch.
- 1653. *December* 16.—Cromwell made Lord Protector.
- 1655. Capture of Jamaica.
- 1658. *May* 24.—Battle of Dunkirk Dunes.
- 1660. Restoration of King Charles II.
- 1661. Blues, Life Guards and Grenadier Guards Raised.
- 1662. The Royal Scots (Royals) taken into the English Service. Tangier and Bombay acquired as dowry of Queen Katharine of Bragança. The Royal Dragoons and the Queen's (Tangier Regiments) Raised.
- 1663. Carolina Settled from Virginia.
- 1664. Capture of New Amsterdam; Rechristened New York. *February*.—War with Holland.
- 1665. The Buffs taken into the English Service. *June* 3.—Naval Victory off Lowestoft.
- 1672. Second War with Holland; Troops Sent to the Low Countries.
- 1674. New York Finally Ceded to England on Peace with Holland.
- 1679. The Guards Sent to Suppress a Rebellion in Virginia.

CHRONOLOGICAL TABLE

1680. The King's Own Royal Lancaster Formed for Tangier.
1681. Settlement of Pennsylvania. The Scots Greys Formed.
1684. Tangier Abandoned.
1685. Monmouth's Rebellion against James II.
　　　Northumberland Fusiliers and Warwickshire taken from the Dutch to the English Service. 1st, 2nd, 3rd, 4th, 5th and 6th Dragoon Guards Raised. 3rd and 4th Hussars Raised. Royal Fusiliers, King's, Norfolk, Lincoln, Devon, Suffolk, Somerset L.I., West York, and East York Raised. Scots Guards Brought into England from Scotland.
1688. 7th D.G. Bedford and Leicester Regiments Raised. William III Drives James II from England.
1689. War with France. The First Mutiny Act Passed.
　　　5th Lancers, Inniskilling Dragoons, 7th Hussars, Royal Irish (now disbanded), Green Howards, Lancashire Fusiliers, Royal Scots Fusiliers, Cheshire, Royal Welch Fusiliers, South Wales Borderers, Scottish Borderers, Cameronians, and First Royal Inniskilling Fusiliers Raised.
1692. William III Begins Operations in the Low Countries. Eighth Hussars Raised.
　　　August 3.—Battle of Steenkirk.
1693. *July* 29.—Battle of Landen.
1695. Siege and Capture of Namur.
1697. Peace of Ryswick.
1701. France accepts the Succession to the Crown of Spain.
　　　1st Gloucester, 1st and 2nd Worcester, 1st East Lancs, 1st East Surrey, 1st Duke of Cornwall's, 1st Duke's, 1st Border, 1st Royal Sussex,

CHRONOLOGICAL TABLE

1701.   1st Hants, 1st South Stafford and 1st Dorset Raised.
1702.   War of the Spanish Succession.
        Marlborough's First Campaign in the Low Countries.
1703.   Marlborough's Second Campaign.
1704.   Marlborough's Campaign in the Danube.
        July 2.—Action of the Schellenberg.
        August 13.—Battle of Blenheim.
        Capture of Gibraltar.
1705.   Marlborough's Third Campaign in the Low Countries.
1706.   Marlborough's Fourth Campaign in the Low Countries.
        May 23.—Battle of Ramillies.
        Operations Begun in Spain.
1707.   Marlborough's Fifth Campaign in the Low Countries.
        Battle of Almansa, in Spain.
1708.   Marlborough's Sixth Campaign in the Low Countries.
        July 11.—Battle of Oudenarde.
        Capture of Minorca.
1709.   Marlborough's Seventh Campaign in the Low Countries.
        September 11.—Battle of Malplaquet.
1710.   Marlborough's Eighth Campaign in the Low Countries.
        Action of Brihuega in Spain.
1711.   Marlborough's Last Campaign in the Low Countries.
        Unsuccessful Expedition against Quebec.
1713.   Peace of Utrecht.
        Minorca, Gibraltar, Nova Scotia and Newfoundland added to the Empire.

CHRONOLOGICAL TABLE

- 1714. Accession of the House of Brunswick.
- 1715. Rebellion in Scotland.
    9th Lancers, 10th and 11th Hussars, 12th Lancers, and 13th and 14th Hussars Raised.
- 1717. 1st South Lancs Formed.
- 1719. Fielding's Invalids (later 1st Welch) Formed.
- 1727. Royal Regiment of Artillery Formed (2 Cos. 1716).
- 1727-8. Gibraltar unsuccessfully besieged by the Spaniards.
- 1739. 1st Black Watch Formed.
    War with Spain.
- 1740. The Expedition to Carthagena.
- 1741. War of the Austrian Succession.
    1st Oxford L.I., 1st Essex, 1st Sherwood Foresters, 2nd Duke of Cornwall's, 1st North Lancs and 1st Northampton Raised.
- 1743. *June 27.*—Battle of Dettingen.
- 1744. Open War Declared between England and France.
- 1745. *May 11.*—Battle of Fontenoy.
    Jacobite Rising in Scotland.
    Capture of Louisburg by the American Colonists.
- 1746. Defeat of the Jacobites at Culloden.
    Battle of Roucoux.
    Capture of Madras by the French.
- 1747. Battle of Lauffeld.
- 1748. British Meet French Troops in India for the First Time. Peace of Aix-la-Chapelle.
    Madras and Louisburg Restored.
- 1749. The Military Settlement of Halifax Founded.
- 1751. Clive's Capture and Defence of Arcot.
- 1752-1754. Sundry Victorious Actions against the French in India.
- 1755. General Braddock's Force Destroyed on March to the Ohio.
- 1756. 1st Royal West Kent, 1st K.O.Y.L.I., 2nd

CHRONOLOGICAL TABLE

1756.   Oxfordshire L.I., 1st Shropshire L.I., 2nd Dorset, 2nd Border, 2nd Essex, 1st Middlesex, 2nd Northampton, 2nd East Lancs, and King's Royal Rifle Corps Raised.
Seven Years' War Begins.
Loss of Minorca.
December.—William Pitt Takes Charge of Affairs.

1757.   2nd Gloucester, 1st Wilts, 1st Manchester, 1st North Stafford, 1st York and Lancs, 2nd Berks, 2nd Hants, 1st Durham L.I., 2nd Welch, 2nd East Surrey, and a Company of Miners Raised.
June 23.—Clive's Victory at Plassey.

1758.   Siege and Capture of Louisburg.
Repulse of the British at Ticonderoga.
Forbes's March to the Ohio.
Capture of Senegal and Goree from the French.
Battle of Condore.

1759.   Capture of Guadeloupe.
August 1.—Battle of Minden.
September 13.—Battle of Quebec.
Storm of Masulipatam.
Action of Badara.
15th Hussars, 16th and 17th Lancers Raised.

1760.   Action of St. Foy; Capture of Montreal.
Actions of Emsdorf, Warburg, and Kloster Kampen.
Battle of Wandewash; Actions of Sirpur and Patna.

1761.   Capture of Belleisle.
Action of Vellinghausen.
Capture of Dominica.

1762.   Action of Wilhelmsthal.
Martinique, St. Lucia, Grenada, St. Vincent, Havana, and Manila Captured.

1763.   Peace of Paris.
Additions to the Empire.—Canada, The Floridas, St. Vincent, Grenada, Tobago, and Dominica.

CHRONOLOGICAL TABLE

1763. Minorca Restored to England.
Colonel Bouquet's Campaign against Red Indians.
Actions of Katwa, Suti, Undwa Nala, and Patna.
1764. Action of Baksar.
1765. Beginning of the Quarrel with the American Colonies over Imperial Defence.
1767–8. Campaigns against Hyder Ali.
1774. Campaign against the Rohillas.
1775. Action of Arass.
The Americans Take the Offensive.
Action of Bunker's Hill.
1776. Capture of New York from the Americans.
1777. Action of Brandywine. Burgoyne's Disaster at Saratoga.
1778. *February.*—France Allies Herself with the Americans.
 1st Highland L.I. and 1st Seaforth Highlanders Raised.
Capture of St. Lucia by the British.
Capture of St. Vincent and Grenada by the French.
The French Repulsed before Savannah.
1779. *June.*—Spain Declares War against England.
2nd Black Watch Raised.
Blockade of Gibraltar Begun.
1780. Capture of Charleston by the British.
Action of Camden.
Capture of Mobile by the Spaniards.
War Declared against Holland.
War with Hyder Ali in India—Disaster to Baillie's Detachment.
1781. Actions of Cowpens, Guilford, Hobkirk's Hill, and Eutaw Springs, and Surrender of Cornwallis at Yorktown.
Actions of Porto Novo, Palilur, and Sholinghur in India.

CHRONOLOGICAL TABLE

1782. Action of Gadalur in India.
Great Attack on Gibraltar Repulsed.
1783. Peace of Versailles.
England Yields Independence to the American Colonies; Senegal, Goree, St. Pierre and Miquelon to France; Minorca and the Floridas to Spain.
1787. Royal Engineers Reorganized as such.
2nd Highland L.I., 1st Gordon Highlanders, 2nd Duke's, 2nd Middlesex Raised.
1788. Foundation of the First Settlement in Australia.
1791–1792. War with Tipu Sahib, First Capture of Seringapatam.
1793. First Two Troops of Horse Artillery Formed.
January.—War of the French Revolution Begins.
Actions before Valenciennes, at Linselles and before Dunkirk.
October.—Operations at Toulon.
2nd Seaforth Highlanders, Cameron Highlanders, 2nd South Stafford, 2nd North Lancs, 2nd South Lancs, 1st and 2nd Royal Ulster Rifles, 2nd York and Lancs, 2nd Shropshire L.I., 1st Royal Irish Fusiliers, 1st Connaught Rangers (disbanded) Raised, also a Wagon-Train.
1794. 2nd Royal Irish Fusiliers (disbanded), 2nd Scottish Rifles, 1st Argyll and Sutherland Highlanders, 2nd Gordon Highlanders, and 2nd Connaught Rangers (disbanded) Raised.
Successful Actions of Beaumont and Willems, and Disastrous Retreat from the Low Countries.
Operations in Corsica.
Occupation of Haiti and Capture of Martinique, Guadeloupe and St. Lucia.

CHRONOLOGICAL TABLE

1794. Naval Action of 1st June.
A Secretary *for* War Appointed.
1795. Loss of Guadeloupe, St. Vincent, Grenada and St. Lucia.
Capture of Ceylon and Cape of Good Hope.
1796. St. Lucia, St. Vincent, and Grenada Recovered.
1797. *February* 14.—Naval Action of St. Vincent.
Capture of Trinidad.
1798. Capture of Minorca from Spain.
Naval Battle of the Nile.
1799. Occupation of Sicily.
Expedition to North Holland.
War with Tipu Sahib and Final Capture of Seringapatam.
1800. Capture of Malta.
First Rifle Introduced.
2nd Argyll and Sutherland Highlanders and Rifle Brigade Raised.
1801. Campaign of Egypt and Capture of the French Army. Peace of Amiens.
1803. Renewal of War with France.
War with the Mahrattas in India—Actions of Assaye, Argaum, Delhi, and Laswari.
Campaign in Ceylon.
Capture of St. Lucia, Tobago, and Dutch Guiana.
1804. Mahratta War—Action of Deig.
1805. Mahratta War—Siege of Bhurtpore.
1806. Capture of Cape of Good Hope.
Battle of Maida.
Expedition to Buenos Ayres.
Mutiny at Vellore.
1807. Unsuccessful Operations at Buenos Ayres and in Egypt.
Expedition to Copenhagen.
1808. Capture of the Danish West Indies.

CHRONOLOGICAL TABLE

1808. Expedition to Sweden.
Beginning of the Peninsular War.
Sir Arthur Wellesley's First Campaign—Roliça and Vimeiro.
Sir John Moore's Campaign in Spain—Action of Coruña,(16 *Jan.* 1809).
January.—Capture of Martinique and the Saints (*April*).

1809. Sir Arthur Wellesley's Second Campaign in the Peninsula—Douro, Talavera.
The Walcheren Expedition.

1810. Capture of Guadeloupe and St. Eustatius.
Wellington's Third Campaign in the Peninsula—Bussaco.
Capture of Bourbon and Mauritius.

1811. Wellington's Fourth Campaign in the Peninsula—Barrosa, Fuentes de Oñoro, Albuera.
Capture of Java.

1812. Wellington's Fifth Campaign in the Peninsula.
Storming of Ciudad Rodrigo and Badajoz, Battle of Salamanca, and Retreat from Burgos.
War Breaks out with the United States.

1813. Wellington's Sixth Campaign in the Peninsula.
Battle of Vitoria; The French Driven from Spain; Battles of the Pyrenees, Nivelle, Nive, and St. Pierre.
October 16–19.—Battle of Leipzig.
American War Continues.

1814. Wellington's Seventh Campaign—Battles of Orthez and Toulouse; Armistice on April 18.
Actions of Chippewa, Lundy's Lane, Bladensburg, and New Orleans in America—Peace with America, *December* 14.
Operations in Holland, and about Genoa.
Beginning of War with Nipal.

CHRONOLOGICAL TABLE

1815. The Campaign of Waterloo.
General peace—*Additions to the Empire.*—Heligoland and Malta in Europe; Tobago, St. Lucia and Trinidad in the West Indies; British Guiana; Cape Colony; Mauritius, Ceylon, and a vast addition to the Indian Territory.
1816. The Nipal War Successfully Ended.
1817. The Pindari War—Battle of Mehidpur.
1818. The Kandyan War in Ceylon.
1819. The Pindari War Successfully Ended.
1824. Siege and Capture of Bhurtpore.
1824–1826. First Ashanti War.
First Burmese War, Annexation of Arakan and Tennasserim.
1829. The Metropolitan Police Established.
1830. The Royal Irish Constabulary Created.
1834. First Kafir War.
1837–1838. Rebellion in Canada.
1838. Transportation of Criminals to Australia Stopped.
Annexation of Aden.
1839. New Zealand Taken under British Sovereignty.
The Afghan War Begins.
The Percussion-Cap adopted for Small Arms.
1840. New Constitution Granted to Canada.
1841. *December.*—Disastrous Retreat of the British Garrison from Kabul.
The First China War Begins.
1842. The Afghan War Ended after a Second British Advance to Kabul.
The China War Ended; Hong-Kong Ceded to England.
1843. The "One Day War" in Gwalior.
The Campaign and Conquest of Sind.
1845. Annexation of Natal.
First New Zealand War.

CHRONOLOGICAL TABLE

1845–1846. The First Sikh War—Actions of Mudki, Ferozeshah, Aliwal, and Sobraon.

1848–1849. Second Sikh War—Actions of Chilianwala and Gujarat.

1850–1852. Second Kafir War.

The Minie Rifle First Tried in Action.

1852. Self-Government Granted to Cape Colony, the Australian Colonies and New Zealand in this and the following Years.

Second Burmese War. Cession of Pegu to England.

1853. First Manœuvres at Chobham. Aldershot purchased.

1854. War Declared with Russia—Invasion of the Crimea—Battles of Alma, Balaclava and Inkerman; Siege of Sebastopol.

The Artillery (previously under the Board of Ordnance), the Militia (previously under the Home Office), and the Commissariat (previously under the Treasury) transferred to the War Office.

1855. *September.*—Fall of Sebastopol After One Unsuccessful Assault on *June* 18.

Army Clothing Department and Enfield Small Arms Factory Established.

1856. *March.*—Peace with Russia.

War with China and Persia

Annexation of Oude.

1857. *May.*—Mutiny of the Bengal Native Army.

September 20.—Capture of Delhi.

November 17.—Relief of Lucknow.

1858-9. Final Suppression of the Mutiny.

1858. *November.*—India Transferred to the Crown; and the European Troops of the East India Company Taken into the Army.

Second Battalion Added to the Queen's and to the 23 regiments next in precedence.

CHRONOLOGICAL TABLE

1860. Third War with China—Kaolun Ceded to England.
1860–1869. Desultory War in New Zealand.
1863. Umbeyla Expedition.
1866. The First Breech-loading Rifle Issued.
1868. The Abyssinian Expedition.
1869. Opening of the Suez Canal.
1870. Introduction of Short Service.
1871. Abolition of the Purchase of Commissions.
1873. The Second Ashanti War.
1878–1880. The Second Afghan War.
1878–1879. Third Kafir War and Zulu War.
1880–1881. Boer War—Independence yielded to the Transvaal and Orange Free State.
1881. The Territorial System introduced; and the Old Numbers and Facings abolished.
1882. First Egyptian Campaign.
1884–1885. First Sudan Campaigns.
1885–1891. Third Burmese War.—Annexation of Upper Burma.
1888. The Army Service Corps Created.
1896. Third Ashanti War—Annexation of Ashanti.
1896–1898. Final Conquest of the Sudan—England exercises Joint Sovereignty with Egypt over the Sudan.
1897. The Tirah Expedition.
1899–1901. War with the Boers in South Africa—The Transvaal and Orange Free State Annexed.
1906. Mr. (afterwards Lord) Haldane Takes in Hand the Reorganization of the Army.
1914. The Great War.

FOREWORD

THIS is a remarkable history of war and achievement which should be read by every young man of the British Empire, at least by those who are proud of the deeds of their forefathers. The history of the British Army is really the history of the British Empire, and for this reason there is much in this book that will interest the youth of the Dominions. It is the traditions of the British Army, with its magnificent achievements, which will one day form the basis of the history of the Dominion Armies.

This book will also, I hope, appeal to a much wider public, and it is sufficiently light and interesting to find an honoured place on every boy's bookshelf; it reads, in fact, more like a romance than history, based as it is throughout on carefully sifted fact and detail. Many, who have not already done so, will, I hope, be induced to read the author's magnificent work, "The History of the British Army," another volume of which has so recently appeared. Sir John Fortescue has

FOREWORD

devoted the greater part of his life and resources to the production of that history, and to researches and travels in connection with it, a task for which the British Army will for all time honour and respect him. He has supplied generations yet unborn with an illuminating account of what the British Empire owes to the initiative, daring and fighting qualities of her soldiers, in spite of the difficulties—raised by both friend and foe— with which they had to contend. This short account of the Army is written more for the junior ranks, but "The History of the British Army" should be studied by every thinking man and woman who proposes to help direct the policy of the Empire.

Among the many interesting features of the book certain national characteristics, both of governments and individuals, stand out very clearly. The British are by nature better at actual fighting than at maintaining armies, and "matters military" have never been given very much attention in times of peace. As a result we have placed such troops as we possessed in a good many "tight places," but in the end our national adaptability has invariably brought us to an honourable conclusion. British Governments, too, seem to have had an instinctive dislike of the good old principle of "concentration of force at the decisive point," and as a result there has always been a great deal of dispersion of effort, with its natural consequence—a prolongation of war. Incidentally, it seems to be this policy which accounts, quite unintentionally, for the extent of the British Empire to-day.

It is a fact well known to the impartial historian that very few, if any, of our British wars have been in any sense wars of aggression; deliberate planning and preparation in time of peace with the object of making war is, in fact, entirely absent from our history. It is also interesting to note that no League of Nations, however ideal in composition and constitution, could possibly have prevented more than a very small proportion of the wars the British Army has been engaged in.

Another characteristic of the nation seems to have been that, although it has entered every war unprepared, it has, on its conclusion, immediately proceeded to reduce the army below its pre-war standard. We have, in fact, treated every great war as if it were the last. And in every case, as history demonstrates, we have been wrong. Unfortunately, too, every great war has its aftermath, and a much-reduced army is liable, as it was a hundred

FOREWORD

years ago, to be hustled about the world in conditions of great discomfort to deal with all sorts and kinds of emergencies which persist in raising their unwanted heads above the waters of everlasting peace.

Among the characteristics of the British soldier, as conspicuous now as centuries ago, is the excellence of his musketry and his steadiness under fire. If combined with this is to be seen a constitutional disinclination to dig, we can only hope that new methods of war may render it unnecessary to do so in the future. The high standard of honour and valour of the British officer has been conspicuous from the earliest times, and for at least a century and a half, if not longer, his care and solicitude for his men have been something quite different from what is seen in other armies. These characteristics, of which the one is no doubt the complement of the other, have undoubtedly won us many victories and saved us from many defeats.

Amongst other points of interest in this book we see how much the British Army, and more especially the private soldier, owes to members of the Royal Family. Of these, one might mention especially Frederick, Duke of York, who, besides founding the Duke of York's School and the Royal Military College, seems

FOREWORD

to have been the real author of the Cardwell System.

It is certainly not generally known that the proportion of the British Nation under arms towards the end of the Napoleonic Wars was fully as great as in the Great War. Nor, indeed, do many realize that at the end of the latter we had not only the largest Navy but also the largest Army, both of which, with the Air Force, could fairly claim a superiority in both *moral* and efficiency over all others.

Of all the features of this book the one that has the greatest appeal to the imagination is the wonderful story of the units of the British Army; the traditions which have survived in spite of re-armament, re-organization, and in some cases temporary disbandment, and which have inspired whole regiments to fall where they stood rather than diminish their glory. These traditions are something unique and, with rare exceptions, have no counterpart in the history of other armies. I do not doubt that in new conditions and with new weapons they will be preserved by existing units, but there can be none who do not read with real regret the story of those regiments—in particular of two famous Corps which founded our Empire in India—which have so recently lost their identity. One day,

FOREWORD

perhaps, they will be revived, but meanwhile they leave behind them a story that may well serve as an inspiration to all, and may do something to alter that entirely British attitude of belittling our own achievements and reserving our admiration for foreign soldiers, and only criticism for our own.

I hope every officer, commissioned, warrant or non-commissioned, and every man in His Majesty's Army, will make the time to study this interesting book, and in their name I heartily thank the author for what he has done for us.

G. F. MILNE, F.-M.

THE EMPIRE AND THE ARMY

CHAPTER I

THE BEGINNINGS

THE British Isles are the gate of the northern waterways of Europe; and by turning this favourable position to account her people have made them the commercial centre of the world. From the shores of those waterways came the Germans and Scandinavians, who were our forefathers; but, having mastered Britain, they were stopped by the Atlantic Ocean and could travel no farther westward. The navigators of old times dared not move out of sight of land, and could only creep along the coast. Let us for a moment do as they did, follow the coast-line southward and see whither it will lead us.

Let us pass along the shores of France, Spain and Portugal, straight to *Gibraltar*, the gate of the southern waterways of Europe, where we shall see the British flag flying at the summit of the Rock. We will not enter the Mediterranean at present, but we will cross the Straits and pursue our way south and westward along the coast of Africa. First we strike Tangier, and two thousand miles farther on the river Senegal, on both of which the British flag flew once, but flies no longer. Then British possessions follow in rapid sequence—*Gambia, Sierra Leone,* the *Gold Coast, Ashanti, Nigeria*—until fifteen hundred miles north of the Cape of Good Hope we strike the vast territory of the *South African Union.* Rounding the Cape we still follow the territory for a thousand miles northward, after which there is a break of seventeen hundred miles as we ascend the east coast until we reach first *Zanzibar,* then *Kenya,* then *Somaliland.* Then, doubling Cape Guardafui we leave the British island of *Socotra* behind us and find a British garrison guarding the southern gate of the Red Sea at *Aden.*

Creeping along the south coast of Arabia we enter the mouth of the Persian Gulf and find at its head the mouth of the Euphrates and *Mesopotamia.* Or we can cut across the mouth of the Persian Gulf without losing sight of land and follow the coast eastward until we find the British flag again at the north-western corner of the *Indian Empire.* It will cost us a long journey to make the circuit of *India* and of *Ceylon* to the south-eastern extremity of Lower Burma, and on along the Malay Peninsula past *Penang* and *Malacca* to *Singapore;* but, so far, we have kept in sight of land, and we can only continue to do so by turning north, rounding Siam, and hugging the Chinese coast to *Hong Kong* and *Wei-hai-wei*. Still, even so, following the track of the mariners of old time we have seen a good deal of the world and of the British Empire.

Now let us leave the timid old coasting navigation behind, furnish ourselves with a compass, and strike boldly across the Atlantic. After sailing for three thousand miles we reach a vast English-speaking Continent. The northern part of it, *Canada*, is, of course, a noble portion of the Empire; the southern is the United States of America. Yet there is a large French-speaking population in Canada; and there are in North America not only French names such as Montreal, Trois Rivières and New Orleans, but also Dutch names such as Haarlem and Hoboken, and Spanish such as Florida, Pensacola and Espirito Santo. South of Canada the British flag flies only over groups of islands—*Bermuda*, the *Bahamas*, and the *Windward* and *Leeward West Indies*, most of them bearing Spanish names—Barbados, Antigua, Trinidad—with *Jamaica* to leeward and just a scrap of territory, *British Honduras*, on the mainland of Central America.

On the north coast of the mainland of South America there is the solid little block called *British Guiana*, and then nothing more until just before reaching Cape Horn we come upon the *Falkland Islands*. The huge continent of America is at once the death-place and new birth-place of the European nations on the Atlantic seaboard. Half of it speaks English, but only Canada remains part of the Empire. Great part of it speaks Spanish, but is lost to the crown of Spain. Brazil is Portuguese, but independent of Portugal. France and the Netherlands retain only French and Dutch Guiana.

So much for the west; let us now turn east, and passing the Straits of Gibraltar enter the Mediterranean. Minorca is one of our lost possessions, but in lieu of it we have *Malta* and *Cyprus* to carry us eastward to Egypt, which though now an independent kingdom, is committed to our charge for defence. To north of it *Palestine* is entrusted to our management, and to south of it we rule over the *Sudan ;* but Egypt's true significance to us is that the Suez Canal—one of the two gates of Asia—is ours, and with it the shortest route through the Red Sea to

India, and beyond. For, with our compass to guide us, we can strike across from Singapore eastward, when we come first to *British North Borneo* and then to *New Guinea*, where we find ourselves with the gigantic island of *Australia* just to south of us, the *Fiji Islands* to east, and to south-east that loveliest of countries, *New Zealand*. Of course, we can sail to India and Australia equally well, though by a longer passage, round the Cape of Good Hope; and then we may call, if we choose, at *St. Helena* in the South Atlantic and *Mauritius* in the Indian Ocean. Go where you will, you encounter the British flag and cannot avoid the British Empire.

It is an enormous family for two little islands. Who made it and built it up? The British trader, escorted and protected at sea by the British sailor, seconded and shielded ashore by the British soldier. Let us see what was the British soldier's part in the business, and first let us glance at his pedigree, and at some other Empires with which England has had to do.

The British Soldier's Pedigree

We British are a strange mixture of fighting races. When Julius Cæsar landed for the second time, in B.C. 54 he found tribes of

Kelts who had themselves displaced an earlier and more primitive people. Britain was a part of the Roman Empire, a colony held by Roman garrisons for four hundred and fifty years, and was then abandoned, though not before there had been born at York one of the greatest of the Roman Emperors, Constantine. Then in 449 came far fiercer invaders, Saxons and Angles, to be followed four centuries later by not less fierce Danes. Under the Danish King Canute England became for a time part of a Nordic Empire, which included Denmark, Norway and the Hebrides. He kept a small standing army of "house-carles," professional soldiers, which at first included Danes only, but later Anglo-Saxons also. The Empire broke up on his death in 1035, and Anglo-Saxon Kings resumed the throne of England, only to be finally cast out by the invasion of Normans, or Northmen, in 1066. The "house-carles," retained by the Anglo-Saxon Kings, perished at Hastings, and so ended the first English Standing Army. Under the first Norman Kings England was almost an appanage of Normandy; under the Angevin Kings, from 1154, it was part of an Empire which included large portions of France. For a full century blood and treasure were misspent in the vain endeavour to build a British Empire in France.

But in the struggle were laid the foundations of the Army which was to win the present Empire.

The Infancy of the Army

In old days every free man between the ages of sixteen and sixty was expected to turn out for the defence of his country, and to bring certain arms with him—mounted or afoot—according to the measure of his property. After the Conquest the Normans introduced the Continental system of binding up the tenure of land with certain obligations of military service; but it was less perfectly developed and was not very efficient in working; and so very early there arose the practice of contracting with leaders to produce a certain number of armed men. Thus England used to be called the home of the soldier, for a soldier is a hired fighting man who fights for *solde, solidus*—the coin for which *s* stands in the sign £ *s. d.* Men went to war in those days in order to make something out of it: the King to acquire new territory, and his followers anything they could lay their hands upon.

Rich men could always afford better weapons than the poor; and by covering themselves with armour and riding good horses, the rich had for a time everything their own way. These mounted mailed men, who carried lance and sword, or battle-axe, were known as men-at-arms. The Swiss first checked them by forming themselves into solid masses or squares of infantry, armed with pikes eighteen feet long. But the English soon afterwards brought the foreign men-at-arms to utter shame. Even before the Conquest it had been the rule for the English men-at-arms to dismount for action; and, by the fourteenth century, there had come into being the English long-bow-men, who could send an arrow through an inch of timber at two hundred yards. The English men-at-arms, dismounted with their lances, formed solid masses of two or three thousand spearmen, while the archers in loose formation on the flanks shot, not at the hostile men-at-arms, but at their chargers. The result was that this formidable cavalry dissolved into a mob of runaway horses; and thus were won the victories of Crécy (1346), Poitiers (1356), and Agincourt (1415). Never before in modern times had shock tactics and missile tactics been so efficiently combined.

Very soon other nations beside the English took to dismounting their men-at-arms for action, and infantry began to be cultivated

MERCENARY BANDS

for its own sake. Firearms had appeared in the fourteenth century, but were as yet very crude—mere tubes of metal on wooden beds which, if light enough to be carried by one man, required him to hold it in one hand and put fire to the touch-hole with the other. The heavier pieces — cannon — were more effective, and by the end of the fifteenth century were already mounted on two wheels, with a trail (then called a limber) to which the team was attached. At about this same time there grew up mercenary bands of professional soldiers in Switzerland, Italy and Germany, whose leaders would accept contracts to fight for or against anyone. These bands were known as companies, and were, in fact, formed on a commercial basis; men of substance investing money according to their means in the buying and equipping of recruits, and taking rank according to the amount of their investment. The profits which they hoped to make consisted of plunder and of ransom for wealthy prisoners; and, when weary of the profession, they sold their shares in the company to anyone who would buy. The companies varied in strength from tens to hundreds, and even thousands, and the symbol of their corporate existence was their flags or colours by which they set great store, especially among the German bands. If by chance any disgrace fell upon a German company, the colours were furled, planted upside down in the ground, and not flown again until the culprits responsible for the crime had been tried and punished by an assembly of the whole company. It is from these companies that fifes and drums[1] and most of our military terms are borrowed; a few of the latter German, others Italian or Spanish, or possibly French, but, at any rate, from a Latin source. Such words are cavalry (Spanish or Italian, *cavallo*, a horse), infantry (the officers called their men their infants, children or boys), artillery (*articularius*), captain (from the Latin *caput*—head), lieutenant (a corruption of *locum tenens*), ensign (a corruption of the Latin *insigne*, standard), and cornet (the horn-shaped flag peculiar to cavalry). Among the men-at-arms a man of inferior rank equipped by a rich master was known as a "serving-knight," *serviens eques*, which word *serviens* was gradually corrupted into serjeant and adopted by the new infantry. A man-at-arms who lost his horse was known as a *lanz spessado*, or broken lance, and served with the infantry; where, being a superior man, he acted as a non-commissioned officer,

---

[1] Drums were an oriental instrument and were brought to Europe by returning Crusaders. Fife is the same word as Pipe, of which the German form is *pfeif*.

and grew to be known as a lance-serjeant or lance-corporal.

The normal formation of a company being in square, it became known as a *quadra* or *squadra;* and a steady old soldier who was placed in the front rank became known as *capo di squadra* or head of the square, from which is derived, through the French form *caporal*, our own term corporal. The words squad and squadron are relics of this square formation.[1] From the German companies we derive our reverence for the colours, the firing of three volleys (in the name of the Trinity) over the dead, and the term *forlorn hope*[2] for a storming party, the actual meaning of the words being the "lost party," and not the lost hope.

Companies and Regiments

At the beginning of the sixteenth century it dawned upon kings that companies levied among their own subjects would be more trustworthy, and not more expensive, than those of hired foreigners, who might sell themselves to a higher bidder on the day of action.

[1] Ships used to go into action in square formation, so the Navy also has squadrons.

[2] Verlorener Hauf. The word *Hauf* (which is the same as our *beap*) becomes in Dutch *Hop*, and we may have borrowed the term either from that source or from some German dialect.

They began to raise them accordingly, and very soon discovered that it was convenient to make companies of uniform strength. The favourite number was, from classical precedent, one hundred, and accordingly a private soldier became known as a *centinel*, one of a hundred. In England, up to the beginning of the eighteenth century, a private centinel was the regular description of a private soldier; but the word, with its corruption *sentry*, had originally nothing to do with watching. The next step was to collect these loose companies into groups under the rule or *regiment* of a single officer who was called the colonel.[1] He retained also the command of his own company, as did likewise his second in command, who, being the staff-officer of the regiment, was known as the serjeant-major, and is now called the major. Therefore, in a regiment of ten companies there were eight captains only, but ten lieutenants and as many ensigns, for each company had its own colour. In an army the captain-general gave his orders to the serjeant-major general, who gave them to the serjeant-majors, who gave them to the serjeants, who gave them to the men.

[1] The word Colonel is a puzzle. It may be derived from *columna*, a column, or *corona*, a crown. It used to be spelled indifferently *colonel* or *coronel;* and we have solved the problem by spelling it in the first way and pronouncing it in the second.

CLOTHING AND ARMS

Uniform Clothing and Arms

Meanwhile, in order to distinguish friend from foe, it had been found helpful to provide soldiers with a coat of uniform colour. This custom seems to have grown up gradually. In England it had been from very early times the practice to give to each man who presented himself for service a fixed sum to pay the expenses of his journey to the general rendezvous. This was known later as conduct-money, and is probably the origin of the King's shilling given to recruits on enlistment. At the end of the fifteenth century we find an additional allowance for "coat-money," that is to say, for a white coat (probably a canvas smock) with the red cross of St. George sewn upon it from collar to skirt. But still more important was uniformity of armament, and about the year 1531 a great step forward was made with hand-firearms. It occurred to some man of genius to fix a lighted match in a catch upon the barrel in such fashion that by the pressure of a finger upon a lever (the trigger) the match could be lowered to the touch-hole, and the charge of powder could be thus exploded. This enabled a man to devote both hands to the weapon. By the addition of a stock he could hold it to his shoulder; and, since the powder was so bad as to require a long barrel in which to burn it all up, he carried also a rest, like a pitchfork, upon which to support it. Thus was born the matchlock, a weapon which has actually been used by regiments that are still with us. Soon it was found essential that matchlocks should be of the same bore, and they came to be known as matchlocks of calibre, a word which was soon corrupted into calivers.[1]

The Germs of the Regular Army

Through most of this time of transition the English had been fighting, first the French, with the result that they had lost all France except Calais, and then each other, until, in 1485, the struggle ended in the accession to the throne of the very strong and able King Henry VII. He at once formed a royal bodyguard, which in its picturesque old dress is still with us as the Yeomen of the Guard. This is the first germ of the British Standing Army; and the choice of scarlet for its clothing and for the Royal livery seems to have been dictated by the red dragon of Wales. Military matters advanced but slowly during the next hundred years, and then chiefly through

---

[1] Arquebus is only a corruption of the German name for the same weapon *Hakenbüchse*, which is literally hook-box, but also means forktube.

voluntary effort. In 1537 the Honourable Artillery Company was founded; and in 1572 the first English volunteers went to Holland to help the Dutch fight their battle of independence against the Spaniards. As time went on, a great many English took service also with the armies of different nations —Spain, Holland, France—and returning home wrote books, showing how backward England was in all military matters. But the most significant movement of the time was the challenging of Spain's monopoly of the new world at sea by such adventurers as Francis Drake and John Hawkins, and the opening of England's eyes to the opportunities that were offered both in the far west and the far east. At the beginning of the seventeenth century there was a positive mania for the formation of companies to exploit North America and the West Indies, with the results that shall presently be set forth. But it will be better first to tell of the growth of the army.

The "New Model." The First Regular English Army

The first settlements of the English overseas had not endured for a generation before the mother-country was torn by the civil strife which was to give birth to the British

Army. We need not go into the cause of the quarrel between King Charles I and the Parliament. Suffice it that the two came to blows, raised casual levies and, during the next three years, fought a certain number of actions without any decisive result. Then, in 1645, Parliament decided that it must raise a permanent force, regularly paid and properly trained and disciplined. On their side Oliver Cromwell, a country gentleman of good family but small means, had raised a regiment of horse; enlisting only men of good character, teaching them their business thoroughly, instilling a high moral standard of conduct, and enforcing strict discipline. This regiment had overthrown every enemy that it had met, and now served as an example of what a regiment should be.

The "New Model" Cavalry

The New Model Army, as it was called, consisted of 11 regiments of horse, each containing 6 troops of 100 men each; one regiment of dragoons, made up of 10 companies each 100 strong; 12 regiments of infantry, each of 10 companies of 120 men; and an artillery-train to which were attached two more regiments of infantry and two companies of firelocks. The infantry regiments had three field-

THE NEW MODEL

officers, colonel, lieutenant-colonel, and serjeant-major or major; the dragoons and cavalry two, colonel and major; and every field-officer had a troop or company. There were therefore 4 captains, 6 lieutenants and 6 cornets to every regiment of horse; 8 captains and 20 subalterns to the regiment of dragoons; 7 captains and 20 subalterns in each regiment of foot. The whole army, for the first time in English history, was dressed uniformly in scarlet, with facings of different colours for the various regiments.

The English cavalry was in advance of the times. The mailed horseman, finding his career checked by the long pikes of the infantry, had taken to the use of pistols as soon as he could get them, and, abandoning shock action, would ride up to the square of pikes and try to shoot the pikemen down. It was customary for these horsemen to be formed eight or ten ranks deep, and the training was for the first rank to fire its pistols, and file away to the rear to re-load, then the second rank and the remaining ranks in succession. But it was found in practice that men who had once filed to the rear were apt to vanish from the field. By 1645 the English cavalry, though still armed with a brace of pistols, were formed in two ranks only, and were trained to trust to their swords in a charge. They wore an iron helmet, with a vertical bar across the face, iron cuirass and heavy jack-boots. By reason of these boots, horse never dismounted for action. There was a trumpeter to each troop, and there were a certain number of trumpet-signals. The rank of serjeant did not exist in the horse. There were only corporals, and to this day there are only corporals in the cuirassed and jack-booted Life Guards and Blues.

The dragoons were simply mounted infantry armed with matchlocks. They were drilled like the foot; their junior subalterns were ensigns and their sound-signals were given by the drum. For action nine men out of ten dismounted, linked their horses by throwing each his bridle over the neck of the next horse, and left them to the care of the tenth man. Their normal formation was in ten ranks deep.

The "New Model" Infantry

The foot were divided into equal portions of pikemen for shock action, and matchlock men, generally called musketeers, for missile action. They were commonly known as the pikes and the shot. The musketeers were dressed in long red coats, technically named cassocks, waistcoats, grey breeches, stockings,

OLD INFANTRY DRILL

shoes and a broad-brimmed hat. They carried their musket, its rest, a bandolier containing twelve charges of powder made up, a powder-flask containing more powder, a box containing a finer powder for priming, a bag of bullets weighing over an ounce apiece, two or three yards of match-cord, and a sword. The pikemen were, at any rate sometimes, equipped with an iron helmet and defensive armour to mid-thigh, which was designed to meet the attack of cavalry with pistols, but was found so heavy that it was gradually discarded. Both pikes and shot were generally formed in six ranks, pikemen in the centre and musketeers on either flank, but these six ranks were generally "doubled" into three for action. And here it must be noted that both cavalry and infantry fell in, not knee to knee and shoulder to shoulder, but with space for one horse or one man between files. At the word "Double your ranks," the second, fourth and sixth ranks stepped into the intervals of the first, third and fifth; and at the word "Double your files," stepped back again into their old places.[1] The drill was thus comparatively simple; but the exercise for pike and musket,

---

[1] Thus, to come to modern days, instead of the word "Form fours," Cromwell would have given the word "To the right hand double your files," and, instead of "Front," he would have said, "To the left hand double your ranks."

especially for loading and firing, was interminable. The words "Order,"[1] "Port," "Trail," and so on, of the modern manual exercise are all relics of the old pike-exercise; and the word "Fire" is an abbreviation of "Give fire," meaning "Press your trigger, and let your smouldering match touch the priming powder." Loading by the muzzle with a long, thin wooden ramrod, fixing the match, and getting the musket on to the rest-fork, was a long business; and it was very difficult to make men load properly in the heat of action. It was not less difficult to keep up a sustained fire. The old system, already mentioned in the case of cavalry, of making the ranks file to the rear in succession as soon as they had fired, was superseded by dividing the companies into small groups, called platoons, of sixteen to twenty men each, and making the odd platoons fire first in succession, and then the even platoons while the odd platoons loaded, and so on. And this platoon-firing lasted as long as the muzzle-loader.

In action, the musketeers opened the fighting at a distance. Their effective range, when their weapons were carefully loaded, may have been three hundred yards. Under cover of

[1] In old days the word was "Order (or trail) *your* arms"; a fashion which still survives in "Rest on *your* arms reversed."

their fire the pikemen advanced to "push of pike," and, after firing a couple of volleys, the musketeers generally fell in with the butt. Then the combat was fought out hand to hand.

As to the artillery, it is impossible to go into detailed description of the guns. They were heavy and clumsy and, being drawn by hired teams, were practically not to be moved when once placed in position. The powder was carried in barrels and loaded into the piece with a ladle; and it was a point of honour that not a grain should be spilled in the process. Before firing, it was the duty of one of the gun's crew to cover up the barrel with a sheepskin to avert any accidental explosion. For this same reason the peculiar escort of the guns were armed with flint-lock muskets, for in a wind the match of the matchlocks flew away in sparks, whereby the muskets of the rear ranks were often fired, with considerable danger to the front-rank men. Such sparks could obviously not be allowed near open powder-barrels.

The "New Model's" Work at Home

The New Model Army, though it had a nucleus of trained soldiers, was filled out by men compulsorily impressed for service. In a few months it had mastered the Royalists; and very soon it was found that the man who could best handle it was Cromwell, who kept it under strict discipline. After breaking down all opposition in England he was sent to Ireland, where, though he dealt sternly with the Irish, he forbade all plunder and paid his way. In 1650 he was sent to fight the enemy in Scotland, and took on his staff a Devon gentleman, named George Monck—a prisoner taken from the Royalists. Being anxious to give Monck a regiment and no regiment being vacant, he made one for him by taking five companies from each of two regiments of the New Model. It is still with us as the Coldstream Guards, and it was present at the battle of Dunbar (3rd September, 1650), when Cromwell, who seemed to be in a desperate situation, saved himself by taking advantage of his adversary's false dispositions, attacking, and winning a brilliant victory. One more victory at Worcester (3rd September, 1651) through an enveloping movement, which is still quoted as a model by German writers, completed his military work at home. Charles I had been executed. His son, with many royal followers, had taken refuge abroad. The army, now fifty thousand strong, could obtain as many good voluntary recruits as it wished. Its discipline, moral tone and efficiency made it the finest and most formidable force in Europe; and it was dreaded accordingly.

The "New Model's" Work Abroad

Then England reckoned with foreign enemies, and first with the Dutch. Three of the Dunbar regiments were taken to serve on board ship, and in 1652, after seven desperate naval actions, we wrested from Holland her supremacy at sea. Meanwhile, the rest of the Army displaced the Parliament and secured the government of England with Cromwell as Lord Protector. Monck, who had served as an admiral in the fighting at sea, then took charge of Scotland, where he fought a masterly mountain campaign in the Highlands. Cromwell, in want of money, sent a filibustering expedition to the West Indies in the hope of taking some from Spain. It was a disastrous failure; but it captured the island of *Jamaica*, which has remained with us ever since. Spain naturally took offence and welcomed the exiled Prince Charles to Spanish Flanders (Belgium), where Cromwell, after concluding an alliance with France, sent, in 1657, 6,000 red-coats to serve with the French under the great Marshal Turenne. On the 24th of May, 1658, a battle was fought at

Dunkirk Dunes, where the English led the attack and drove the Spaniards to retreat. One small body of hostile infantry alone stood fast, until, finding itself left in isolation to meet the whole of the Army, it laid down its arms. They proved to be the loyal English gentlemen who had followed the exiled King Charles over sea and had made themselves his guards.

On the 3rd of September, 1658, Cromwell died, and after several months of confusion Monck concentrated his Scottish troops at Coldstream, and marching from thence to London restored the Monarchy. In May, 1660, Charles II reached London; and from this point we enter upon the history of the present Standing Army, and of the Empire which, principally, called it into being.

CHAPTER II

THE FOUNDATION OF THE STANDING ARMY

THE first step after the Restoration was to disband Cromwell's army, which had very nearly been accomplished when an insurrection in London, early in 1661, showed the need of an armed force to protect the King and his capital. Accordingly, the King raised a regiment of Foot Guards out of the Royalists who had been present at Dunkirk Dunes, supplemented by others at home, also a regiment of Horse and two troops of Life Guards. These are still with us as the Grenadier Guards, the Blues and the Life Guards. Further, Monck's regiment of foot alone among those of the New Model was not disbanded, and survived with the new title of the Coldstream Guards. Moreover, there was in the French service a regiment of Scots which had been drawn originally from a Scots brigade that had served under that great soldier, Gustavus Adolphus of Sweden. Charles II asked that it might be returned to him; and in 1662 it came over to England as the

Royal Scots or Royals, the senior regiment of the Infantry of the line. In that same year Charles married a wife, Princess Katharine of Portugal, who brought him as her dowry, Tangier, practically a port in the Mediterranean, and Bombay, the most important harbour on the west coast of India. Tangier, being surrounded by fierce and aggressive Arabs, required a garrison, and for this purpose there were raised a regiment of Foot and a regiment of Dragoons, still with us as the Queen's and the Royal Dragoons.

The Growth of the Empire in the Seventeenth Century

But apart from these new possessions the Empire had grown apace since the beginning of the seventeenth century. An East India Company had been formed in 1599, and received a charter granting it fuller powers in 1660. It had then already settlements in Bengal and Madras, and had very early formed independent companies of soldiers to defend them, which were the germ of the Dublin Fusiliers in Madras and Bombay, and of the Munster Fusiliers in Bengal. It had also taken *St. Helena* in 1651. In the west, British possessions beyond sea had increased far more rapidly. *Bermuda* had been settled since 1609, and had sent colonists to the *Bahamas*. *Barbados* had been British since

1627, and Cromwell had made it his base of operations against Jamaica. *Antigua, Montserrat, Nevis* and *St. Kitts* were also British. In Central America the British had formed a tiny community for the cutting of logwood— to the great indignation of the Spaniards—ever since 1630, and this was the beginning of British Honduras. But the most important Colonies were those which now form part of the United States. Virginia was the earliest of these, dating from 1606. Farther north the Pilgrim Fathers had landed in 1620 and, not a little through hard quarrelling among themselves, had spread themselves over what are called the New England States. Maryland also had been settled since 1634. Virginia sent an offshoot to Carolina in 1663.

Altogether there was a promising line of colonies along the North American coast, but they signified no real hold upon the country. The true gates of North America were Quebec on the St. Lawrence and New York upon the Hudson, both of which throw open waterways to the great lakes, and from them to the great rivers which traverse the vast continent from north to south. The French had founded Quebec in 1608, and some English adventurers captured it for King Charles I in 1627; but he sold it back to the French five years later.

New York, then called New Amsterdam, was in the hands of the Dutch. Any power which secured both Quebec and New York would be mistress of the whole continent; and that is the secret of all our fighting in North America.

Additions to Empire and Army under Charles II

Let us now look at the work done for the Empire by the Army under Charles II.

Fighting began early, and the first quarrel arose out of a contest for the West Coast of Africa. The British had long traded, chiefly in the matter of negro slaves, in Gambia and the Gold Coast; and the Dutch, who were their rivals, tried to oust them by force, not only there, but in the East Indies. In 1665 Charles II declared war against Holland, with many interesting results. The first was that an English regiment in the Dutch service—a remote representative of the volunteers that had gone to fight for the Dutch in 1572—refused to bear arms against their mother-country and were received into the English infantry, where they still remain as the Buffs. The next was a great naval victory off Lowestoft, where some of the Guards served on board the fleet. The third was the dispatch of an expedition which captured New Amster-

WILLIAM III AND JOHN CHURCHILL

dam. When peace was made, New Amsterdam was kept by the English and granted by Charles to his brother, James, Duke of York, whereupon New Amsterdam became New York. Thus one gate of the North American continent was gained; and the colonization of Pennsylvania in 1681 gave the English a connected coast-line from New England to Carolina.

A second war against Holland, in alliance with France, took a British force to the Low Countries in 1672, under the command of Marshal Turenne. The troops were new levies grouped round a nucleus of the Guards, and amongst the officers was a certain Captain John Churchill, who had joined the First Guards in 1667 at the age of seventeen, had later gone through savage warfare at Tangier, and was now to learn his business with marked distinction under the great captain, Turenne. On the Dutch side was another remarkable man, of the same age as Churchill, William, Prince of Orange, the future King William III, of whom we shall see more. When the war ended in 1674, William was allowed to form three English regiments for the Dutch service out of the disbanded men. Two of these we shall see again. During the rest of Charles II's reign there was no more fighting except at Tangier, where it never ceased; and it was necessary to raise another regiment for the garrison in 1680, which is still with us as the King's Own. In 1679, a rebellion in Virginia compelled the dispatch of a detachment of Guards across the Atlantic—the first instance of the use of the Army as Imperial police—and in 1680 yet another detachment of both regiments was sent to Tangier. That post, in fact, demanded more men than could then be spared, and in 1684 it was abandoned, leaving England without any port in the Mediterranean. Meanwhile, some odd troops of horse, raised in Scotland in 1675, were supplemented and made, in 1681, into a regiment of dragoons, which is famous under the name of the Scots Greys. Thus we have brought our army up to some troops of Life Guards, one regiment of horse (the Blues), two of dragoons, the First Guards, the Coldstream Guards, the Scots Guards (already more or less in being in Scotland), and four regiments of infantry.

CHAPTER III

THE COMPOSITION AND NATURE OF THE STANDING ARMY

LET us now summarize the nature and duties of the Standing Army during its first period, for they are typical of a state of things which was to undergo little change for about two centuries.

In the first place, there were three different establishments, for England, Scotland and Ireland, with different rates of pay. These were reduced to two after the union with Scotland in 1707, and to one after the union of Ireland in 1801.

Next, it was not an army at all, but only a collection of regiments. Each regiment was built up on the model of the old mercenary bands. The officers bought their commissions, which were virtually shares in a commercial venture. Every field-officer and captain was the proprietor of his troop or company, and every colonel the proprietor of his regiment. All received pay indeed, but that pay allowed them only a small sum over and above the interest on the cost of their commissions. The pay of the field-officers was set forth in the establishment-lists as a mere allowance additional to their pay as captains. It mattered not if, as was frequently the case, the colonel were a general officer, for a general received no pay as such in time of peace. If he were a member of the headquarter-staff (a rather later development), or if he were sent away on active service, then a special estimate was drawn up for his remuneration, but not otherwise. A general might be, and very often was, the poorer for his promotion, unless he obtained the post of a governor of a fortress or was appointed colonel of a regiment.

There were some thirty fortresses on the establishment, most of which, even as late as the middle of the nineteenth century, were worth less than £1 a day in salary. The colonel of a regiment made a profit, if he could, by clothing his regiment out of a fund created by the stoppage of twopence a day from the pay of every man; but it frequently happened that he sustained loss. Nevertheless, under a system in which everything, including accountancy, was done regimentally, the colonel enjoyed great powers and much independence. His regiment's precedence was fixed, but it was known by his name, not, until the latter half of the eighteenth century, by a title or a number. For financial business he had a clerk, called an agent, the germ of the later banking firms of Army agents. The regimental surgeon and the regimental chaplain, for whom he received pay, were practically his servants. Every allowance made to him or to his officers figured on the muster-rolls as the pay of fictitious men. In fact, so closely was every item of administration penned up within the four corners of the regiment that the War Office consisted only of a few clerks—not above a dozen even at the end of the eighteenth century—to check the regimental accounts.

The purchase-system, as it was called, ensured a regular flow of promotion, but officers had their drawbacks as well as their advantages under it. In the first place, captains had to keep their troops and companies up to establishment; and recruits very often cost more than the bounty, or levy-money, granted by the country, in which case the captain had to find the balance out of his own pocket. Remounts, again, were for the same reason a heavy tax upon cavalry officers. If officers got into debt, they had no alternative but to sell their commissions. But the hardest measure dealt out to them lay in the fact that, if they died, or were killed in action, they forfeited the price of their commissions, and that there was no pension for their widows. They were, therefore, obliged to raise a fund for such pension out of their own pockets, the State giving no contribution towards this fund but the pay of one fictitious man, known as a "widow's man," to each troop or company. If an officer were cashiered by sentence of court-martial he forfeited the value of his commission; and thus he was practically bound over to good behaviour in a bond to that amount. Half-pay, granted upon the disbandment or diminution of a regiment at the close of a war, was a retaining fee designed to build up a reserve of officers.

The men were enlisted for life and, to save officers from the expense of replacing those that were past work, were generally kept in the ranks as long as they could stand. They paid, out of stoppages from their wages, for their food, their clothing, and for their right to claim a haven in Chelsea Hospital, which was set apart for old soldiers by Charles II. There were practically no barracks in England, so the men were billeted in public-houses at a fixed tariff. Thus, like any other labouring man, they paid for their board, lodging and clothing out of their wages; but they were supplied with their arms—the tools of their trade.

There was no uniformity of drill. Colonels were obliged to dress their men more or less according to fixed pattern, and inspections were held to see that their muster-rolls were true; but commanding officers were free to train their men as they thought best. Two new weapons came into use in Charles II's reign. The first was the bayonet, the invention of which enabled the musket and the pike to be blended into one, and gradually drove the pike out of use, until, by the end of the seventeenth century, it had practically disappeared, leaving only the name *piquet* behind it. With the pike vanished defensive armour for infantry, though a relic of it survived, in a scrap of metal called a gorget, which was worn more than a century later by officers on duty. The other new weapon was the hand-grenade, which brought about, in 1678, the formation of a grenadier company in each regiment. When throwing a grenade the grenadiers slung their muskets across them; and, since they could not do so without knocking off their broad-brimmed hats, they were provided with a tall mitre-like cap. All through this time, however, the flintlock was steadily driving out the matchlock. At first, when both weapons were in use, the flintlock was known as a fusil, and a regiment of fusiliers (which did not last long) was formed, like the two companies of firelocks in the New Model

Army, for duty with the artillery only. Being also required to sling their weapons, fusiliers likewise wore a long narrow cap, generally of fur. They and the grenadier companies did not recognize the rank of ensign, so their subaltern officers were second lieutenants.

There was as yet no regiment of artillery, but such gunners as there were belonged to a different department from the cavalry and infantry, being subject to the Board of Ordnance, just as the Navy is and for long has been subject, through the delegation of the Sovereign's powers, to the Board of Admiralty. All transport and supply were matters of contract and were, therefore, as a purely financial matter, the business of the Treasury. For nearly two hundred years from the Restoration every British Army in the field was subject to three different departments.

Further, it must be borne in mind that to the very end of the eighteenth century the first duty of the Army upon the declaration of war was to man the fleet.

It remains only to notice one more point in which the practice of the eighteenth century differed more and more from that of the seventeenth. It was always assumed, in the latter period, that the garrison of a place was inalienably attached to it. All of the thirty

FOREIGN GARRISONS

fortresses [1] which possessed Governors harboured also some little body, often not exceeding a dozen or twenty soldiers, which remained in them until the men were in the last stage of decrepitude, and never left them. So, too, when a new Colonial possession was acquired, a fixed garrison was sent out there and kept there. Thus, when New York was taken, the Duke of York formed two independent companies and sent them thither, where they remained for two generations; and the same practice was followed in some West Indian islands. In India, as we have seen, the East India Company adopted the same system, enlisting not only British but native recruits. But the East India Company's European troops were enlisted not for life but for a limited term. They were the first British soldiers engaged for short service.

All other settlements were supposed to raise militia and defend themselves after the English fashion; and for a time they did so, even in West Indian Islands. But, as shall be seen, the Colonies very soon began to appeal to England for help, thus raising the whole question, not yet finally settled, of Imperial Defence.

Apart from that, the chief bond of union

[1] Windsor Castle was one of them; and when I went there in 1905 there was still an old gunner who for forty years had climbed up to the top of the Round Tower to hoist and strike the flag. His normal dress was undress uniform with carpet-slippers, a strange survival of bygone times.

within the Empire were Acts, passed early in Charles II's reign, prohibiting the importation of Colonial produce into England except from the British Colonies, and the importation of European goods into the Colonies except through England, and forbidding all commerce between mother-country and Colonies except in ships built in England and manned in some proportion by English crews. These Acts of Trade and Navigation, as they were called, built up the English mercantile marine; but the Acts of Trade were bitterly resented by the Colonies and, indeed, could not be enforced. The reader should bear these two questions of close trade within the Empire and Imperial Defence in mind, against the time of our quarrel with the American Colonies.

These details are given at some length because they held good, for the most part, during the next century and a half. The bayonet and flintlock were still the weapons of the infantry when Queen Victoria came to the throne. Within the same period there were a few changes in the cavalry, though rather more in the artillery, which shall be noted in their place; but there was very much more in common between the Army of 1661 and that of 1850, than between that of 1850 and that of 1900.

CHAPTER IV

THE BEGINNING OF THE FIGHT FOR EMPIRE

King James II and the Army

CHARLES II died in 1685, and was succeeded by his brother James, a good soldier, a good sailor, and a very able administrator, but a bigoted, narrow-minded and vindictive man. He at once took the military forces at home in hand, and endeavoured also to unite the American Colonies in order that they might successfully resist the French in Canada. The rebellion of the Duke of Monmouth in 1685 gave him an excuse for augmenting the army, and he began by recalling the British regiments recently raised for the Dutch service, two of which endure to this day as the Northumberland Fusiliers and the Warwickshire. He then added a regiment of fusiliers as escort to the artillery, now known as the Royal Fusiliers, and eight more regiments of Foot, now called the King's, the Norfolk, the Lincoln, the Devon, the Suffolk, the Somerset Light Infantry, the West York, and the East York; of which the Devon and the Suffolk were actually raised in those counties. He also formed six new regiments of horse, now known as the First to the Sixth Dragoon Guards, and two of dragoons—now the Third and Fourth Hussars. He further called down from Scotland a regiment expanded in 1681 from certain companies which had for some time existed as the King's bodyguard in that Kingdom, and which is still with us as the Scots Guards. Lastly, in 1688, he hastily raised further additional regiments, of which two came into being and are now the Bedford and the Leicester.

Altogether he increased the Army, all told, to 20 regiments of foot, 7 of horse and 4 of dragoons; but he alienated most of them, as of the rest of his subjects, by endeavouring to force upon them acceptance of the Roman Catholic faith; and, in 1688, he was driven from his Kingdom by the invasion of his son-in-law, William of Orange, from Holland, who with his consort Mary succeeded him as King William III. France at once espoused the cause of the dethroned King, James II, and declared war against Holland; and therewith began the long struggle between England and France which was ultimately to decide the possession of the New World and establish the British Empire.

THE MUTINY ACT

The First War for Empire; New Regiments and the Mutiny Act

Ireland had embraced the side of King James; and the French King helped him there with officers and money. William, therefore, was at first obliged to turn the main strength of his British forces to the reconquest of Ireland, which occupied him until 1691. Hence, 6 regiments only were sent over to the Low Countries in 1689, under the command of General John Churchill, now Lord Marlborough. Of these the Royal Scots, not relishing forced change of allegiance from a Stuart and a countryman to a Dutchman, mutinied and refused to embark. They were overpowered, and their action brought about the passing of the first Mutiny Act, upon the annual renewal of which, in one form or another, the existence of the Standing Army is supposed to depend.[1] The Mutiny Act was the first statutory admission of the fact that military discipline is a thing apart from the law that governs civilians; and this, though it came nearly thirty years after the Standing Army had been in existence, was a step in advance.

---

[1] I say "supposed" because the Mutiny Act was more than once allowed to lapse for months, and once for a whole year (1699). Yet the Army went on without it.

THE EMPIRE AND THE ARMY

Great numbers of regiments were now raised to support the new dynasty and to fight the French, of which a goodly number survive. Ireland furnished a regiment of Protestants, the Royal Irish (which, after over two centuries of life, were recently disbanded), the Inniskilling Fusiliers, the Fifth Lancers and the Inniskilling Dragoons, the three last named being all originally derived from Enniskillen. Scotland produced the Royal Scots Fusiliers, developed from independent companies, which had existed since 1678; the Scottish Borderers, which were raised in two hours; the 1st Cameronians, which went into action at Dunkeld when they were three months old and, in spite of cruel casualties, behaved like veterans; and the regiment of dragoons, which is now the Seventh Hussars. England supplied the 7th Dragoon Guards, the regiment which is now called the Green Howards,[1] the 1st South Lancashire (first raised in Devon, and for years a Devon regiment), the Cheshire, the Royal Welch Fusiliers (raised on the Welch marches) and the South Wales Borderers. Some of these had begun life more or less in 1688, but were not placed on the establishment until 1689.

---

[1] The name dates from 1738 when there were two Colonels Howard, one of whom commanded the Buffs, which were known as the Buff Howards; and the other the old 19th Foot which, in virtue of its facings, became the Green Howards.

William III's Campaigns in the Low Countries. Campaign of 1692

By 1691 William had done with Ireland, and in 1692 he was able to take 23,000 British troops across with him to the Low Countries. It is quite impossible to make the operations intelligible without endless details, so it may briefly be said that the French were invading what is now called Belgium, but what was then the Spanish Netherlands, very much along the line of the present northern frontier of France, and that William and his allies were doing their best, so far with indifferent success, to keep them back. Belgium was a favourite fighting ground in those days of scanty roads and difficult transport, for, being fertile, it could feed armies in the field, and it had waterways which were useful for the transport of supplies and stores. The country was so well known that it was mapped out into camping grounds like a chess-board, and the southern frontier was studded with fortresses, great and small. War was not conducted in those days as in these. The sovereigns of Europe were proud of their standing armies; but they found them very expensive, and were, therefore, inclined to treat them rather as showy toys in times of peace—a tendency which was soon to lead to ridiculous but imposing uniforms—

and to be careful of risking them in time of war. The system preferred was to invade an enemy's country, entrench yourself there to the teeth and live there at his expense. From time to time you manœuvred to make him weaken the garrison of some neighbouring fortress and, if you succeeded, you laid siege to it with a part of your force and covered the siege with the rest. Your enemy, meanwhile, entrenched himself opposite you and looked at you until want of food or forage forced him to move. In due time the besieged town surrendered; and by that time the summer was ended, and you and your enemy both went into winter-quarters; you feeling proudly conscious that you had made a great campaign. Then the regimental officers went home to raise recruits for the replacement of casualties, and next spring the same game began once more. Thus wars lasted for years, until one side or both were financially exhausted; but it was a rigid rule never to fight a pitched battle except with enormous odds in your favour. It was much better to "subsist comfortably" on your enemy's ground and at his cost, until you drove his subjects into revolt and himself into bankruptcy.

William was more of a fighting man than many of his time, and in 1692 he was nettled by seeing the French Marshal Luxemburg besiege and capture Namur under his very nose. He therefore laid a plan to surprise the French Army, which was rather carelessly dispersed about Steenkirk (3rd August). Ten British battalions and two Danish bore the brunt of the attack, which was at first successful; but being unsupported, through some blunder, they were beaten back after very obstinate fighting with cruel losses, the 1st Guards and the Warwicks being terribly punished. However, the troops had done admirably, and in the winter they were supplemented by the raising of two regiments of dragoons, one of which survives as the Eighth Hussars.

Campaign of 1693. Landen

In 1693 Luxemburg took his revenge. William offered battle at Landen (29th July), in a position too extensive for his 50,000 men, and with an unfordable and insufficiently bridged river in his rear. All the most important points were held by the British, and, though Luxemburg had 80,000 men, it was only after two attacks had been repulsed with bloody losses that he succeeded at last in carrying them. The Coldstream Guards and Royal Fusiliers, even in the third attack, held their own for some time against five brigades of French infantry in their front and the famous French Household Cavalry on their flank. But the odds were too great; and, though William in person charged repeatedly at the head of the British cavalry (Life Guards, 1st, 3rd, 4th, 6th Dragoon Guards) to cover the retreat of the infantry, the battle ended in the rout of his army. However, the British had shown their quality; and they increased their reputation at the siege of Namur, in 1695, where the Guards greatly distinguished themselves in the first attack upon the outworks, the three battalions of the brigade losing 32 officers. Moreover, the Royal Irish gained at Namur their title of Royal, with a Latin inscription on their colours which is, so far as the writer knows, the first instance of a "battle-honour" upon any British colour.

Colonial Wars, 1692-1697. The Peace of Ryswick

In 1697, being utterly exhausted, France agreed to the Peace of Ryswick, which left matters very much as they were. No addition was made to the Empire, and the only expedition sent overseas was to the West Indies, where the naval commander and the commissary allied themselves together to wreck

FRENCH OFFENSIVE IN AMERICA

the operations of the military commander, in order to deprive him of any share in the prize-money. The result was naturally abject failure. The naval commander, the commissary and most of the troops died, and the military commander returned with the wreck of his force to tell the tale. But in North America the French in Canada took the offensive at once. They had between 2,000 and 3,000 regular troops, and with these they descended upon the borders of New England and New York and made frightful havoc. The Americans in those states alone could have raised 10,000 to 12,000 militia; but the Revolution of 1688 on that side of the Atlantic upset all the wise measures of James II and of his Governors; and the Colonies were fain to cry to England for help. William could spare them none, so they sent a small expedition by land against Montreal and by sea against Quebec. That by land broke down on the way owing to dissension, indiscipline and disease, and the naval force failed miserably before Quebec. Fortunately, Louis XIV could spare no reinforcements for Canada, and so New York escaped capture; but the French inflicted great damage elsewhere, simply because the various English provinces were too selfish and too jealous to work together.

United, they could have overpowered Canada with ease, for they had vast superiority in numbers; but they preferred to appeal for help to England and to require her to do the work which they might very well have done themselves.

However, the war was morally not unprofitable. Cromwell's army had been the terror of Europe, but it had hardly been seen on the Continent; and it was under William III that the new red-coats first made their mark in the contest with France. They had more experience of defeat than of victory, for William was no great general, but they had proved themselves to be formidable.

CHAPTER V

THE WAR OF THE SPANISH SUCCESSION

PEACE lasted only until 1701. In that year Louis XIV accepted for his grandson Philip, Duke of Anjou, the crown of Spain, which had been bequeathed to him by his great-uncle King Charles II of Spain. All Europe stood aghast. The union of all the dominions and resources of Spain and France in a single hand promised to make France the mistress not only of Europe but of the world. The possession of Spain alone sufficed to exclude the English and Dutch fleets from the Mediterranean, while that of the Spanish Netherlands (Belgium) laid bare the southern frontier of the Dutch Netherlands and gave France the ports of Ostend, Nieuport and, above all, Antwerp, as bases for an invasion of England. Furthermore, the Spanish dominions in Europe included Naples, Sicily, the Tuscan ports and the Milanese in Italy, which gave overpowering strength in the Mediterranean. By astute diplomacy France added to these advantages

THE EMPIRE AND THE ARMY

alliances with Portugal, which was the only base from which Spain could be attacked by land; with Savoy, which secured communications between France and Italy; with the Elector of Bavaria, whose domains, astride the Danube, opened the road to Vienna; and with the Elector of Cologne, whose territory cut off communication between the Dutch Netherlands and the Upper Rhine. Lastly, in February, 1701, a French army crossed the northern frontier of France and seized the barrier-fortresses with their garrisons—15,000 of the best Dutch troops—by surprise and without resistance.

William III, in the face of such danger, formed a coalition of Austria, Prussia, minor German states, Denmark, Holland and England. Seventeen new regiments of infantry were raised. Of these there survive the 1st Gloucester, 1st Worcestershire (both of which had originally been formed in 1694 and, though disbanded, could recall most of their officers from half-pay), the 1st East Lancashire, the 1st East Surrey and 1st Duke of Cornwall's (which, with the 1st East Lancashire, began life as marines), the 1st Duke's, the 1st Border, the 1st Royal Sussex, the 2nd Worcester (these two last raised in Ireland), the 1st Hants, the 1st South Stafford and the 1st Dorset. Before they were nearly complete William had died, leaving his sister-in-law, Anne, to reign in his stead, and recommending to her John, Earl of Marlborough, as the person best fitted to carry on his work.

Marlborough, his Plans and his Difficulties

Marlborough was a man who combined supreme ability as statesman, administrator, diplomat and general with amazing tact and irresistible personal charm. His ideas of war were quite modern. He had no patience with the pottering methods of his contemporaries, and wished from the first to beat the French armies in the field and march straight upon Paris from the east, by the valley of the Moselle, where there was no such nest of fortresses as on the Belgian frontier. Had he been permitted to do so, he would have finished the war in two, or at most three, campaigns; but he was thwarted throughout by the jealousy of his allies and the prejudices of their generals. The Dutch were the worst in this respect. They always sent civilian deputies with their armies to see that nothing rash was done, and, since a general might not handle the Dutch troops as he would without their consent, his task was heartbreaking.

THE EMPIRE AND THE ARMY

The Campaigns of 1702 and 1703

Marlborough's first campaign of 1702 was conducted on the eastern frontier of Belgium; and four several times the Dutch deputies interposed to prevent him from attacking the French with the practical certainty of sweeping success. The campaign of 1703 was wrecked also by Dutch timidity and incompetence. Marlborough spent eighteen days vainly trying to persuade the deputies to allow him to attack, and a great opportunity was lost.

Campaign of 1704. Blenheim

In 1704 the danger of Vienna became so desperate, under the joint pressure of the French and Bavarians, that Marlborough had no choice but to leave the Dutch to defend the Low Countries, and lead the rest of his army to the Danube. With amazing skill he deluded the enemy as to his intentions and was clear away before they could stop him. The redcoats (14 squadrons of cavalry and as many battalions of foot) impressed everyone with the smartness of their appearance and their exemplary behaviour on the march. Foreign jealousy had ordained that Marlborough and a German Prince should command in chief on alternate days. Marlborough wanted the

BATTLE OF BLENHEIM

bridge over the Danube at Donauwörth, to gain which he must attack the enemy in a strong position called the Schellenberg. He contrived within 24 hours to take his men over 15 miles of execrable road, and to storm the position out of hand. The English were highly distinguished in the action and suffered heavily, the 1st Guards losing 12 officers out of 17, while they, the Royal Scots and the Royal Welch, each had over 200 casualties.

Marlborough then overran Bavaria until a French army under Marshal Tallard came down to join the Elector, and took up a position at Blenheim, on the Danube, across Marlborough's line of communications. Marlborough had got rid of his German Prince for the time, and had been joined in his turn by Prince Eugene of Savoy, a splendid soldier in the Austrian service; their united force numbering 52,000 men against the enemy's 56,000. To the great astonishment of the French and Bavarians, Marlborough and Eugene attacked; and Marlborough, passing his cavalry over a boggy stream, cut the enemy's line in two, while the British infantry by a series of assaults on the village of Blenheim kept twice their number of French battalions engaged. The victory was overwhelming; the French loss in the action and subsequent pursuit amounting to 40,000 men and 100 guns. The casualties of the Allies numbered 13,000, and those of the British alone over 2,000; the Carbiniers and the Cameronians being apparently the greatest sufferers.[1]

Blenheim shattered the military fame of France; and this was not the only gain of the campaign. Marlborough had sent expeditions to the Mediterranean, both in 1702 and 1703, which, though they accomplished no great things, at least detached Portugal and Savoy from the French alliance and so threw open Spain itself to attack. In 1704, a third expedition attacked and took *Gibraltar*, which added a permanent post in the Mediterranean to the Empire.

Campaigns of 1705 and 1706. Ramillies

In 1705 Marlborough hoped at last to begin his march on Paris by the Moselle, but his Allies never presented themselves at the rendezvous; and he was obliged to prosecute operations in Flanders, which were once again wrecked by the jealousy of the Dutch generals

[1] Regimental lists of casualties are rarely to be found at this period. The number of officers killed and wounded is given, for that was a matter for the State. The casualties among the men (though, of course, returned to the general in the field) were a matter for each colonel, who had to make them good. *Nominal* lists of rank and file, killed and wounded, were not sent to the War Office till 1793. At Blenheim the Sixth Dragoon Guards lost ten officers and the Cameronians twenty.

and the timidity of the deputies. In this year a few troops were sent to the Spanish Peninsula to uphold the claim of the Austrian Archduke Charles to the throne, and did some marvellous feats under that eccentric genius, Lord Peterborough. But the main sphere of action for the British was still the Low Countries, where, in 1706, Marlborough, having at last found complaisant Dutch deputies, engaged the French at Ramillies (12th May) and beat them thoroughly, with a loss of 13,000 men and 50 guns. The British infantry were employed only for a false attack, but the British cavalry led the pursuit and pressed it hard. Within a fortnight the Spanish Netherlands—Belgium—had been cleared of the enemy, saving a few small fortresses, up to the sea. These little strongholds were reduced before October; and so ended the great campaign of Ramillies.

Campaign of 1707

Unfortunately this success was not properly followed up. The Austrians wrecked Marlborough's plans for the campaign of 1707; and he was relegated once again to Flanders. A very rainy season made all operations difficult—men were actually drowned in mud, as at Passchendaele in 1917—and the Dutch depu-

ties intervened on the one occasion when
Marlborough was about to strike a heavy
blow. In Spain also, earlier in the year,
things went wrong. Lord Galway, advancing
with 15,000 men from Murcia upon Madrid,
encountered Marshal Berwick with 25,000 at
Almansa. Half of Galway's men were un-
disciplined Portuguese, who ran away at once.
The other half, chiefly British, with some
Dutch and Germans, utterly defeated the
enemy in their own front, but were presently
attacked on all sides by superior numbers,
and after a desperate fight were nearly all
cut down or captured. The British officers
killed numbered 88. The Warwicks had 21
officers killed and wounded out of 23, and the
Norfolks 25 out of 26; so that the red-coats
at least did their duty.

Campaign of 1708. Oudenarde

Encouraged by the respite of 1707, the
French made extraordinary exertions for the
campaign of 1708. By bribing the authorities
in Ghent and Bruges they recovered both
places, and then turned against Oudenarde.
Marlborough, having moved his 80,000 men
28 miles in 24 hours, was there before them,
and attacked at once with his leading troops,
throwing the rest into action as they came up.

LILLE, MINORCA, MALPLAQUET

Darkness alone saved the French from utter disaster, but they escaped with the loss of 15,000 men. Marlborough then turned to what contemporary judges deemed the most extraordinary of all his feats. With 84,000 men he besieged and captured Lille, the most powerful fortress in France, under the eyes of a French army of 94,000. Ghent and Bruges were then recovered; and meanwhile, Marlborough, who never forgot the Mediterranean, planned a descent by some of the British troops in Spain upon Minorca, which was easily captured by General Stanhope, and remained a British possession for over 70 years.

Campaign of 1709. Malplaquet

In 1709, Marlborough was opposed in Flanders by Marshal Villars, a man — like him — with modern ideas of war, and a very able and gallant commander. Yet Marlborough twice outwitted him, besieging and capturing Tournai first, and then investing Mons. Villars followed him and entrenched himself in an immensely strong position at Malplaquet; and here, on the 11th of September, was fought one of the bloodiest battles in history. Marlborough's plans were all but wrecked because, contrary to his order, the Prince of Orange insisted on leading 16,000 Dutch infantry straight into a strongly entrenched re-entrant angle, whereby he lost half of his men and very nearly lost the battle. Marlborough managed to drive the French out, but his casualties numbered 20,000 against the French 12,000. Twenty British battalions were engaged at Malplaquet, of which the Buffs and the Coldstream Guards suffered most heavily. The operations ended with the capture of Mons. It would have been a great campaign for any general but Marlborough; yet it was not satisfactory to him. The prolongation of the war, which was none of his doing, had strengthened his enemies both at home and in his own camp, and he could now afford to take no risks.

Campaign of 1710

The campaign of 1710, therefore, was limited to the siege and capture of Douai, Béthune, Aire and St. Venant, each of them a strong fortress, which cost the Allies altogether some 15,000 casualties. Such a feat would have made a great reputation for any other general, for Villars dared not attempt to interrupt Marlborough; and the operation had a solid value for opening up the navigation of the Lys and clearing the way to Paris. Meanwhile, in the same year, there had been another reverse in Spain. An advance of the

Allies from Portugal upon Madrid brought down upon them by surprise a French force, composed of the garrisons upon the Spanish frontier. The French, marching with incredible speed, came upon the Allies before their commander, an Austrian, had any idea of their proximity, and cut off their rearguard, which was composed entirely of British. The British general, Stanhope, threw himself into the town of Brihuega, and there, with 2,500 men against 20,000, he held his own through four hours of desperate fighting until ammunition failed and he was fain to surrender. The British casualties numbered 600; those of the enemy 1,800. The behaviour of all the troops was superb, but Stanhope could not refrain from giving special praise to the Scots Guards.

Campaign of 1711

By the end of the year 1710, the British Ministry, which had so far supported Marlborough, had fallen, the Queen had turned against him, and the new administration betook themselves to a new policy of what are now called "side-shows." They withdrew from Marlborough five of his best battalions and sent them, under command of Colonel Hill—brother of the Queen's favourite, Mrs. Masham—to go up the St. Lawrence and capture

Quebec. The ships went astray while sailing up the river. Eight transports were wrecked; over 700 officers and men were drowned; and Hill returned home having effected nothing.

Meanwhile, Marlborough, surrounded by spies and enemies, was left to do what he could in the presence of Villars, whose army was numerically stronger than his own by about one-third. Knowing that the new English administration would soon make peace, Villars had ensconced himself behind fortified lines of extraordinary strength along the marshy ground of the Canche and the Scarpe from the sea to Bouchain, and refused to come out and fight. He boasted that he had brought the great Marlborough to a dead halt, but he did not know his adversary. Marlborough turned all the domestic enemies around him to good account; but there is not space to describe his wiles here. There was one fort, barring a passage across the lines which he particularly wished to be destroyed; and he beguiled Villars into destroying it himself. He affected to lose his temper and gave wild orders for the movements of his troops, all carefully designed to deceive the enemy and further his own objects. He induced Villars to move the bulk of his troops to the west, and took out all his generals for

MARLBOROUGH'S LAST CAMPAIGN

a reconnaissance to show them their points of attack in that quarter. He deceived his own army so completely that they were in despair and said that he had gone mad. Then at the last moment, at nightfall, he issued a complete set of new orders, and by a forced march eastward of 40 miles in 18 hours, passed quietly through the impregnable lines and took up a position within striking distance of the three fortresses of Bouchain, Cambrai and Arras. Half the infantry fell out during the march, and some died; but most of them came in during the next day. Villars was frantic, and galloped after him so fast with a few cavalry that he blundered into Marlborough's outposts, lost the whole of his escort, and narrowly escaped capture himself. He hurried his army to the threatened spot, and offered battle. The treacherous Dutch deputies now pressed Marlborough hard to fight, hoping for his defeat; but Marlborough would not oblige them. Outmanœuvring Villars, he sat down before Bouchain, besieged it and took it under the Marshal's very eyes. It was the climax of a wonderful military career.

The Peace of Utrecht, 1713. Additions to the Empire

His reward was to be recalled in disgrace, dismissed from all public employment, accused of every kind of crime, and within a year driven from England, to all intent a banished man. The English Ministry was already negotiating with France; and in March 1713 was concluded the Peace of Utrecht, whereby it was conceded that Louis XIV's grandson should, after all, be King of Spain, but that France and Spain should never be united under one crown. Thus the object which the war had been waged to prevent was tamely granted at the last, though France had been beaten to her knees. For the rest, the Empire received the solid addition of *Gibraltar*, Minorca, *Nova Scotia* and *Newfoundland*, which last had been for years a mere fishing place, without any settlement ashore, for English and French alike. It was not a great increase; but the war had shown what a British Army could do.

Accession of the present Royal House; the Death of Marlborough

Queen Anne died in 1714 and was succeeded by George I, the first King of the present dynasty. The Ministers who had disgraced Marlborough hastened to fly abroad, and Marlborough returned from exile, but took no further share in public life. He died in 1722 and was honoured by a great military funeral, at which, for the first time, were heard the

SERVICES OF MARLBOROUGH

words of command: "Reverse your arms," "Rest on your arms reversed." The earlier years of his career were marred by a duplicity which remains a blot on his character. Still he was, perhaps, the greatest soldier that we have ever produced; and while conducting his marvellous campaigns he found time also to look after political business at home, and to conduct endless diplomatic correspondence and missions abroad. It was he, in fact, who kept the Coalition together by his miraculous tact and patience. Could he have directed the military forces of the Coalition, or even of the troops under his own command, with full powers, he would have dictated peace at Paris by 1704. He raised the fame of the British Army in Europe to the height which it had enjoyed under Cromwell, and it could not be raised higher. In France his name was one of terror. By his own soldiers he was adored by the name of Corporal John. Though a very strict disciplinarian, particularly where the population of a foreign country was in question, he looked studiously to the comfort and well-being of his men; and his care for them, his irresistible charm, his extraordinary coolness and gallantry in action and the confidence which he inspired as a leader made him loved as few generals have been. He had nevertheless some queer characters to deal with. Owing to the constant demand for recruits, men were enlisted for short service, which brought in a good class of soldier; but besides these, there was considerable impressment of unemployed, ne'er-do-wells and downright criminals. When Marlborough was deprived of his command, these bad characters mutinied, and the entire force felt inclined to mutiny. But the good predominated, the mutineers were suppressed; and to the last Marlborough's veterans approved themselves worthy of Corporal John. His name must ever be honoured by the British Army.

CHAPTER VI

THE INTERVAL OF PEACE, 1714-1739

THE new King had not been a year on the throne before there broke out, in 1715, a rebellion in Scotland in favour of the exiled Stuarts. The greater part of the Army had been disbanded, but the regiments now called the 7th and 8th Hussars were hurriedly saved from disbandment, and there were further raised 13 new regiments of dragoons and 8 of foot, all of which were presently dissolved, excepting 6 of dragoons, which are now known as the 9th and 12th Lancers, and the 10th, 11th, 13th and 14th Hussars. The rebellion was easily suppressed, as was also another little rising in 1718 which was countenanced by Spain. War had broken out with Spain in that year, but came to an end after no very serious operations in 1720; and thenceforward there were twenty years of unbroken peace.

In those years the Standing Army was only with the greatest difficulty maintained in the face of bitter attacks in Parliament; and, the King being rarely in England, its control passed mainly into the hands of its political head, the Secretary for War, with much prejudice to its discipline. But the greatest difficulty was that raised by the need for supplying garrisons for the newly-acquired possessions of the Empire, and also for some of the islands in the West Indies. The old system of attaching garrisons permanently to places was breaking down, and the whole question of sending out regiments and relieving them came up. There arose, also, the still more serious matter of accommodation for these garrisons. In England the troops were billeted in ale-houses; but even in Ireland there were so few ale-houses that it had been found necessary to erect barracks. At Gibraltar, in Minorca and in the wild and remote settlements of North America, there were, of course, no ale-houses; and, what was worse, in Nova Scotia there was no ale, and no drink for the garrison but water. This condition of things puzzled the civil authorities in England a great deal. Soldiers in those days dreaded going abroad to a strange country in time of peace, and they soon learned to dread it the more when they found that they had no decent roof over their heads, no decent bedding to keep them warm, no decent food to eat. Moreover, a regiment ordered to

FOREIGN GARRISONS AGAIN

a garrison oversea could never tell when it might be relieved. It might wait for twenty or thirty years. The 1st South Staffordshire went to the West Indies in 1706 and was not relieved for sixty years. The result was that a regiment destined for a foreign garrison was weakened to extremity by desertion before it embarked, and generally ended by incorporating the greater part of the regiment which it was meant to relieve—old soldiers who had taken a liking to the wine or the women of the foreign country and were content to stay abroad. There were many petty mutinies on foreign stations at this period, and it cannot be said that they were inexcusable.

However, the authorities blundered on between the old system and the new, and managed slightly to augment the Army. Four independent companies were told off as a permanent garrison to Nova Scotia, and as many to Newfoundland; and in 1717 these were united into a regiment which is now the 1st South Lancs. In the first alarm of the war of 1718, too, Chelsea Pensioners were called out for service, and ten companies of them were incorporated, in March, 1719, into a regiment which began life as Fielding's Invalids and continued to be Invalids for seventy years, but are now known as the 1st Welch.

In 1727 came a far more important addition—the Royal Regiment of Artillery—called into existence because, when guns and gunners were asked for on the outbreak of the Scottish rebellion of 1715, the Board of Ordnance could produce neither the one nor the other. The new regiment were a peculiar people. The purchase-system did not obtain in it; a commission in it was not to be bought with money; the men were clothed not by a colonel —who was expected to make profit out of the transaction—but by the Board of Ordnance; and promotion went by seniority. Their officers were carefully trained to their business, and in 1741 a Royal Military Academy was established for that purpose. The result was that, whereas in the cavalry and infantry you might, and did, find officers who had studied their profession, in the Artillery you could be sure that every officer knew his duty. Thus, for the best part of a century, the officers as a body were far superior in military knowledge and military science to the rest of the Army; though, when first it was proposed to put an artillery officer as general in command of a mixed force of all arms, there were grave doubts whether it could be done. For the rest, the gunners had still no trained drivers, and in war depended upon hired teams

FIRST HIGHLAND REGIMENT

and wagoners. They had no flags, for their guns were their colours, and they were dressed in blue. In fact they were, once more, a peculiar people, but their chief distinction was their superiority.

One other legacy came to the army from this same Scottish rebellion. General Wade, who was sent up to the Highlands to disarm the Highland clans, had statutory powers to impress all clansmen who declined to surrender their arms as recruits to serve beyond sea. This was a harsh measure; but it was suggested that, if Highlanders so clung to their arms, they might bear them in the service of the King. There had been odd companies of such Highlanders ever since 1710, and now four permanent companies were raised which, wearing a kilt and very dark tartan, became known as the Black Watch. In 1739 these were expanded into a regiment, which still bears the name of 1st Black Watch.

George I, a very able man, whose diplomatic influence was most powerful in Northern Europe, was too little in England to accomplish much for the Army, but he checked abuses, particularly illegal stoppages from the pay of the men, drew up a uniform system of drill, instituted a regular system of inspection of regiments by general officers and—a very important reform—provided the infantry with steel ramrods. His son, George II, who had distinguished himself at Oudenarde, was unfortunately infected by the example of his brother-in-law, King Frederick William of Prussia, with the passion for dressing his soldiers like dolls and manœuvring them like puppets. Military fashions always follow civil fashions in dress; and now the simple long scarlet frock of Queen Anne's time was slightly shortened, and the points of the skirt in front were doubled back, so that the facings extended in a broad band from thence up to the collar. The sensible old long-flapped waistcoat remained, together with the breeches and shoes, unchanged; but the old-fashioned stockings were now covered with long white buttoned gaiters reaching from mid-thigh to the foot. These gaiters, still worn by the drum-majors of the guards on certain state occasions, were called spatterdashes (the origin of the modern word *spats*) and were furnished to the men by the captains out of the company funds. Lastly, the old broad-brimmed hat had its brim turned up in three places and was thus converted into the three-cornered hat still worn by state-coachmen. The men were clean-shaved and had their hair made into a pigtail and powdered; but Grenadiers, as a rule, grew long whiskers, just as, within the writer's life-time, the pioneers of infantry battalions used to wear beards. The caprices of colonels supplemented the sartorial proclivities of the King, at least one providing his entire regiment with ruffles at wrist and bosom. Everything was sacrificed to smart appearance on parade. The gay clothes were an attraction to recruits, and little thought was given to the fitness of this fine raiment for war.

The War with Spain, 1739. Carthagena

Hostilities came in 1739, as the result of 50 years of quarrelling with Spain over her claim to exclusive rights of trade with her vast possessions in South America. The English nation had known no serious war since Marlborough's time, and was now intoxicated with the speedy prospect of plundering the wealth of New Spain. Recruits flowed in so readily that officers could pick their men; and it was decided, on the recommendation of Admiral Vernon, to send a fleet and troops against Carthagena, in South America. As usual, two regiments were needed to help man the ships. The military force consisted of a number of newly-enlisted marines, very raw and imperfectly disciplined, and two old regiments (West York and South Wales Borderers); besides which the English Colonies in North America were called upon to furnish four battalions, making the number of troops up to about 13,000 in all.

Owing to great confusion in the preparations, the expedition did not sail until November, 1740—four months late; and by the time it reached Jamaica in January, 1741, it had already lost Lord Cathcart, who was commander-in-chief, 17 other officers and 600 men dead from sickness. In March the fleet and army came before Carthagena. The General, Wentworth, an excellent man in time of peace, was so irresolute that he wasted a month in feeble operations before he delivered his assault, which was so unskilfully managed that, though the men behaved well, it failed with heavy loss. Of 1,500 troops engaged, 43 officers and over 600 men were killed and wounded. The soldiers were already dying fast of yellow fever, and this reverse took all the remaining spirit out of them. In four days the strength of the effective men fell from 6,600 to 3,200. There were hospital-ships, but few doctors, no hospital orderlies and no hospital comforts. The men wallowed in filth until they died, when they were thrown

A DISASTROUS FAILURE

overboard, only to rise to the surface in a few hours and poison the whole harbour. In May the expedition was abandoned and the troops returned to Jamaica, reduced to 1,700 men fit for duty. Within a week of leaving Carthagena, 1,100 men died, and at Jamaica the deaths were still 100 a week. By the beginning of December there were not 300 privates fit for duty. In February, 1742, a reinforcement of 3,000 men arrived, and in March the expedition put to sea to attack Porto Bello. Only picked men were taken; but within three weeks 1,000 of them were prostrate or dead, and the enterprise was given up. Of the men who had originally sailed with Cathcart not one in ten returned. Hostilities were simply extinguished by yellow fever, the Spanish army being as hopelessly paralysed by it as the English. The story is one of the most ghastly in the history of war. Its only effect in England was to reveal the grossest mismanagement in all departments, the guns and ammunition being in particular very defective. Its worst consequence was to embitter the hostility between the British Navy and Army; the Navy alleging that they could have managed affairs much better for themselves if their admiral had been left in supreme command.

The War of the Austrian Succession

Meanwhile a quarrel of a different kind had arisen in Europe, once again over the succession to a vacant throne. In 1740, the Austrian Emperor Charles IV died, leaving his dominions by bequest to his daughter, Maria Theresa. The rival claimant was the Elector of Bavaria; and France, mindful of her old friendship with that house, supported his cause, hoping ultimately to divide the Holy Roman Empire into four weak kingdoms: Bavaria, Saxony, Prussia and Hungary, all of which should be dependent upon herself. She was trying once again to secure predominance in Europe. England and Holland—the Maritime Powers as they were called—favoured the side of Maria Theresa. Parliament voted money for the dispatch of over 16,000 men; and King George II went over to Hanover to assemble the troops of his German subjects also. Eleven new regiments of marines and of foot were raised in 1741, and seven of the latter are still with us as the 1st Oxford Light Infantry, 1st Essex, 1st Sherwood Foresters, 2nd Duke of Cornwall's L.I., 1st North Lancs and 1st Northamptons. The situation was complicated by the fact that King Frederick of Prussia, by an act of unblushing brigandage, had invaded

WAR OF AUSTRIAN SUCCESSION

Maria Theresa's dominions and seized Silesia, which distracted the main strength of the Austrians to that quarter and enabled a strong French force to advance into Bohemia and thence to threaten Vienna. Lord Stair, a veteran of Marlborough's wars, who was in command of the British force, wished to assemble his army in Belgium (now become the Austrian Netherlands) and hold them ready to march straight upon Paris, trusting that the Empress would come to terms with Frederick, and then turn all her strength against the French in Bohemia. The Empress, after her troops had been twice defeated by Frederick, did get rid of him by yielding Silesia to him; and then all went forward as Stair had hoped. The Austrians drove the French from all their posts in Bohemia, holding the enemy's army closely besieged at Prague. The French troops assembled for the defence of their northern frontier were obliged to hurry to the rescue of their comrades at Prague; and the road to Paris lay practically open. But King George raised objections to Stair's project on the ground that England and France were not yet at war. Both had put troops into the field and were prepared to fight each other, but only as auxiliaries— England of the Empress and France of the

Elector of Bavaria. Thus the whole of the year 1742 was wasted by the British.

Campaign of 1743. Dettingen

Things went no better in 1743. The Austrians insisted that King George should move into Germany in order to overawe some of the minor German princes into alliance with them. He accordingly took up a position above Aschaffenburg; a French Army, about 70,000 strong under Marshal de Noailles, lying some 40 miles to south of him. De Noailles manœuvred skilfully to intercept the King's supplies of food and forage, and, knowing that the King must consequently retire very soon, laid his plans to make an end of him. The King had only one line of retreat, down the right bank of the Main, which involved passing, by the village of Dettingen, through a defile not more than a mile wide between rugged woody hills and the river. At this point De Noailles posted a strong force to bar the King's way. He also erected batteries on the other side of the river to play upon his flank as he marched; and finally, he threw another detachment across his rear to prevent him from countermarching. In fact he made very effective dispositions to catch the King, as he said, in a mousetrap.

BATTLE OF DETTINGEN

Great was the confusion in the King's Army when he found his retreat cut off and the French artillery tearing into his flanks. However, he formed his army for battle to his front, posting his 12 British battalions in two lines on his left with the 3rd Dragoons (now Hussars) filling up the space between their left flank and the river. To the right of the British infantry stood an Austrian brigade of horse and 4 regiments of British cavalry in first line, and 5 regiments of British cavalry in second line. The action practically was confined to a desperate attempt of the French Household cavalry to bear down the British left and turn its flank. They were repulsed by the steady and deadly fire of the Royal Welch and Royal Scots Fusiliers, and above all by the repeated charges of the 3rd Dragoons which, with only two squadrons present, fought on until three-fourths of their men and horses were down. The French infantry behaved badly and would not face the English fire; and, after the defeat of the Household cavalry, they ran away in disgraceful panic. Thus, after four hours of sharp work, King George fought his way out of the mousetrap with no further mishap than 826 casualties among his 16,000 British troops and 2,500 in all, against at least 5,000 killed, wounded and prisoners on the French side. This was the last battle in which a King of England commanded in person. George II's horse bolted with him to the rear at the opening of the engagement, so on regaining the front the King dismounted saying: "Now I am sure that I shall not run away." His son, the Duke of Cumberland, was also run away with by his horse into the middle of the French lines, but he escaped with a bullet in the leg. Altogether Dettingen was a curious rather huggermugger affair, redeemed by the destructive fire of the British infantry and the spirit of the Austrian and British cavalry. But the heroes of the battle were the 3rd Dragoons.

Campaign of 1744-1745. Fontenoy

The result of Dettingen was to put an end to the French operations in Bohemia and to shift the main scene of action to Belgium, as most convenient to the British, whose base was at Ostend, and to the Dutch who, after much trouble, had at last been persuaded to join them. But a Marlborough was needed to make the coalition work together, and there was no Marlborough. Stair had resigned after Dettingen. Wade, his successor, after trying in vain to get something done during 1744, resigned likewise; and, in 1745, William,

BATTLE OF FONTENOY

Duke of Cumberland, not yet twenty-five years old, took over the command. His opponent, Marshal Saxe, easily out-manœuvring him, laid siege to Tournai. Cumberland advancing found Saxe, on the 11th of May, in position by the village of Fontenoy. Saxe's right rested on the Scheldt, whence his line ran forward for a mile and a half to a salient angle at Fontenoy, and then back for another mile from Fontenoy, which was strongly fortified, over a perfect natural glacis to three strong redoubts, armed with cannon. Saxe, one of the great generals of the day, had 56,000 men and Cumberland 50,000, of which 25,000 were British and the remainder Dutch and Austrians. Cumberland ordered the Dutch and Austrians to attack the salient at Fontenoy, but they would not face it, the Dutch troops being worthless. Cumberland then ordered the British—20 battalions—and the Hanoverian infantry to attack the re-entrant between Fontenoy and the redoubts. They advanced in three lines, the first two British, the third Hanoverian. They moved steadily over half a mile of open ground through a furious cross-fire of artillery, met the flower of the French infantry at the crest, held their fire till they were within thirty yards and then blasted them off the field. Saxe, judging the battle lost, entreated the French King, who was present, to retire at once; while, to gain time, he hurled two lines of cavalry at the red-coats, which shivered them likewise to fragments with their terrible fire. However, Saxe meanwhile managed to bring forward his reserves. The Dutch would not move, and Saxe was thus able to turn the bulk of his army against the British and Hanoverians. The British cavalry came forward to cover their retreat, and the infantry fell back slowly and in good order, the rear repelling a furious charge of the French Household cavalry. Of 15,000 British and Hanoverian infantry, 6,000 had fallen in the fight, the casualties of the British being just over 4,000. The Suffolks and the Welch Fusiliers had each of them over 300 killed and wounded.

Campaign of 1746. Roucoux

Fontenoy was a defeat, but a glorious defeat; and it was the end of the campaign. The bulk of the British troops were hurried back to England to meet Prince Charles Stuart's invasion. There is no need to re-tell the story of his successes over raw English recruits at Coltbridge and Prestonpans, of his astonishing advance as far as Derby, of his retreat, of his third success at Falkirk in January, 1746, and of his final defeat at

BATTLE OF ROUCOUX

Culloden on the 27th April. Suffice it that this petty rebellion paralysed the Allied operations in Flanders for twelve months and that before they were resumed, Marshal Saxe had mastered most of the Austrian fortresses on the southern frontier of Belgium. He was now working to secure the line of the Meuse, so as to sever the communication between the British and their Austrian Allies, and to operate by that river for the invasion of Holland. As a means to that end he was threatening Namur; and the Allies took up a position about the village of Roucoux, just to north of Liège, in the hope of saving it. Here Saxe attacked them on the 11th October, 1746. The brunt of the action was borne by 16 battalions, 4 of them British, 4 Hanoverian and Hessian, and 8 Dutch, all of which behaved superbly, repelling attacks from ten times their numbers of French and finally retiring steadily and in good order. The 1st Oxfordshire L.I. on this occasion lost 200 killed and wounded, first in defence, then in successful counter-attack, and finally in a stubborn stand to cover the retreat.

Campaign of 1747. Lauffeld

The campaign of 1747 opened even more unprosperously than the last. The Dutch were

THE EMPIRE AND THE ARMY

behindhand in all their preparations. Saxe, having taken Namur in the previous campaign, was threatening Maastricht, and Cumberland prepared to take up a position to protect it. Before he could occupy it Saxe, having marched 50 miles in two days, was upon him; and Cumberland hastily formed his line of battle on a front of some five miles, the key of the defences being the villages of Vlytingen and Lauffeld on the left. These were held by the British (14 battalions) and Hanoverian infantry, with 4 regiments of British cavalry; the Dutch occupying the centre and the Austrians the right. Saxe, having enormous superiority of numbers, launched 11 brigades, covered by the fire of 40 guns, to the attack of Vlytingen and Lauffeld. They were repulsed with heavy loss. Bringing up two more brigades he renewed the assault and was again beaten back. He then called up yet another two brigades, including 6 battalions of Irish, to a third onset, and drove back the British to the edge of Lauffeld village, only to be thrust out once more by a counter-attack. All was going well with the British when some Dutch squadrons in the centre, seized with panic, galloped straight into the flank of the red-coats and threw the whole line into confusion. Saxe seized the moment to throw three more brigades

BATTLE OF LAUFFELD

against Lauffeld, and the village was lost. Order being restored, the British infantry turned about and began a steady retreat, General Ligonier charging into the entire mass of the French cavalry with the Greys, Inniskillings and a regiment of Hanoverian dragoons. He broke through the whole depth of the French squadrons and fell upon the infantry beyond; but his men, being assailed on all sides, were broken past all rallying. He was taken prisoner, and Cumberland, who had galloped into the thick of the fight in the hope of reforming his dragoons, narrowly escaped the same fate. Taking command of the 4th and 7th Dragoons (now the 4th and 7th Hussars) he covered the retirement of the infantry, which was effected in good order without further loss. The British troops had one and all behaved so well that Cumberland could not single out any one regiment for particular praise. Their casualties numbered 2,000, of which 160 fell on the Greys alone. They were not well supported by the Austrians and Dutch and, in fact, they, the Hanoverians and Hessians, bore the whole brunt of the fight. The total loss of the Allies was about 6,000, and the French acknowledged the loss of 10,000. Though accounted a defeat, the battle of Lauffeld saved, for the time, the fortress of Maastricht.

Throughout the war the Dutch had proved themselves apathetic and unstable, while the Austrians had never furnished the troops that they had engaged to provide in return for the money supplied by England. In fact, the Allies would have been driven out of the field had not the French troops at this period been, from various causes, of very inferior quality. Both sides were exhausted; and the war was ended on the 30th of April, 1748, by the Peace of Aix-la-Chapelle, which, but for two small details, left things very much as they were.

The Situation in America

But these two small details lead us away both west and east to watch the building up of the Empire oversea. Let us turn first to America.

It was always the shrewd practice of the French, when they found themselves the neighbours of the English upon any continent, to leave the possession of most of the coast-line to the English and, reserving some good points of access for themselves, to spread themselves down in rear of their rivals and occupy the back-country behind them. In North America they never ceased to bicker with the English colonists on the frontier, with continual encroachments, whether in time of peace or of war. In the early part of the 18th century they still considered the greater part of the North American Continent to be their own, and possessing, as they did, one of its main gates at Quebec, they did their utmost to make their pretensions good. The principal English access to the Great Lakes and so to the great rivers that flow through the heart of the continent, lay up the River Hudson from New York and thence through Lakes George and Champlain to the St. Lawrence. The French sealed up the passage into Lake Champlain by erecting a fort at Crown Point, upon territory which was claimed by the province of New York, and another fort at Niagara to block the pass between Lake Ontario and Lake Erie. This was well and wisely imagined; but, irritated by the loss of Nova Scotia under the Treaty of Utrecht, the French did also a very foolish thing. They betook themselves to the island of Cape Breton, immediately to north of Nova Scotia, and there they built an elaborate fortress of masonry, called Louisburg, to protect a harbour from which French privateers and cruisers could prey upon British commerce, and French expeditions could raid British posts. If Louisburg could have provisioned itself from the island of Cape Breton, something might have been said for it, but it could not. It was dependent upon the sea for its supplies, and therefore, without supremacy at sea, was a hostage to fortune. Moreover, the masonry was most costly to keep in repair, for the summer was too short to allow the mortar to set, and the winter so severe that the frost split mortar and stones and brought the walls to ruin every year.

However, the French were very proud of it and the colonists very much afraid of it; and in 1744 part of the garrison of Louisburg embarked and overpowered without difficulty two little English military posts in Nova Scotia. Thereupon the colonists of New England resolved to attack Louisburg. By good luck a British squadron from England joined them; and, with the help of the gunners and some guns from the men-of-war, the colonists by great good fortune succeeded in capturing Louisburg after a siege of six weeks, on 17th June, 1745. The colonists then begged for help from England for a regular attack upon Quebec in 1746, and three regiments were actually sent over from England for the purpose; but the project came to nothing. Two French expeditions for the recapture of Louisburg also failed, one through misfortune, the other through defeat by a British fleet off the coast of France; and the war ended with the

INDIA IN THE 17TH CENTURY

British flag still flying over Louisburg. The fortress was, however, restored to France, under the peace of 1748, in exchange for Madras, and very wisely, for, as has been said, Louisburg was useless without superiority at sea.

The Situation in India

Now let us turn to the East and look into this question of Madras. Since the beginning of the 17th century the Mohammedan invaders had mastered the greater part of India, and for 200 years a succession of strong men—known to history as the Mughal or Mogul Emperors—had ruled over it. But Hindu champions had arisen against them, notably the Mahrattas and the Sikhs, and when the last of the great Emperors died in 1707, the Empire fell to pieces and was partitioned among their late viceroys and other adventurers, notable and obscure. If there had been no Europeans in India the Mahrattas would certainly have mastered it, for the military power of the Sikhs was not to ripen until the 19th century; but four European nations, England, France, Holland and Portugal, had, all of them, trading stations in the country; and the issue was, which of the more powerful, England or France, was to be mistress in India. The French had taken the initiative by founding in 1735 a thriving colony at Mauritius as a base for military operations, and by establishing at their settlement of Pondicherry a little force of Mohammedan natives, drilled and trained after the European fashion. By judicious intervention in the quarrels of the Indian princes, who were contending for the fragments of the Mughal Empire, the French extended their power and influence widely; and, when the war of 1742 broke out, they were represented by a very able and ambitious man, Jean François Dupleix.

French Capture of Madras. Robert Clive

In 1746 he sent 1,100 European soldiers and 400 Sepoys to besiege Madras and took it without difficulty, the English garrison numbering only 200. Dupleix failed to prosecute his success against the English; in 1747, reinforcements arrived from England with a very capable commander, by name Major Stringer Lawrence; and in June, 1748, English troops met French in India for the first time in a little action close to Pondicherry, and beat them. On the other hand, an attempt to capture Pondicherry in the same year by a mixed British force under Admiral Boscawen was a complete failure, and is worth mentioning only because a young clerk in the East

India Company's service, named Robert Clive, distinguished himself greatly in the course of the operations. Major Lawrence took this young clerk in hand, becoming a second father to him, and taught him all that a good old soldier could teach to a promising young subaltern.

Fighting in India. 1751-1754

Madras was restored to England, as has been told, by the Treaty of Aix-la-Chapelle; but the peace did not prevent the English and French from continuing to fight as allies of native princes. Things went ill for the English until 1751, when they were so desperate that as a last chance Clive was sent away with 200 Europeans and 300 Sepoys to attack the chief native enemy's capital at Arcot. He took it without resistance and held it for 51 days against superior numbers, though with the loss of half of his men. Then, being reinforced, he sallied out, beat the French with inferior numbers in the open field (14th February, 1752), and again before Trichinopoly (27th April, 1752), until in June, 1752, a final great success in that same quarter seemed to secure the permanent predominance of the English. But the French were not beaten yet. There was constant fighting during the remainder of the year, always with success to the British, for Clive had the gift of turning the worst and rawest recruits into heroes; and in 1753 and 1754 the contest resolved itself into a series of little actions of 1,000 or 1,500 men a side, fought with the tactics of the parade-ground before Trichinopoly. Lawrence won three such actions with great skill, in person; and a fourth, in which the French had double the number of the English—about 6,000 men against 2,000— was brilliantly carried to victory by one of his junior officers, Captain John Caillaud. After so many defeats Dupleix was recalled to France in disgrace, and the long struggle between the two nations in India was brought to a close for the moment by a conditional treaty. But the issue had not been decided yet, though one great point had been gained—the French had learned to dread meeting the English in the field.

The Fighting in America

But it was not in India only that English and French abroad had come to blows while their mother-countries were living in peace at home. In North America the English Government had done nothing in counterpoise to the establishment of the French at Louisburg, except to found, in 1749, a military settlement —the only thing of the kind in our history—

BRADDOCK'S DISASTER

of some 4,000 disbanded soldiers and sailors at Halifax. In that same year, both English and French traders met on the river Ohio, the great waterway which, rising near Lake Erie, leads into the Mississippi and so to the Gulf of Mexico; and the two peoples fell at variance forthwith, for the French, true to their constant policy, designed to shut off the English from the interior of the continent, and had no idea of admitting them to the Ohio. The English Governors of the Colonies wished to erect fortified posts on the river, but the Colonies would do nothing but talk; and, meanwhile, the French constructed a chain of little forts to secure their object, and sent the English on the Ohio about their business. This was an act of war, but nothing would induce the majority of the Colonies to move a finger for their own defence; and the burden was, as usual, thrown upon the mother-country. Two battalions were sent from England in January, 1755, the 1st Essex and the 1st Northampton, both miserably weak, with General Edward Braddock of the Coldstream Guards to command in chief. They landed in Virginia in March. The colonists were very obstructive in the matter of providing transport; and it was June before Braddock was able to march with his two English battalions, now each swelled to 700 men by Virginian recruits, 450 Virginian militia and one excellent Virginian officer, Colonel George Washington.

Braddock's Defeat near the Ohio

A forest campaign in a strange country was a novelty to Braddock and to the troops which he had brought with him from England. He had seen service with Cumberland in Flanders, and attempted to apply the principles of Flanders to the backwoods of America. In 12 days he traversed no more than 42 miles, and then, on 8th July, he came upon his enemy and found himself in a ring of fire from unseen Indians. The Virginians at once took cover, but Braddock insisted that all of his men should stand up in array as if they had been at Fontenoy. Falling fast, but unable to perceive any foe, they fired into the air and presently broke in panic. Braddock, after five horses had been killed under him, ordered a retreat, but he was mortally wounded, and his force was practically annihilated. Of 86 officers only 26, and of 1,373 men only 459, escaped unharmed.

This was a real disaster; and other operations of the colonists against the French posts on the Great Lakes in the same year came to naught. The news caused great dismay in

LOSS OF MINORCA

England, but the Ministry in power was utterly resourceless and incompetent. They hesitated even to declare war, being terrified of a French invasion, which they had no idea of meeting except by the hire of Hanoverians and Hessians. They did, however, in January, 1756, raise 10 new regiments, which remain with us as the 1st Royal West Kent, 1st K.O.Y.L.I., 2nd Oxfordshire L.I., 1st Shropshire L.I., 2nd Dorset, 2nd Border, 2nd Essex, 1st Middlesex, 2nd Northampton and 2nd East Lancs. They also ordered the formation of a regiment of four battalions from among the foreign population in America; and these, originally called the Royal Americans and later the 60th, now survive among us as the King's Royal Rifle Corps. But the Ministers had no very clear idea what they should do with them, and meanwhile they had shamefully neglected their foreign garrisons. The French, being quite aware of this, laid siege to Minorca with 16,000 men. The Governor of Minorca, General Blakeney, was one of Marlborough's veterans and past 80 years of age, but he had so few officers with his garrison of 2,800 men that he was obliged to do most of the work himself. For ten weeks he held out gallantly, himself never changing his clothes nor going to bed from the first day to the last. Then, not having men enough to man his guns, he, on 28th June, surrendered. The Government thereupon shot Admiral Byng, because they had not given him a fleet strong enough to relieve Minorca, and dismissed the Governor of Gibraltar because, most pardonably, he had refused to weaken his garrison in order to man Byng's ships. This was one of the most disgraceful years in our history.

The Seven Years' War

In May, 1756, nearly a year after Braddock's disaster, England at last declared war against France, and a couple of battalions were sent to America. Such a reinforcement was too small to accomplish anything, and accordingly nothing was done. Meanwhile, towards the end of the year, France, Austria, Saxony, Russia and Sweden combined together to crush Frederick the Great and to partition Prussia; and all Europe was plunged into what is known in history as the Seven Years' War. The Coalition threatened Hanover, and for this and other reasons England sided with Frederick.

In December, 1756, the incompetent Ministry made way for William Pitt, whose energy put a new face on affairs. He sent back all foreign troops from England to Hanover. He passed, to provide for internal

THE ADVENT OF PITT

defence, a Militia Act under which the whole manhood of England was to be trained to arms as militia-men in periods of three years' service. He raised at once 15 new battalions, of which there still remain the 2nd Gloucesters, 1st Wilts, 1st Manchester, 1st North Stafford, 1st York and Lancs, 2nd Berks, 2nd Hampshire, 1st Durham L.I., 2nd Welch and 2nd East Surrey. He formed also two regiments of Highlanders—a new experiment in those days. He increased the Royal Artillery and added to them a company of Miners— the first germ of the Royal Engineers. Lastly, whereas the late Government had ordered one battalion to North America, he sent off no fewer than eight. These, however, arrived too late to do any serious work; and the campaign of 1757 in America, which was confined to some trifling operations on the lakes, ended once again to the advantage of the French. In Europe nothing was attempted but a feeble raid on the French coast, which failed completely and should never have been attempted. The only good news for the year came from India, but that must be told later.

The Campaign of 1758. Louisburg

In 1758, Pitt planned three main operations in America—the siege of Louisburg; an advance upon Montreal from the side of New York; and an advance upon the Ohio to make good Braddock's failure. Louisburg was entrusted to General Jeffery Amherst, with 14 battalions, and to a fleet under Admiral Boscawen. The operations began on 8th June with the forcing of a disembarkation in the presence of a prepared enemy—the first operation of the kind in the history of the Army. It was successfully accomplished under the direction of General James Wolfe, after which the siege was carried on with no great loss until, on the 27th July, Louisburg and its garrison of 5,600 men surrendered. The advance upon Montreal failed owing to the incompetence of the General. Quite unnecessarily he hurled his troops against an impregnable position at Ticonderoga; and, though they assaulted again and again with amazing gallantry and resolution, they were beaten back with heavy loss. Seven battalions were engaged, and their casualties numbered 1,600, those of the 1st Black Watch alone amounting to 500. The advance upon the Ohio was successfully carried out by General Forbes in the face of appalling difficulties of transport and supply. The column was engaged once with the French on the way, but found the French post on the Ohio abandoned and replaced it by a new fort, which was christened Pittsburgh in honour of William Pitt. The name is still retained by the huge industrial city, which now covers the site. In Europe nothing was done beyond some abortive raids upon Brittany; but on the West African coast a British expedition captured the French settlement at Senegal and the island of Goree.

The Year of Victory, 1759

At last, in 1759, Pitt's military plans were fully developed. They included (1) an attack on the French West Indies, (2) attacks on Canada from the side of New York by land and the side of Quebec by sea, (3) sundry operations in India, (4) operations in Germany to keep French troops in Europe and to assist Frederick the Great, whose hands were already overfull. Let us glance at each of these in turn.

The West Indies

(1) Six battalions and a squadron of ships reached Barbados in January, 1759, and sailed at once to the French island of Martinique about 100 miles away. The General, dismayed at the sight of the mountainous, forest-clad island, looked at it helplessly until, fortunately, he died. His successor, General Barrington, though crippled by gout, noticed that in the neighbouring French island

of Gaudeloupe the commander had dispersed his troops over all the coast, trying to defend every point. Barrington, therefore, overwhelmed these posts one after another. It was an operation of great hazard, for his protecting squadron had been called away, and a single French man-of-war could have sent all his transports to the bottom; but he took the risk. On the very day that he mastered Guadeloupe, a French fleet and army came up before the island, twenty-four hours too late to save it, and sailed away again. This was a very smart piece of work.

Canada. Quebec

(2) In June a fleet under Admiral Saunders, convoying 8,500 men under General Wolfe, sailed up the St. Lawrence to the attack of Quebec. For six weeks Wolfe sought in vain for a favourable opening; but his only attempt against the French was repulsed with the loss of some 500 men, and he despaired of success. Then Admiral Saunders came to his help. Day after day he sent his ships up the river above Quebec with the flood-tide and down with the ebb, threatening a disembarkation at any moment, keeping the French on the march continually to prevent it and wearing out the nerves of their com-

BATTLE OF QUEBEC

mander. At last, in the early morning of 13th September, Wolfe did disembark, and drew up his troops for battle over against the landward fortifications of Quebec. He could not have kept them there, and if the French commander, Montcalm, had only left him alone, Wolfe must have withdrawn them. But Montcalm, losing his head, came out to fight Wolfe, and, though he had slight superiority of numbers—about 5,000 against Wolfe's 4,500 —his men were no match for the British in a duel of musketry. Two British volleys fired at thirty yards' range decided the battle in a few minutes. Montcalm and Wolfe were both mortally wounded. All was confusion among the French after Montcalm's fall, and on the 18th September, Quebec surrendered. It is noteworthy that in this action the East Yorks were formed in double instead of the usual triple rank—the first example, so far as the writer knows, of this formation in the history of the Army. The casualties of the British were 630.

Ste. Foy and Montreal, 1760

Meanwhile, General Amherst, making his way along Lakes George and Champlain, did not reach the St. Lawrence and Montreal before the winter ended his campaign. Thus the French were left still in force at their capital. The British garrison of Quebec, unprepared for the intense cold of a Canadian winter, suffered much from frost-bite and still more from scurvy. By the middle of April, 1760, 700 men had died, and only 3,000 were fit for duty, when a force of 7,000 French, half of them regular troops, appeared before Quebec. Such was the contempt in which the British held the French that General James Murray, on 28th April, marched out to meet them in the open, and fought a very severe little action at Ste. Foy. He was beaten, with a loss of 1,000 killed and wounded, but even so he could hardly make his men obey the order to retreat. Then it was his turn to be besieged at Quebec; but his officers took pickaxe and spade and shared all work and hardship with the men, until the 16th of May, when British frigates sailed up the St. Lawrence, destroyed the transports and supply-vessels of the besieging force and compelled them to retreat, leaving forty guns behind them. In July, Murray moved upon Montreal from the east, while Amherst came down upon it from the west. The French force had melted away through discouragement and desertion and only 2,500 demoralized men were left. On the 8th of September,

VICTORIES IN INDIA

Montreal surrendered; and thus was accomplished the conquest of Canada. It put an end to the menace which had kept the British Colonies in alarm for the best part of a century.

India, 1756-1760. Plassey, Condore, Badara, Wandewash

(3) It will be remembered that, in 1755, the French and English in India agreed for a time to a truce. In that same year the first regiment of the King's Army[1] arrived in India—the 1st Dorsets, who still bear the motto *Primus in Indis*—and they were very soon wanted. Bengal, Orissa and Behar had passed under the rule of a prince named Siraj-ud-Daoula who, hearing that the French and English were likely soon to be at war again, attacked and took Calcutta in May, 1756. When the news reached Madras, Clive was at once sent to Calcutta with 900 Europeans, including some of the Dorsets, and 1,500 Sepoys. After some preliminary operations, Clive attacked and beat Siraj-ud-Daoula on 23rd June, 1757, at Plassey, with little difficulty or loss, his troops including detachments of the Dorsets, Munsters and Dublins. The action was trifling, but the victory gave the British dominion over Bengal, Orissa and Behar.

Then the scene of operations was shifted

[1] The Dublin and Munster Fusiliers were originally of the East India Company's army and remained so until 1859.

to the south, where the French for a time had the upper hand about Madras; but the balance was restored by Clive, who sent a small force under Lieut.-colonel Forde of the Dorsets to make a counterstroke against the French in the Northern Circars. Forde gained a brilliant victory over the French at Condore, on 9th December, 1758, and followed this success up by storming the French fortress of Masulipatam, with extraordinary daring, in April, 1759. Then the Dutch entered the field against the British in Bengal, and Forde, attacking them at Badara on 25th November, with inferior numbers, destroyed them after a fight of an hour. Forde, on coming up with the Dutch, had written to Clive and the Council of Government for orders. Clive, who was playing whist, laid down his hand and wrote, "Dear Forde, fight them at once. I will send you the Order-in-Council to-morrow." This victory put an end to Dutch competition. On 22nd January, 1760, Colonel Eyre Coote of the Dorsets won a decisive action against the French in the south at Wandewash; and in April the French flag ceased to fly in India.

Germany, 1759-1760. Minden, Warburg

(4) To make clear the nature of the British operations in Germany without much detail

BATTLE OF MINDEN

and special maps is quite impossible. It must suffice that Frederick of Prussia, being engaged with Saxons and Austrians in the south and Russians on the east, needed protection from the French on the west. This protection was afforded by a mixed army of British, Hanoverians and Hessians under a very able commander, Prince Ferdinand of Brunswick, which acted, so to speak, as Frederick's right flank-guard. Being inferior in numerical strength, it was Ferdinand's business to avoid general actions as a rule, and to manœuvre in the space between the sea on the north, the Main on the south, the Weser on the east and the Rhine on the west. Still, he did fight a battle or two; and of these some account must be given.

The first was the battle of Minden on the 1st August, 1759. In this action the French were drawn up with a mass of cavalry in their centre, and with infantry on their wings. The British infantry—six battalions—with three Hanoverian battalions attached to them, were in Ferdinand's centre, and by some mistake they conceived that they had been ordered to attack. They advanced accordingly, Suffolks, 1st Hants, Royal Welch in front line; Lancashire Fusiliers, 1st K.O.Y.L.I. and Scottish Borderers in second line; three Hanoverian battalions in third line. They passed through a cross-fire of artillery to the first line of the French horse, smashed it to pieces, continued their advance, shattered the second line of French horse, turned and beat back four brigades of French infantry which threatened their flank, and finally routed the third French line of horse. It was, perhaps, the most astonishing feat ever accomplished by British infantry; and, had Lord George Sackville, the commander of the British cavalry, taken advantage of it, the result would have been an overwhelming victory instead of a mere success. Sackville was tried by court-martial and cashiered for disobedience of orders; but this could not make good the opportunity lost. The casualties of the six battalions, which went into action 4,434 strong, were 1,330; those of the Lancashire Fusiliers being 320 and those of the Suffolks, 302.

At the end of the year 1759, there were raised, for the first time in the history of the Army, six regiments of light dragoons—three of which have survived as the 15th Hussars, 16th Lancers and 17th Lancers. The 15th went straight out to Germany on active service, and at the action of Emsdorf, on 16th July, 1760, they hunted a body of French infantry 20 miles, charged through them three times, captured one battalion single-handed and were chiefly instrumental in taking 2,600 French prisoners. They lost 125 men and 168 horses in this their first action. A fortnight later, at Warburg, on 31st July, the British cavalry, under Lord Granby, had the chance of removing the reproach of Minden, by galloping down upon a large body of French infantry and practically annihilating them. In October, on the other hand, an attempt to surprise a French detachment at Kloster Kampen, with numerical odds of three to two in favour of the French, was foiled with heavy loss to the British battalions engaged; though in this action, as at Minden, the deadliness of the British musketry fire was the amazement of foreign officers.

The campaigns of 1761 and 1762 were chiefly campaigns of manœuvre. The French fought a feeble general action against Ferdinand, at Vellinghausen, on 10th July, 1761, and chance gave the British, and particularly the Northumberland Fusiliers, an opportunity for distinction at Wilhelmsthal on 24th June, 1762; but to enter into further detail is impossible.

Other Operations of the Seven Years' War

Even now, however, we have not completed the work of the Army during the Seven Years'

War. In April, 1761, a small expedition captured the island of Belleisle on the French Atlantic coast, as a place of refreshment for the British blockading fleet, and in June troops from America were brought down to the Caribbean Sea, where they captured first Dominica and then, at the beginning of 1762, Martinique, St. Lucia, Grenada and St. Vincent. Meanwhile, war had broken out with Spain, which had come to the rescue of France; and the troops in the West Indies, having been further reinforced from America, proceeded to the attack of Havana, which fell in August after a siege of two months, during which the British buried 5,000 men dead from sickness alone. In the east, the Indian Government sent an expedition to Manila, which surrendered, after ten days' battering, on 5th October. Lastly, the Spaniards having invaded Portugal on pretext of her friendship with England, 7,000 men were sent to defend Lisbon.

In fact, British troops were scattered about all over the world. Under the energetic impulse of Pitt, the Army had risen in 1762 to 150,000 British and 65,000 Hanoverians and hired Germans in 1762. But the British recruits had been raised, for the most part, by very vicious methods, and at that time no battalion in the West Indies lasted more than

THE EMPIRE WON

two years. By 1763 all the combatants were hopelessly exhausted in men, and most of them in money. Peace was made. The British, while giving back Havana and Manila to Spain, recovered Minorca and took over Florida. From France they kept the whole of French North America and, in the West Indies, St. Vincent, Grenada, Tobago and Dominica. The Empire had been won.

CHAPTER VII

THE BURDEN OF EMPIRE

India. 1760-1776

NOW came the problem of providing for the Empire's defence. The first troubles came to India, almost before Eyre Coote had completed the conquest of the French. Though the Empire of the Mughals had been broken up, there was still a titular Emperor, who, early in 1760, marched down to recover the provinces of Bengal, Orissa and Behar. Clive had gone to England on leave, and the danger was great, but was averted by the victories of Colonel Caillaud at Sirpur (22nd February) and of Captain Knox before Patna (16th June). A new native ruler, Mir Kassim, was appointed for the three provinces by the East India Company, and he at once began to form an army trained and disciplined by Europeans.

The reader should take note of this, for in all parts of the world the native inhabitants, having once felt or observed the prowess of the British Army, either imitated their methods or called in the aid of foreign officers to train their troops for them. In India, apart from the prince above mentioned, the latter method was adopted successfully by Hyder Ali, by the Mahrattas, by the Gurkhas and by the Sikhs. The general principles of discipline were also borrowed by the Zulus in South Africa and by the Ashantis in West Africa. Mir Kassim was only the first of many enemies who were rendered formidable by the example of the British themselves.

Undwa Nala and Baksar

Owing to the misconduct of the East India Company's servants in Bengal during Clive's absence, Mir Kassim turned against the British in 1763, took a part of their force there by surprise and at a stroke destroyed a fourth of their army. The peril was desperate, but Bengal was saved by the genius of Major Thomas Adams, who with a handful of men defeated Mir Kassim's troops at Katwa (19th July), Suti (2nd August), Undwa Nala (5th September), and Patna (6th November). Worn out by fatigue, Adams, a marvellous officer, died in January, 1764, but his work was completed by Major Hector Munro at the battle of Baksar (23rd October, 1764). Early in 1765 Clive returned to India, and his statesmanship brought the struggle to an end. The Munsters and the Dublins, one or the other, bore the brunt of all these actions, which were not the less critical because many of them are not ranked as battle-honours.

Hyder Ali and the Mahrattas. 1767-1776

Unfortunately the East India Company's Government at Madras was as corrupt as that of Bengal and contrived to quarrel with Hyder Ali, a Mohammedan soldier of fortune, who by sheer ability had made himself master of Mysore and of great part of Southern India. Happily there was an officer, Colonel Joseph Smith, who was competent to deal with him; and, after two campaigns in 1767 and 1768, the Madras Council concluded peace with Hyder Ali upon the basis of mutual restitution of conquests, an ignoble result which was due chiefly to the foolish interference of the Council with the direction of operations in the field. But Hyder remained always on the border, a dangerous neighbour who was destined for long to be a thorn in the side of Madras.

In 1772 new trouble arose from dissensions among the Mahrattas, the most formidable of the rivals to the British in India. As an incident in the confused situation thereby brought about, came a short campaign on the side of Bengal against the Rohillas, which was decided by a single victorious action on 23rd April, 1774, and is remembered chiefly by the part that it played in the impeachment of Warren Hastings. But it was on the side of Bombay that British intervention in the disputes of the Mahrattas was most active. There was only one serious engagement in the field —at Arass on 18th May, 1775—which very nearly turned to disaster, but was saved by a supreme effort of the commanding officer, Colonel Keating. Of 14 British officers present at this little affair 7 were killed and 4 wounded, which is sufficient evidence of the strain thrown upon them. There was, however, the gain of the small islands immediately to west of Bombay to be set against the cost of the operations, which were brought to an end by a treaty of peace in March, 1776.

Thus, practically ever since the final defeat of the French in India, one or more of the three presidencies had been at war, necessarily or unnecessarily, with native princes; and this process was to go on with little intermission for another century. The story of these earlier wars is little known and not very interesting to read; and the work done fell mainly upon the East India Company's regiments which were not admitted to the King's Army until

1859. Nevertheless they all form part of the history of the consolidation of the British Empire in India, the accomplishment of which has been one of the principal tasks of the British soldier.

The Dispute with the American Colonies over Imperial Defence

But while the Empire was growing in the east, it was to suffer grievous loss in the west. Hardly had the French been expelled from Canada than a lawyer in Boston began to agitate against the restrictions imposed upon American trade by the Parliament in London. This individual later went mad; but a great many important movements in the world have been started by men who were not quite sane. The New England Colonies had very early shown signs of ambition for independence, and not unnaturally. Men who cross the ocean into the wilds and found settlements by sheer industry, courage and determination, may reasonably claim to be left alone to manage their own affairs. But the weak points in the attitude of the Colonies was that, though quite strong enough, if united, to have driven the French out of Canada, they had preferred to quarrel among themselves. and to beg the mother-country to bear the brunt of the contest for them. No sooner had the mother-country finished the work than they turned against her.

Colonel Bouquet's Red Indian Campaigns, 1763-1764

Now, the conquered territory of America demanded a number of garrisons, not only for the main stations of New York, Quebec and Halifax in the north, and of Mobile and Pensacola in the south, but also for a vast number of posts upon the Great Lakes and upon a line of some three thousand miles from the St. Lawrence to the lower Mississippi. These internal posts were needed for protection against the Red Indians; and the need for them was proved by a very formidable Indian rising about the Great Lakes in 1763. The Colonies at first flatly declined to furnish a man for its suppression, and Colonel Bouquet of the King's Royal Rifle Corps was obliged to collect sick British soldiers from hospital to meet the danger. Marching out with 500 men, chiefly of the 1st Black Watch and King's Royal Rifle Corps, he was attacked by the Indians in force on 5th August, 1763, and only succeeded in beating them off after 48 hours of continuous fighting, which cost him a fourth of his force killed and wounded. The campaign was prolonged until October, 1764, when the power of the Indians was at last broken; but the brunt of the work was borne by British troops, the Americans being obstructive rather than helpful. Perhaps the most memorable thing about this little campaign is a set of tables for the transport and supply of his force which was printed by Bouquet at Philadelphia, the first thing of the kind in the history of the Army, and therefore of special interest to the Army Service Corps.

The Breach with the Americans

The attitude of the Americans was not promising for solution of the problem of Imperial Defence, which the British Government approached in 1765. America needed 10,000 men in all for her garrisons; and the British Government quite equitably asked the Colonies to contribute to the expense. The Colonies admitted the justice of the claim in principle, but they were so much divided by their squabbles that they could not agree to give a voluntary contribution; and the British Government thought to get over the difficulty by passing an Act to obtain revenue from the Colonies by Stamp Duties. To their amazement the Act called forth a storm of protest in the Colonies, and a beginning of physical violence at Boston. The Act was repealed, but the right to tax the Colonies was affirmed; and the Colonies adroitly shifted the ground of dispute from the concrete policy of Imperial Defence to the abstract question of the taxation of any British subjects who were unrepresented in the British Parliament. Factious politicians at home took up the cry, William Pitt being one of them; and the dispute is generally represented as a picture of loyal colonists goaded into rebellion by oppression. This is a mistake. The affair was certainly mismanaged at home; but the agitation against England had begun four years before the Stamp Act was passed; and the movement was really less against any definite grievance than towards independence. The centre of the revolution was Boston, where a minority of not very reputable men overawed the peaceable majority by the most brutal violence. Had this minority been early put down with a high hand, it is just possible that a reasonable arrangement between mother-country and Colonies might have been arrived at. But this was not done; and the party of brute force gathered impetus from impunity. At last, in April, 1775, the militia of Massachusetts and the British soldiers came openly to blows; and the American rebels thereupon fell upon the British posts on the Lakes with a view to attack on Canada. At Boston, in June, 2,500 British troops attacked an American force in an entrenched position at Bunker Hill and drove them from it, but at cost of 1,054 casualties—89 of them officers—which rendered the British powerless until reinforced. Meanwhile, other Americans pressed on against Quebec, which they assaulted on 31st December, but were repulsed with heavy loss; and so ended the operations of 1775.

Campaign of 1776

The Army in England being underpaid, recruits were difficult to obtain for America, besides which every Englishman would have preferred not to fight the Americans. However, troops were somehow scraped together and sent across the Atlantic; and by June the Americans were driven headlong out of Canada with heavy loss to themselves. In July, 1776, the American Colonies declared their independence; and, in September, General Sir William Howe, with some 25,000 British and Hessians, recaptured New York and drove the American army in rout and demoralization into Pennsylvania. Had not the campaign been begun so late, owing to the tardiness of preparations in England, and had it been prosecuted with sufficient energy by Howe, the struggle might almost have been decided in England's favour in 1776.

Campaign of 1777. Saratoga

In 1777, however, the British Government by a blundering scheme of operations gave the Americans the opportunity that they needed. New England being the home of the revolution, it was resolved that a force under General Burgoyne should advance southward along the line of the Hudson towards New York, and that a force under Howe, from New York, should advance up the Hudson to meet him, thus securing the line from the St. Lawrence to New York and cutting off New England completely from the rest of the Colonies. The plan was sound enough but, by some extraordinary blunder, the Government ordered Howe also to proceed to Pennsylvania and to prosecute operations there. Howe went to Pennsylvania accordingly, defeated Washington completely at the Brandywine River (3rd October), and established himself in Philadelphia for the winter. But, as Howe could not be in two places at once, Burgoyne upon reaching the head-waters of the Hudson found himself isolated and alone, unable to keep open his communications from the weakness of his numbers, and with enemies closing in upon him from every side. He struck out right and left, and his troops behaved nobly and were never beaten in the field. In one action at Bemis Heights on 19th September, the Lancashire Fusiliers, Royal Scots Fusiliers and 1st Wilts, together only 800 strong, with 48 gunners and 4 guns, held their own against overwhelming numbers for many hours, until darkness put an end to the fight, at the close of which the three battalions had lost 350 officers and men, and the gunners all their officers and 36 men. But all this gallantry was unavailing. Burgoyne had started with 7,000 troops; on 17th October he found himself surrounded at Saratoga by 18,000 Americans, having barely 3,500 men fit for duty. He had no alternative but to surrender, upon the condition that he and his men should be shipped to England and should serve no more in America. The American Congress, despite of strong protests from Washington and other of their generals, violated this capitulation, kept all the prisoners except Burgoyne in America, and tried their utmost by hardship and ill-treatment to drive them to enlist in their own service.

The Americans Ally themselves with France

From the beginning the Americans had sought for the help of France, which had

FRENCH ALLIANCE WITH AMERICANS

already given them much clandestine assistance. The English Government, after the disaster of Saratoga, offered to suspend all Acts relating to America which had been passed since 1763, and virtually to concede all that England had been fighting for since 1775. Fearful of losing the opportunity of damaging her old rival, France, on the 6th February, 1778, signed a treaty of alliance with the revolted Colonies; and from that hour the reconciliation of mother-country and Colonies became impossible.

The spirit of the British nation was roused by the intervention of France; and several new regiments were raised, of which the 1st Highland L.I. and 1st Seaforth Highlanders still abide with us. The English Government now resolved to evacuate Philadelphia, to stick only to the vital points which they held in the American Continent, and to attack France in the West Indies. In July, 1778, a French fleet with 4,000 troops on board appeared off the American coast; but after four months they accomplished nothing, with the result that French and American seamen could not meet ashore without coming to blows. As in their former wars, the colonists expected most of the unpleasant work to be done for them.

St. Lucia, 1778

Meanwhile, in September, the French had taken the British island of Dominica; but the British counter-stroke in the West Indies was soon to fall. On the 4th November a squadron sailed from New York for Barbados convoying 59 transports with about 5,800 troops on board, under General Grant. On the very same day the French fleet, under Count d'Estaing, sailed from Rhode Island, without any encumbrance, for Martinique, 100 miles to leeward of Barbados. The British fleet reached Barbados on the 10th December, waited there only one day and sailing straight for St. Lucia, which lies just to windward of Martinique, captured the island almost without resistance. The British flag had hardly been hoisted, when d'Estaing's fleet, twice the strength of the British, appeared in the offing. Admiral Barrington tucked the transports away in a bay, and anchored his men-of-war across the entrance in an unassailable line, while General Grant posted a detachment of his troops on the heights above, to prevent the French from bringing up guns to drive Barrington from his anchorage. The rest of his men Grant placed in the forts on either side of the harbour to deny the entrance to the French fleet.

D'Estaing waited until he had collected

ST. LUCIA, 1778

12,000 men, with which, on 18th December, he attacked the British post on the north side of the harbour. The access to it lay across an isthmus less than 300 yards broad, and here the British—1,300 men under General Medows—were drawn up to meet them. The action lasted for four hours, and at the critical moment the British ammunition failed, and the order was given to cease fire. Instantly, in all the heat of battle, the men brought their muskets down from their shoulders undischarged. Then a gun, captured by the British in the forts, fired its last round. The French column wavered. The British fired their last cartridges in a single volley and counter-attacked with the bayonet; and the French, giving way, retired from the combat. Their casualties numbered 1,600, or 300 more than the whole of the British force engaged. Those of the British did not exceed 171. The operations are memorable, first for the finest example of fire-discipline in the history of the Army, and secondly as the most signal instance of perfect co-operation between Army and Navy. The French forces, both by land and sea, were just double those of the English. If the Army had failed, the men-of-war would have been driven into the jaws of the French fleet; if the Navy had failed, the troops would have been cut off and compelled to surrender from starvation. By working most skilfully and heartily together they held St. Lucia until made safe by reinforcements, and with St. Lucia a harbour which commanded the French naval base at Fort Royal, Martinique.

Operations in America, 1778

At the very end of 1778, a small British force was sent to Georgia to rally the loyalists in the south and to check Americans' raids upon the British territory in Florida. Savannah was taken after a smart little action on 29th December, and to all intent the King's authority was restored in the province. The idea seems to have been, even thus early in the struggle, to retain a hold upon some at least of the Southern Colonies, even if New England and possibly other of the Northern Colonies should be lost. The officer commanding the expedition, General Augustine Prevost,[1] then invaded South Carolina, and after fighting a brisk little action in which, with a cost of only 16 casualties to himself, he dispersed an American force with the loss of 600 men and 7 guns, he pushed forward upon Charleston.

---

[1] On his march from Florida to Georgia, preparatory to this expedition, Prevost had to feed his men for days together upon oysters.

CAPTURE OF SAVANNAH

He was, however, forced to retire by the arrival of d'Estaing with the French fleet and army from the West Indies, where in July they had captured St. Vincent and Grenada; and in September Prevost found himself besieged by the French and Americans in Savannah. On 9th October, d'Estaing assaulted the defences in great force and was defeated with heavy loss, the casualties of his own troops and the Americans numbering 900, whereas Prevost's did not exceed 54. The honours of the day lay with a detachment of the 2nd King's Royal Rifle Corps, who bore the brunt of the action. D'Estaing then sent part of his fleet to the West Indies and the remainder to Europe; and thus, for the second year in succession, the French forces in America accomplished absolutely nothing, while even in the West Indies they had achieved very little.

Spain declares War; Danger at Home, 1779

Elsewhere in America, General Clinton concentrated all his troops about New York, from which he made successful little raids by sea upon American depots; but he could accomplish no more from want of troops. The danger, in fact, was far greater at home than abroad in this year; for in June Spain had seized the moment to declare war against us, and for a few weeks the united fleets of France and Spain were masters of the Channel. Many new regiments were raised, of which one only, the 2nd Black Watch, has survived, and there was great alarm in England; but the danger passed away, not again to recur. It was, however, certain that the Spaniards would try to recover all of their lost possessions, having no other pretext whatever for declaring war; and in fact, in this same year, she began the blockade of Gibraltar which was not finally to be raised until 1782. In the New World her possession of New Orleans was a standing menace to the British garrisons in Florida, and it was only a question of time before she should attack not only them but probably also Jamaica.

Operations in America, 1780

Grievously overmatched, with not nearly enough ships or troops to guard the widely scattered Empire, the English Government, instead of concentrating to hold the really essential stations, decided not only to endeavour to hold all possessions, but even to add to them fresh vulnerable points. Clinton had just men enough to make New York and Canada secure; but the Government determined that his one small army should, moving by sea,

CAPTURE OF CHARLESTON

do the work of two, and ordered him to open the campaign of 1780 by the siege of Charleston in Carolina. His transports were dispersed by a storm, and it may be mentioned, to give an idea of his difficulties, that two of his ships were blown across the Atlantic, one to Falmouth in Cornwall, and the other to Gibraltar. However, on 9th May, Charleston surrendered with its garrison of 6,600 men, having cost Clinton no more than 265 killed and wounded. The war in Carolina then, for a time, took the form of raids and surprises by small bodies of irregular troops, mostly enlisted Americans, the two most prominent of the British leaders being Banastre Tarleton and James Simcoe, the forerunners of such men as Herbert Plumer and Julian Byng in the South African War of 1899–1902. But the menace of a more solid American force demanded in July the presence of a corresponding British military body, which was supplied by 4,000 men, nearly half of them British regular regiments. On 16th August, Lord Cornwallis routed the Americans at Camden, and then, flushed with success, he invaded North Carolina. On 6th October, one of his advanced detachments, 1,100 strong, under Major Ferguson, was surrounded and utterly destroyed by a party of about 1,000 American backwoodsmen—all of them skilled marksmen and without their peers in forest-fighting—and Cornwallis was fain to retreat.

In other spheres of operations little was accomplished in 1780. The Spaniards from New Orleans, in March, captured the little garrison of 300 sickly soldiers which held Mobile, but were driven back by a British squadron before they could take Pensacola. Gibraltar manfully held its own; and for the third consecutive year the French fleet on the American coast proved itself absolutely impotent.

Operations in America, 1781. Yorktown

In November, 1780, two of Cornwallis's irregular detachments sustained serious reverses, and in December he found himself confronted by the American General, Nathaniel Greene, a fine fellow, and a really able fighting soldier. However, having received a small reinforcement from Clinton, he again invaded North Carolina in January, 1781. On the 17th a strong flanking detachment, which he had sent out under Tarleton, was destroyed by the American leader, Morgan, at Cowpens, and thereby his force was reduced by at least one-fourth. However, he continued his advance with 2,300 men, and on the 15th March

BATTLE OF GUILFORD

met 5,000 Americans under Greene, at Guilford. After a very severe action he drove Greene back, but at a cost of at least one-third of his force. A detachment of the three regiments of Guards, 481 of all ranks, lost 206 killed and wounded. Such a victory was no victory, and Cornwallis retreated to his base on the sea at Wilmington. Greene thereupon advanced upon Cornwallis's old line of communications with Charleston, but was checked by Lord Rawdon—the future Earl of Moira and Marquess Hastings—who stood up to him at Hobkirk's Hill with 900 men against 1,200, outmanœuvred him and, after a very sharp little action, beat him back, though at a loss to himself of 270 killed and wounded. Rawdon then retreated upon Charleston, and Greene swallowed up one after another of the posts on the British line of communications. By chance, three British regiments, intended for New York, landed at Charleston in June, and with these Rawdon rescued a certain number of the remaining posts, until sickness forced him to return to England. The command then devolved upon Lieut.-colonel Stuart of the Buffs who, on 8th September, fought a very bloody but indecisive little action against Greene at Eutaw Springs. Stuart had about 1,800 men and Greene about 2,000, and each side lost about 900 killed, wounded and prisoners.

Meanwhile Cornwallis, at the end of April, marched with 1,600 men into Virginia, where he picked up reinforcements from New York which raised his strength to about 7,000 men. He spent a month hunting a mixed force of 5,000 French and Americans under the Marquis de la Fayette, when Clinton received warning that Washington was preparing for a great attack upon New York, and asked Cornwallis to send him back troops immediately. Cornwallis did not obey, and the situation remained confused until the end of August, when the French fleet under Count de Grasse arrived off the coast of Virginia in overwhelming force, and secured, for the time, command of the sea. Cornwallis, though aware of this, neither attacked Lafayette nor retired to Carolina, but fortified himself at Yorktown on the Virginian coast. Clinton was obliged to await naval reinforcements before he could sail to Cornwallis's assistance, and meanwhile Washington marched down by land from before New York to join Lafayette. Their joint forces, 16,000 men, penning Cornwallis into Yorktown, compelled him, on 19th October, to surrender. The French fleet, after three years of failure, had at last, in the fourth year,

Minorca and Gibraltar

The war continued, however, with France and Spain, and also with Holland, which had been ignobly dragged into the quarrel by France. Minorca, after a heroic defence of six months, surrendered in February, 1782, the garrison being reduced at last to 600 starved and sickly men who had hardly the strength to march out and lay down their arms. The 1st K.O.Y.L.I. and 2nd Gloucesters were of this noble garrison, whose courage and endurance make the siege of Minorca for ever memorable. Gibraltar continued to defend itself stoutly, repelling in September a very formidable attack with great loss to the French and Spaniards. In the West Indies, St. Kitts was shamefully surrendered by the planters; but on 12th April, Rodney, based upon St. Lucia, won his great victory over Count de Grasse at the battle of the Saints and saved the whole situation in those seas. But there was yet one more sphere of operations of which we have so far seen nothing, and to which we must now give attention.

THE EMPIRE AND THE ARMY

Operations in India, 1778-1782. Hyder Ali and Tipu Sahib

In India, the Governments of Bengal and Bombay became entangled, partly through French intrigue, in a quarrel with the Mahrattas in 1778; and their troops were fully engaged against this enemy in the field when news came of the French declaration of war. Sir Hector Munro at once advanced from Madras and reduced the whole of the French settlements with little difficulty; but Hyder Ali claimed to be the protector of one of these settlements and invaded British territory with some 90,000 men, of which 15,000 were infantry trained on the European model, and 400 were French soldiers. Owing to Munro's faulty dispositions a detachment of 3,850 men under Colonel Baillie was, in September, 1780, isolated and overwhelmed after a desperate resistance, in which detachments of the 1st Highland L.I. and 1st Dublins covered themselves with glory. Of 86 British officers only 16 were taken unhurt, to suffer a bitter captivity. In alarm, the Madras Government called in the veteran Sir Eyre Coote to take command, but even Coote, owing to the appearance of a French fleet on the coast in February, 1781, was in imminent danger for five long days of seeing his army starve, or being compelled to surrender. Happily, the French fleet sailed away, and Coote, still in a most dangerous situation, attacked Hyder Ali at Porto Novo, on 1st July, 1781, and beat him despite numerical odds of ten to one against him. Twice more he attacked and defeated Hyder at Palilur and Sholinghur, until want of transport, which had crippled him throughout, compelled him in November to retire to Madras. Meanwhile two small expeditions attacked the Dutch settlements and gained the harbour of Trincomalee for the British fleets; but Hyder Ali had not yet been decisively defeated, as he was very soon to prove.

In February, 1782, Hyder Ali succeeded once more in surprising and destroying an isolated detachment of 1,600 Sepoys, as well as in doing other mischief, which Coote, from want of transport and owing to the uncertainty of his communications by sea, was unable to prevent. The campaign of 1782 dragged on with varying fortune but no decision, and at its close Hyder Ali died and Coote resigned his command, to die at Madras a few months later. The French and British fleets on the coast fought action after action without any great advantage to either side; but French troops were landed to the total number of 3,000 infantry, which with 3,000 French Sepoys and 5,000 of Hyder Ali's troops under M. de Bussy were entrenched in a strong position at Gadalur. These were attacked by General Stuart, Coote's successor, on 13th June, 1783, and after a sharp action driven from some of their defences. A naval engagement on the 20th left the French temporarily masters of the sea, and the situation was most perilous, when on the 28th arrived news that peace had been concluded with France. Operations were continued for a year against Tipu Sahib, Hyder Ali's son, until March, 1784, when a treaty was concluded with him upon the basis of a mutual restitution of conquests; and so at length this long and desolating war came to an end.

Under the terms of peace, England granted independence to America; restored St. Lucia and ceded Tobago, Senegal, Goree, St. Pierre and Miquelon to France; and yielded to Spain Minorca and the Floridas; all other captures by either side being restored.

Reflections on the American War

Regarded solely from an European point of view, the American War of Independence was practically a continuation of the Seven Years' War—a counter-attack by France and Spain to redeem the humiliation which they had suffered at the peace of 1763. The American rebellion gave them their opportunity and they seized it.

LOSS OF AMERICAN COLONIES

Without France the Americans would never have won their independence by force. They were not sufficiently in earnest about it. Had they been of one mind, the conquest of three millions of people across 3,000 miles of ocean would have been far beyond the power of England or of any other nation at that time. But, as usual, the colonists were divided; and the war was, in fact, a civil war, in which the American loyalists recruited by the English fought, if anything, better than the American rebels. Yet the action of France was slow. Only in the fourth campaign after her entry into the war, when England had not only France but Spain and Holland upon her back, did the French fleet at last, after many failures, accomplish anything for her allies; and by that time the Americans were at the last gasp. "We are at the end of our tether," wrote Washington in April, 1781, "and now or never our deliverance must come." Nor were the French, even so, the most formidable helpers of the revolted Colonies. Ireland also was in a state of rebellion, and provided the French fleets with the salt provisions without which they could not have gone to sea. The West Indian Islands were disloyal from greed of gain. Most powerful of all was the opposition in Parliament, which left no stone unturned to encourage the rebels and thwart every measure of the Government. In fact, if either the Americans or the British had been united, either could have beaten the other without difficulty. France just, but only just, inclined the balance in favour of the Americans, and she paid for her intervention only seven years later with her ruin.

From a military point of view the fault of the English was excessive dispersion of force in the effort to second the loyalists in too many places. It is nearly always a mistake to invade a hostile country in reliance upon a friendly party within it. Had the English held New York, Quebec, and a post on the Chesapeake, and relied on naval operations only, they might possibly, by harassing the coasting trade of the Colonies, have brought them to reason with much less trouble and expense. The best military authorities in England advocated this course, condemning all military operations as hopeless of ultimate success; and they proved to be right.

Lessons learned in America

For the rest the Army learned many useful lessons in America. Matched against a cunning and elusive enemy, very often in dense forest, they had to rely upon bullet rather than bayonet, and upon the individual initiative and marksmanship of each man rather than on the solid discipline of the company or of the battalion in line. The infantry worked in double rank, so as to gain a greater front of fire, and, except possibly for purposes of parade, seems never to have reverted to triple rank. At the same time greater attention was given to rapidity in loading which, by experts, was carried to extraordinary perfection. Major Ferguson, who fell in action in October, 1780, could load and fire a muzzle-loading rifle eight times in a minute, throwing more than half of his bullets on to a target of the size of a man's head at 100 yards. John Moore, the future general, as a boy of fourteen could load and fire a musket five times in a minute. All this meant speedier consumption of ammunition; and accordingly the soldier's waistbelt was transferred to his right shoulder to carry an additional pouch of cartridges, and the number of rounds borne in the two pouches was raised to fifty-six. But no practical improvement was wrought in the clothing, though some at least of the irregular corps in America had their hair cut short and wore short jackets. Possibly sheer necessity may have forced some of the regular regiments to do likewise, for unpractical clothing is generally thrown off without ceremony on active service. The old spatterdash had already been discarded in favour of black woollen gaiters in 1767; but the uniform coat was still long in the skirt, though more cut away in front. The hat had changed for the worse, being turned up in front and behind instead of on three sides, so that it gave no shade to the eyes nor protection to the neck. One or two small changes however, are worth mentioning, which belong to this period. Hitherto there had been no distinction of dress to mark the various grades of regimental officers. All alike wore the crimson sash round their waists; and there was nothing to mark off the subaltern from the field-officer until 1791, when field-officers were required to wear epaulettes. Serjeants had always worn round the waist a sash of crimson striped with the colour of the regiment's facings; and this remained unchanged. Officers of Grenadiers took to wearing the badge of a grenade upon their epaulettes, and officers of Light Infantry a bugle horn. The bugle had apparently crept into use by imitation of some of the German Jäger (Hunter) regiments in the Seven Years' War, though without official recognition. It was certainly used in St. Lucia in 1778. But, before the epaulette had been introduced by regulation,

STARVATION OF THE ARMY

officers had taken to wearing shoulder-knots of ribbon, which those of the Light Infantry sometimes turned into a fringe. This was the origin of the "wings" later worn by the officers of the flank-companies of all battalions. It is evident that regiments were still very much a law to themselves in all such matters.

The Ten Years of Peace, 1783-1793

The short period that intervened between the American War and that of the French Revolution was one of the most dismal in the history of the Army. The British Empire seemed to have come to an end; the country was overburdened with debt; and there appeared to be little occasion to keep an army at all. The soldier was so miserably paid that he could not keep body and soul together, and the subaltern officers, especially in the cavalry, were even worse off than the men. Something was done for the relief of the soldiers, but nothing for the officers. Yet improvements of one kind or another went forward all through this interval. The last of the old regiments of Horse were turned into the 1st, 2nd, 3rd and 4th Dragoon Guards in 1788; the Life Guards were changed from odd troops to two regiments in the same year; and the Light Dragoons, between 1775 and 1783, were augmented from three regiments to eleven by the conversion of the 7th, 8th, 9th, 10th, 11th, 12th and 13th Dragoons into Light Dragoons, which henceforth were uniformly clothed in blue. More important was the introduction, in 1792, of an uniform drill-book for the whole Army, and of regulation bugle-calls (composed by the great master, Joseph Haydn) a year or two later. The Royal Engineers, a corps consisting of officers only, was reorganized as such in 1787. The two first troops of Horse Artillery were formed in 1793; and still earlier, in 1787, the 2nd Highland L.I., 1st Gordon Highlanders, 2nd Duke's and 2nd Middlesex had been called into existence for the urgent needs of India. So, after all, it appeared that the Empire had not quite come to an end, and we must see what was this new trouble in India.

The War in Mysore. The First Capture of Seringapatam, 1792

It was, in fact, renewed aggression by Tipu Sahib of Mysore who, stimulated to mischief by the French, had attacked an ally of the British in Southern India. After a preliminary campaign for the capture of Tipu's frontier fortresses in 1790, Lord Cornwallis, the Governor-General, took the field in person in 1791, and invaded Mysore. On the 21st March, he

CORNWALLIS AT SERINGAPATAM

took Bangalore by assault and marched upon Seringapatam, but was foiled by lack of transport and of forage; Tipu's light horse hovering all round him, burning all the country ahead of him, and pouncing remorselessly upon any small party or broken-down wagons. Cornwallis, with great difficulty, advanced within nine miles of Seringapatam, and there fought an action which, he hoped, would make an end of Tipu's army; but the stroke failed, chiefly owing to a violent thunderstorm, and he was compelled to destroy his siege-train and retreat with his army in a state of starvation to Bangalore. From thence he was able to take by storm three of Tipu's most formidable fortresses to secure his line of communication in the next campaign, and in January, 1792, he again moved upon Seringapatam from the side of Madras with 22,000 men, while General Robert Abercromby, with 9,000 more, marched upon it from the side of Bombay. Once again Tipu burned every human dwelling on the line of the advance; but, on the 6th February, Cornwallis attacked him in an entrenched position before Seringapatam, and after thirty-six hours of sharp fighting defeated him utterly and compelled him to sue for peace. This was not yet the last of Tipu, for in due time we shall record the second and final capture of Seringapatam.

CHAPTER VIII

THE WAR OF THE FRENCH REVOLUTION

THE news of peace restored in India had not long reached England before Europe was again plunged into war. In France the cost of the American War had, among other causes, brought about financial difficulties which had ended in the overthrow of the established Government and to the transfer of power to theorists, fanatics, and even to downright rogues. Their mismanagement had reduced the country to chaos, bankruptcy and starvation; and in the autumn of 1792 the reigning faction decided to sally forth to the plunder of their neighbours. They invaded the Austrian Netherlands—Belgium—with an eye, above all, to an attack upon Holland and the plunder of the Bank of Amsterdam. The Government of the Dutch Netherlands had reached the last stage of inefficiency and impotence; and Austria, though concerned for the defence of her territory in the Netherlands, was distracted by a revolution in Poland, which interested not only her, but also her rivals, Prussia and Russia, very much more in Eastern than in Western Europe. This diversion in Poland was, in fact, the salvation of revolutionary France, for it left her very soon, as shall be seen, with only a single formidable enemy, England, to westward.

The Younger Pitt's Military Policy

England is always rightly nervous as to the control of the navigation of the Scheldt by a strong naval power, and she was pledged by treaty to keep it in the hands of the Dutch and to maintain Austria in the possession of Belgium. In January, 1793, the British Government severed diplomatic relations with France, and France responded at once by declaring war upon England and Holland. The military impotence of England at the moment was extreme. Owing to the miserable pay granted to the soldier, all regiments were below strength; and, after providing for foreign garrisons and for Ireland, which was in a state of veiled rebellion, there were not more than 15,000 regular troops available to defend and maintain order in Great Britain and the Channel Islands, to man the fleet, and to undertake any offensive operations that might be projected. William Pitt, who was then Prime Minister, was persuaded that a country in such financial difficulties as France could not long maintain a war, and that the best method of reducing her to submission was to capture her possessions in the West Indies and so destroy all of her colonial trade. This task promised to be the easier, since the French Revolutionary Government had proclaimed the equality of black men with white, with the result that the blacks had risen against the whites, and the whites were prepared to welcome anyone who would restore to them their property and their dominance. Moreover, the mastery of all French possessions in the West Indies promised not only the transfer of their wealth to England, but also much relief to the British Navy in its task of protecting British commerce. It was to the West Indies, then, that Pitt designed to direct such military strength as England possessed, ignoring the fact that in that climate, as has already been mentioned, two years' service, even in time of peace, was sufficient to destroy a battalion.

Operations in the Low Countries, 1793

But, meanwhile, the Dutch showed such helplessness and apathy in their own defence, that in March a brigade of Guards and three battalions of the line were hastily sent over to Holland under the Duke of York. The Austrians were already assembling on the French frontier under Prince Josias of Coburg-Saalfeld; and after much haggling it was agreed that this tiny British force, together with a contingent of Hanoverians and hired Hessians, which were also placed under the Duke of York, should act with the Austrians, on condition that the capture of Dunkirk should be effected as soon as possible, and that the fortress should be handed over to England.

The campaign opened in May, two brigades of British Light Dragoons joining the Duke of York soon afterwards; and, after some feeble preliminary operations, Valenciennes was besieged and taken. The only brilliant little action came on the 18th August, when the brigade of Guards under Colonel Gerard Lake, no more than 1,100 strong, attacked 5,000 French in a fortified position, at Linselles, routed them and captured 12 guns. The Duke of York then moved down to the siege of Dunkirk, in itself an utterly unprofitable operation, found that the Government had provided him with no naval assistance, and, after striving for three weeks to cope with greatly superior numbers, was compelled to abandon his siege-train, and to make a very dangerous retreat, having suffered a loss of 10,000 men. Nothing material was accomplished during the remainder of the campaign, owing to this squandering of strength upon a useless object.

Toulon, 1793

Meanwhile, a counter-revolution in the South of France had, in August, thrown Toulon into the hands of the British fleet; and four battalions, being part of the fleet's complement, were landed there to hold the place with the help of Spanish and other foreign troops. In October these were reinforced by two more British battalions; but meanwhile a young artillery officer, named Napoleon Bonaparte, had come upon the scene. The perimeter of the defences was far too great for the small numbers of the British and their Allies to hold with security. The French, steadily reinforced to greatly superior strength, pressed them harder and harder, and in December the British fleet and army evacuated Toulon, having suffered considerable loss.

The West Indies, 1794

Owing to dispersion of force. therefore, nothing was accomplished in Europe in 1793; and the expedition to the West Indies, having been detained for a time owing to the serious situation created by the failure before Dunkirk,

WEST INDIAN CONQUESTS

did not sail until the end of November, two months too late. But in that quarter, too, the British had undertaken a new and unexpected task, for the French planters at Haiti had invited the Governor of Jamaica to send troops to take possession of the French Colony; and the Governor, in September, had dispatched 700 men of his weak garrison, which would, of course, need to be reinforced. The expedition from England, under General Grey and Admiral Sir John Jervis was, however, designed to take the French islands to windward, and, in February, 1794, it attacked Martinique. The troops, some 7,000 strong, were the cream of the Army. The two chiefs, both of them very able men, were on most affectionate terms; and the Fleet and the Army worked heartily together. Martinique fell after a month of skilled operations; St. Lucia was taken with little difficulty in two days; Guadeloupe was mastered by the end of May; and four battalions of the force were then sent to leeward to reinforce Haiti. All had gone as well as possible; but here were four new garrisons to be supplied in a very deadly climate.

Corsica, 1794

Yet the British Government never dreamed of reducing the number of its spheres of operations. The troops at Toulon were at once moved to Corsica, whither they had been invited by a section of the inhabitants. The operations, owing to dissensions between Admiral Lord Hood, who wished to direct everything himself, and the military commanders, did not prosper until May, 1794, when General Charles Stuart arrived from England, put an end by tact and firmness to the friction between the two services, and by equal ability and energy mastered every stronghold held by the French in Corsica. His chief assistants were Captain Horatio Nelson of the Navy, and Colonel John Moore of the Army; but his success was all his own, and the powers that he manifested were sufficient to prove that England possessed at least one general of the first rank.

Corsica signified the absorption of yet more British troops in an isolated garrison; but the Government was none the less bent on prosecuting the campaign in the Lower Countries. New regular regiments had been raised in 1793; the 2nd Seaforth Highlanders, the Cameron Highlanders, the 2nd South Stafford, the 2nd North Lancs, the 2nd South Lancs, 1st and 2nd Royal Ulster Rifles, the 2nd York and Lancaster, the 2nd Shropshire L.I., the 1st and 2nd Royal Irish Fusiliers and the 1st Connaught Rangers, being all of them survivors of that year. Moreover, the two first Horse Artillery batteries, with their own trained drivers, had actually come into being; and, lastly, there was formed a corps of wagoners, rather over 600 strong in all ranks. This latter was the first attempt at a military organization of the transport-service, and though it was a failure (for the men were drawn from so bad a class that they were known as the "Newgate Blues"), it has an interest as the first forerunner of the Army Service Corps.

In the course of 1794 there were added, among other regiments which have not survived, the 2nd Scottish Rifles, the 1st Argyll and Sutherland Highlanders, the 2nd Gordon Highlanders and the 2nd Connaught Rangers, the last named being formed of Scots from the Dutch service.

The Low Countries, 1794

Unfortunately, in its main effort to gain recruits, the Government resorted to the vicious system of the elder Pitt, offering commissions of all grades, from lieutenant-colonel to ensign, to any who would produce a given number of men. The result was to stimulate a wild speculative traffic in recruits, to elevate actual schoolboys to the rank of lieutenant-colonel, and to fill the Army with the half-witted, the immature and the decrepit. These, however, took no share in the earlier part of the campaign of 1794, which was distinguished at the outset by some great cavalry actions. On 24th April, the 15th Hussars and a single regiment of Austrian hussars swept away 1,000 French cavalry and 3,000 French infantry at Villers-en-Cauchies. On the 26th, at Beaumont, near Le Cateau, six Austrian and twelve British squadrons attacked and utterly dispersed 20,000 French infantry, capturing 22 guns; and on the same day, in another part of the field, two Austrian and four British squadrons broke into another column of French infantry and captured 10 guns.

On the 10th of May, 22 squadrons of British and two of Austrian cavalry charged into three French squares, killed or captured 1,500 men and took 13 guns. But in a pitched battle near Tourcoing, on the 17th–18th May, the Austrian Commander deliberately left the Duke of York's troops in isolation; and only with great difficulty could they make good their retreat with the loss of 26 guns. Having contrived this reverse as an excuse for withdrawing from the Netherlands, the Austrians presently departed to look after Poland; and the Duke of York, reinforced by 18 British battalions of newly-raised men to a strength of about 40,000, was left to keep 150,000 French out of Holland if he could. Naturally he failed. The army was obliged to retreat in the depth of an Arctic winter to the Ems. With the bad class of officer and man lately acquired, all discipline broke down; and only the wreck of the force was, early in 1795, re-embarked in the Ems for England. It was the most disastrous European campaign in the history of the Army. Not only were the troops raw and of poor quality, but every department was defective. The guns with their carriages and equipment were obsolete; the transport arrangements were faulty, and the medical arrangements simply infamous. This, it may be noted, was the first campaign in which Colonel Arthur Wellesley took part, in command of the 33rd (1st Duke's); and he made note of it as an example of the way in which things should not be done.

Operations in the West Indies, 1794-1798

In the West Indies matters went fully as ill. Not a man was sent to Grey to make good his casualties in action and through sickness, not a scrap of stores, not a shred of clothing, not a pair of shoes. French agents stirred up the negroes in all quarters to revolt. The troops, much reduced in numbers by the climate, wore out their remaining strength in the effort to meet them. Guadeloupe was lost in September, 1794; the British islands of St. Vincent and Grenada were practically mastered by the negroes early in 1795; and St. Lucia was evacuated in May. A driblet of reinforcements, sent out in the spring of 1795, was too weak to recover the lost territory; and this was only accomplished with some difficulty by a fresh expedition of some 18,000 thoroughly bad troops under Sir Ralph Abercromby in 1796. As to Haiti, it simply devoured soldiers as fast as they were poured into it. Year after year operations were undertaken and carried gallantly forward during the cool months; and year after year the troops were destroyed by yellow fever and left impotent during the hot season. But the British Government was still insatiable of West Indian Islands; and, in 1797, Abercromby was sent out again, this time to attack Spanish possessions, for Spain had since August, 1796, leagued herself with France against England. He captured Trinidad with little trouble, but could effect no more, for most of the troops on the spot, which he was expected to use, were dead. At last, in 1798, General Thomas Maitland had the great moral courage to evacuate Haiti; and so at last England was delivered from

CAPTURE OF THE CAPE

West Indian operations. They had cost her probably not far short of 100,000 men of the Army and Navy; had done France no material injury, and had brought England nothing but St. Lucia, Martinique and Trinidad—additional garrisons which might be counted on to destroy at least 1,000 soldiers a year through yellow fever.

Events in Europe, 1795-1797

In Europe, throughout this time, the British military efforts after the evacuation of the Low Countries were as futile as abroad. There were foolish little raids upon the French coast in 1795, which failed altogether of their object. One of these, to the Isle d'Yeu, off the Atlantic shore, was positively criminal in its absurdity and recklessness, and should have brought the responsible Minister to impeachment. Corsica proved to be a hornets' nest and was evacuated. In fact, practically nothing to the serious injury of the French was accomplished in any quarter, if we except the capture of the Cape of Good Hope in 1795, a little enterprise which is interesting chiefly as an example of the difficulty of executing even the smallest operation without land-transport.

And, meanwhile, a great general had risen up among the French in the person of Napoleon

Bonaparte, who after a succession of victories against the Austrians in Italy had forced them to conclude, in April, 1797, a treaty which made over Belgium and a great part of Italy to France, and left England to continue the struggle alone. A bad year for England was 1797. There was a mutiny in the fleet; there was an acute financial crisis in the City; and Pitt was so much dismayed by the general outlook that he tried, though unsuccessfully, to obtain a respectable peace with France by offering to her corrupt rulers a bribe of £450,000. The only consolation for all these disasters was Sir John Jervis's naval victory off Cape St. Vincent on the 14th of February, a great action in which the 2nd Welch took a prominent part. A private of that regiment was the first man to board the Spanish ship *San Nicolas* from the British ship *Captain*, taking precedence of Horatio Nelson himself. The only promise for the future lay in a tiny body of 2,000 British and 4,000 foreign troops sent to Lisbon in June to protect it against the Spaniards who, under French influence, were striving to induce Portugal to close her ports to the British. This, owing to the squandering of her military resources upon secondary objects, was actually England's only striking force; and two-thirds of it—the foreign

BATTLE OF THE NILE

troops—were, from mismanagement and indiscipline, practically worthless. But the man appointed to command them was Sir Charles Stuart, and he very quickly made good soldiers of them.

Operations in the Mediterranean, 1798

The year 1798 opened a little better than 1797. A ridiculous little raid upon the coast of Holland resulted in the capture of the whole of the 1,200 soldiers employed in it. A rebellion in Ireland followed, and a tiny column of French regular troops, which was landed there in August, met with initial successes which were most disgraceful to the English name,[1] before it was overwhelmed by superior numbers. The rebellion was suppressed, and meanwhile the tide began to turn. The rulers of France, anxious to get rid of so dangerous a rival as Napoleon Bonaparte, sent him off in command of an army to Egypt. He captured Malta on the way and made an easy conquest of Egypt; but Nelson followed him, and catching his escorting fleet at anchor in Aboukir Bay, on 1st August, annihilated it. Thus Napoleon's army was cut off from France, and could be dealt with as an isolated body at leisure. The victory was of transcendent

[1] The old 5th Dragoons was disbanded for misconduct and its name left blank on the Army List as a perpetual reproach.

importance at the moment, for all Italy, owing to oppression of the French, was ready to rise against them, while the capture of Malta by Napoleon had excited the hostility of the Tsar of Russia towards France. The Court of Naples, at the instigation of Nelson, declared war against France prematurely and was at once driven by French troops out of the mainland of Italy into Sicily. Almost at the same time General Charles Stuart embarked four British battalions from Lisbon and Gibraltar for Minorca, and by sheer skill and magnificent "bluff" cowed the Spanish commander into surrender. As Stuart had not above 3,000 men and had only six light field-guns, whereas the Spanish garrison numbered 3,600 within powerful fortifications, his performance may be accounted one of the most astounding pieces of audacity in the history of the Army.

British soldiers were not fond of digging in those days, but under the magical impulse of Stuart's personality they soon made Minorca nearly impregnable against recapture; and then Nelson appealed to him for a couple of British battalions to secure Sicily. Stuart embarked them at once and sailed with them to Palermo, where he landed on the 10th March, 1799. Within forty-eight hours he had the whole population at his feet. He also drew up a skilful plan for the defence of Sicily by its own peasantry, and pointed out to the British Government the advantages of Sicily as a base from which to operate against the French upon either coast of Italy. He then visited Malta, which was under blockade by a British squadron, and in May sailed for England with his health utterly broken down by hard work. He had done more to shape a sound military policy for England in six weeks than the British Cabinet had accomplished in six years.

The Expedition to North Holland, 1799

Meanwhile a new Coalition against France had been formed by England, Austria, Russia and Turkey; and all that England needed was a striking force. The Government, instead of turning the manhood of England to account by passing it through the Militia, had frittered it away into endless independent corps of fencibles (regulars enlisted for home-service only), yeomanry and volunteers, the last named being of no military value; while the rest, excepting the yeomanry, simply competed with the regular army for recruits. However, there was now no danger of invasion, and it was resolved to offer militiamen a bounty to join the regulars. In this way the regular battalions were filled up with good men; and it was determined to send 30,000 British to operate in conjunction with 40,000 Russians for the recapture of Holland. The Government had no information whatever about Holland, and they expected their general to dispense with such a thing as land-transport. However, after making strong protests, Sir Ralph Abercromby sailed with 12,000 men for the Dutch coast, and forced a landing a little to the south of Helder on the 27th of August. This was the second important disembarkation in the face of an enemy in our history and, though successful, taught many lessons for such an operation in future.

Immediately after the landing, the Dutch evacuated Helder, which gave the British a safe port and base for the rest of the campaign, and Abercromby took up a strong position among the dykes (for this part of the country is all land reclaimed from the sea) to cover it. Here he was attacked, on the 10th September, by the French in force, but repulsed them with a loss of 2,000 killed, wounded and prisoners, his own casualties little exceeding 200. The Lancashire Fusiliers were greatly distinguished in this action.

A few days later the rest of the army appeared, under the supreme command of the Duke of York; and, 12,000 Russians having

EVACUATION OF NORTH HOLLAND

also arrived, a general attack was made, on 19th September, upon the French, who had taken full advantage of a strong position offered by the dykes. The Russians having little training or discipline, and the British battalions not having had time to assimilate their militiamen, the operation failed. Another attack on 2nd October gained a little ground, and the success is commemorated under the name of Egmont op Zee. On 6th October a small isolated movement brought on a third confused general action, which ended decidedly to the advantage of the French. The Duke of York then retreated and was thankful to re-embark for England under a capitulation, his army having come to the end of its supplies. The campaign had cost about 10,000 casualties; and in a country where movement was impossible except along causeways, progress against a resolute enemy, except with enormous superiority of numbers, was hopeless. The Government had once more chosen the wrong theatre of war for its army, and had moreover so contrived matters that the troops arrived there first, then their supplies, and last of all their transport.

However, this campaign in North Holland brought into existence a new Wagon-Train of 600 men and 514 horses, though it landed too late to be of service. The Horse Artillery also came into action for the first time, and the Chestnut battery received its baptism of fire. The new Army—for it was nothing less —had come into existence. The Duke of York, appointed Commander-in-Chief in 1795, was beginning to collect an effective Staff at Headquarters, to reduce chaos to order, and to restore discipline; and there was at least some prospect that British troops might intervene effectively in the war in Europe.

India. The Final Capture of Seringapatam

Meanwhile French emissaries had stirred up Tipu Sahib to fresh enmity in India, and it had been necessary, in 1798, to reinforce the troops there with one of Charles Stuart's battalions from Lisbon and two more from the Cape. Accordingly, in March, 1799, 33,000 troops, of which 5,000 were European and 6,000 irregular cavalry, advanced upon Seringapatam from the side of Madras under General Harris, while 6,000 men, of which about 2,000 were European, under General James Stuart, moved from the side of Bombay. Harris's army, encumbered by a vast number of followers, marched in a hollow square three miles broad by seven miles deep, taking a zigzag route so that Tipu's cavalry, deceived as to its direction, might not destroy all the forage on the way. With enormous difficulty it reached Seringapatam, and after a week of preliminary siege-operations, stormed the great fortress on the 4th of May. Tipu was slain, his dynasty was brought to an end; and there was no more trouble with Mysore. It may be mentioned that Colonel Arthur Wellesley commanded a division of Harris's army and was left to restore order and put down gangs of banditti in Mysore, which he very effectually did; also that the assaulting column was led by Colonel David Baird, who had been taken prisoner by Tipu with Baillie's detachment in 1780, and had shared also in Cornwallis's successful advance against Seringapatam in 1792.

The Great Opportunities Lost in 1800

This same year, 1799, brought about a vital change in the fortunes of France. Napoleon managed to evade the British cruisers and return to Paris where, in November, he overthrew the existing Government and became himself sole ruler with the title of First Consul. Russia also had quarrelled with Austria and withdrawn from the Coalition, but her General, Suvorof, had gained great successes against the French in Italy, and the Austrians were confident of driving the French out of Italy in 1800. Charles Stuart proposed the concentration of 20,000 men at Minorca, from which they could operate against the flank of the French on the Riviera while the Austrians attacked them in front; and, had his advice been followed, the career of Napoleon might have been ended in 1800. As things fell out, the British Government frittered away its force in meaningless and futile operations on the French Atlantic coast during the time when its intervention might have been decisive, and finally divided their 20,000 men into two parts, with the idea of attacking Cadiz and Ferrol. And meanwhile Napoleon crossed the Alps, won the battle of Marengo on the 14th June, restored the whole situation of the French in Italy, conciliated Russia and Spain, and came to terms with Austria. The British Government had lost a great opportunity, with the less excuse since Charles Stuart had pointed out to them what they should have done. He resigned his command in the Mediterranean in disgust upon the rejection of his plans, and died shortly afterwards. His name is little known in the Army, but he was the only one of our Generals besides Marlborough who combined great general ability with profound military knowledge, irresistible personal charm, and magic of leadership. The organization of such little forces as were entrusted to him was sought out in every detail as a model by the Duke of York, and, had Stuart lived, he would have been fully competent to do the work afterwards done by Wellington.

The First Rifle

The year 1800, therefore, passed disgracefully away. There was nothing to show for it but the fall of Malta in September, after a year's blockade. However, the 2nd Argyll and Sutherland Highlanders were raised; and in January was introduced the first rifle—a straight-grooved weapon. This led to the formation of an experimental corps of riflemen which began life as the 95th, but is now known as the Rifle Brigade. They were not quite the first riflemen in the Army, for in 1797 a 5th battalion of foreigners, armed with rifles, had been added to the 60th (now King's Royal Rifle Corps); but these had at first been designed for service in America only, though they found their way to Ireland during the rebellion of 1798. This battalion was from the first clothed in green, as also was the new 95th, green being the accepted colour for gamekeepers employed in forests, who were the model for riflemen.

The Campaign in Egypt, 1801

Late in 1800 the Government bethought themselves of the isolated French Army in Egypt and ordered Sir Ralph Abercromby to embark 16,000 men in the Mediterranean to attack them. They also summoned a small force from India to co-operate by way of the Red Sea. Concentrating at Malta, Abercromby sailed to Marmaras Bay on the coast of Asia Minor, and there very carefully trained his force to the work of disembarkation, so that all battalions might land complete, and form line with the least possible disorder. He then sailed to Aboukir Bay; and on the 8th March, 1801, the troops in flat-bottomed boats were rowed by blue-jackets under a cross-fire of artillery to the beach, where they formed up steadily. Sir John Moore at once led three battalions against a sandhill which was the key of the position and stormed it out of hand. The French Commander, through neglect or misapprehension, had stationed only 1,600 infantry, 200 cavalry and 15 guns to oppose the landing; and, though the cavalry gave some trouble, they were beaten off by the 1st Black Watch who, though they had lost heavily in the boats, were perfectly formed almost as soon as they stepped on the beach. Thus the disembarkation was very quickly accomplished at a cost of no

BATTLE OF ABOUKIR

more than 650 casualties, of which over 170 fell on the 1st Black Watch and 97 on the Coldstream Guards. This is the classical model of a landing in face of an enemy, which was not forgotten at the Dardanelles in 1915.

The French now concentrated 5,000 men with 21 guns to oppose the British advance along the narrow peninsula which leads from Aboukir to Alexandria; their inferiority in numbers being in part made good by the fact that they had cavalry and horses to draw their guns, whereas Abercromby had no mounted troops, while his cannon were painfully dragged through the sand by seamen. On 13th March he thrust the French back with a loss of 500 men and 3 guns, but at a cost of 1,300 casualties to himself; and then, being totally ignorant of the full strength of the enemy in Egypt, Abercromby entrenched himself about two miles from a French fortified position which covered Alexandria. There, on the 21st March, the French attacked him with 10,000 men and 41 guns, and after a hard and well-fought action were utterly defeated. They left 1,000 dead and 600 wounded on the field, and their total loss must have been at least 4,000. Their prisoners, some of them veterans of Napoleon's army of Italy, declared that they had never known the meaning of a fight and of musketry fire before. The British casualties numbered 1,473; and it was in this action that the 1st Gloucesters, facing their rear rank about to meet attacks in front and rear, won the privilege of wearing their number (28th) on both back and front of their head-dress. The Scots Guards had 200 casualties, and a regiment of Minorquins, which Charles Stuart had taken over as a rabble and turned into soldiers, behaved superbly, losing 13 officers and over 200 men. But the heroes of the campaign were the 1st Black Watch who, out of a total strength of 800, lost in the three actions 23 officers and 481 men killed and wounded, and were never beaten.

Abercromby was mortally wounded in this decisive action and thus honourably ended a fine and patriotic career. His place was taken by General Hutchinson, who had little difficulty in reducing the remainder of the French in Egypt to surrender. They had managed their affairs badly, for they had numbered 25,000 when Abercromby landed, and had allowed themselves to be beaten in detail by 17,000. Immediately afterwards, Baird's contingent from India appeared on the Nile, having marched 100 miles across the desert from the Red Sea. They arrived too late to take any share in the operations: but the occasion is

BATTLE OF ABOUKIR

memorable, which brought troops from the two great British military bases—the British Isles and India—to meet together in a theatre of war midway between them.

All combatants being now thoroughly exhausted, a truce was patched up in 1801, which is known as the Peace of Amiens.

CHAPTER IX

THE MAHRATTA WAR IN INDIA

The War of the French Empire, 1803-1814

NAPOLEON had little thought of preserving peace. In 1802 he sent an emissary to make trouble in India; and French officers in the service of the Mahrattas threatened to revive the old French rivalry in that country. After long forbearance, Lord Mornington, the Governor-General, declared war upon the Mahrattas, and in August, 1803, sent two armies against them under his brother General Arthur Wellesley in the south, and under General Gerard Lake in the north. Wellesley began by storming the fortress of Ahmednagar to give himself an advanced base. Then moving forward he came, on 23rd September, upon the army of the Mahrattas, drawn up in order of battle near the village of Assaye, with one stream in their front, another in their rear, and their left flank near the junction of the two waters. Never supposing that the Mahrattas would have the tactical skill to change position, Wellesley forded the water to attack

ASSAYE AND ARGAUM

their left flank, only to find himself confronted by the entire Mahratta host, some 18,000 infantry, trained by Europeans, 15,000 to 20,000 irregular cavalry, and over 100 guns served by trained artillery-men. He himself had 7,000 men, of which 2,000 were British infantry, and 400 British cavalry of the Company's service (now the 19th Hussars) with 14 guns; but he had committed himself so far that he could not draw back. The course of the battle was critical, for a grave blunder was made by one of his subordinates; but his British regiments saved him, and the battle ended in a complete victory for Wellesley and the capture of 98 guns. His casualties numbered nearly 1,500; and the heroes of the action were the 2nd Highland L.I., who lost every one of their 17 officers killed or wounded, and 384 men out of 550. Never did any regiment behave more nobly. A second and far less severe action at Argaum, on 29th November, continued the discomfiture of the Mahrattas, and the capture by assault of the fortress of Gawilghur, on 15th December, brought Wellesley's adversary to sue for peace.

In the north, Lake took the field in August with nine regiments of horse, of which three were British, 14 battalions of foot, of which the 2nd Duke's only was British, and 65 light guns. First he stormed the fortress of Aligarh on 3rd September; and then on 10th September, with 4,500 men, he attacked 19,000 Mahrattas under a French leader near Delhi, defeated them with great loss and captured 68 guns. Following up the remaining forces of the Mahrattas, he overtook them after a march of 25 miles at Laswari, on 1st November, and fell upon them at once with the 2nd Duke's, four battalions of Sepoys and one regiment of British cavalry, the enemy having 17 trained native battalions, 4,000 or 5,000 horse and 72 guns. The action was very severe and at the crisis of the battle Lake's horse was shot under him. His son, who was his aide-de-camp, gave him his own horse, and had hardly done so before he was wounded, to all appearance mortally, before his father's eyes. For one moment Lake hesitated, then turned his horse away and, resuming the direction of the fight, overthrew the Mahrattas utterly. The enemy fought with desperation to the last, and at the close of the combat nothing remained of the 17 battalions but 2,000 prisoners, while every Mahratta gun was captured. Lake's casualties numbered 824, the 2nd Duke's being the regiment that suffered most. In the three affairs of Aligarh, Delhi and Laswari they had lost 18 officers and 428 men killed and wounded, and were still unconquerable.

DEIG AND BHURTPORE

Lake, in 1804, turned against the Mahratta chief Holkar, sending a detachment of five and a half Indian battalions upon an extremely hazardous expedition, which returned discomfited with the loss of half of its numbers. This reverse undid the effect of Lake's previous successes and compelled him to take up the pursuit of Holkar in person. After extraordinary marching he succeeded in surprising and dispersing Holkar's cavalry with great slaughter on 17th November. Four days earlier, on 13th November, General Fraser with 6,000 men attacked Holkar's infantry before Deig, advancing through a cross-fire of batteries, posted one behind the other, for a distance of 2,500 yards, utterly defeating the 14,000 Mahratta infantry and capturing 87 guns. Fraser was mortally wounded early in the action by a cannon shot, but Colonel Monson, taking his place, by sheer personal courage gained the victory, the 2nd Duke's once again doing most of the work and losing 162 killed and wounded. The fortress of Deig was then, after a few days' cannonade, assaulted and taken by storm at a cost of 220 casualties, on Christmas Day, 1804.

Lake then turned upon the Raja of Bharatpur (Bhurtpore), who had seconded Holkar, and tried to master the very powerful fortress of that name by such primitive methods as he could devise. He had not nearly men enough to invest it, for its perimeter was of eight miles, and he could not batter a proper breach in the wall, which was of immense thickness and height, because it was built of mud and simply crumbled into loose dust under the stroke of shot instead of falling to ruin like a wall of masonry. Four several assaults did Lake deliver at various points within seven weeks, all of them unsuccessful; and then, having lost 3,000 killed and wounded, he came at last to the conclusion, which he should have reached at first, that he had neither men enough nor guns enough for the task. However, he now took the field against Holkar with his cavalry only and hunted him with indefatigable persistence till, in December, he dictated to him his own terms. He and Wellesley had in great measure broken the power of the Mahrattas.

The Campaign in Ceylon, 1803

While these important operations were going forward in India there had been trouble also in Ceylon, where the Kandyans in the mountainous centre of the island were perpetually threatening the European settlements on the plain. A small expedition of about 3,000 men accordingly marched up to Kandy, in February,

1803, meeting with little resistance for the Kandyans were miserable cowards, but with enormous difficulties, owing to the ruggedness of the country and the prevalence of jungle-fever. Kandy was taken and occupied; but the garrison's communications were soon cut off, and after repelling an attack the commandant agreed to evacuate the city under a capitulation. The Kandyans violated the agreement, attacked the garrison as it marched away, and virtually annihilated it. It was impossible at once to avenge this treachery, for epidemic sickness had destroyed the greater number of the troops, both British and native, in Ceylon, and few could be spared from India. So the subjugation of Kandy was remitted to future years, though it came in due time.

Operations in the West Indies

At home, the peace was broken by Napoleon's persistent ignoring of past treaties, and in May, 1803, England declared war against France. Addington, who had succeeded Pitt as Prime Minister in 1801, had no idea of changing Pitt's military policy; and since the West Indian garrisons were strong, he employed a part of them to capture St. Lucia, Tobago and Dutch Guiana. This was easily accomplished, and thus garrisons in sickly stations were multiplied. But Napoleon now made ostentatious preparations for an invasion of England, and the Government had to organize the manhood of the country for its defence. In doing so they made every mistake that they possibly could, producing such a confusion of different conditions of service for volunteers and militia and regular soldiers that Pitt lost patience, displaced Addington, and came into office again in May, 1804. His measures for strengthening the Army were as futile as Addington's; but he formed a new coalition of Russia, Austria, Sweden and England against France.

In February, 1805, Napoleon, as part of a general scheme to distract the British Government, sent an expedition to the West Indies which attacked Dominica. The little garrison, less than 1,000 strong, made a most spirited defence, 300 men of the 2nd Cornwalls setting a fine example; and Dominica was saved. The French armament accomplished nothing more in the West Indies, and in September Napoleon broke up the camps which he had formed for the invasion of England and marched eastward for the Danube.

Operations in Europe

One thing had at least been done for the British Army in England while she stood on the defensive. Sir John Moore had trained a brigade consisting of the 1st and 2nd Oxfordshire L.I., and the Rifle Brigade to the work of light infantry, and introduced a new regimental system into those battalions. Every captain was to educate his company, officers as well as men, and thus these battalions were not to be dependent, as British battalions always had been and for the best part of a century were still to be, on the excellence or worthlessness of their colonels, but were to maintain their high standard in despite, if necessary, of their commanding officers. This was a novelty in the British Army.

England was now in a position to take the offensive if she could produce a striking force. Up to the year 1804 she had done no more than send a small detachment of about 7,000 men to the Mediterranean, whose commander, Sir James Craig, after many wanderings, finally deposited it at Naples in October, 1805. The Mediterranean was the quarter, as Charles Stuart had repeatedly pointed out, where the British could act most effectively; and the way was cleared for them by the destruction of the naval power of France and Spain by Nelson at Trafalgar on the 21st October, 1805. But Napoleon was making rapid progress against his enemies in South Germany.

An army of 30,000 Austrians had surrendered to him at Ulm on 20th October, and he was pressing on to meet the Russians. Hanover had been made over by him to Prussia; and the British Government, with some idea of recovering it, or of attacking Holland, sent 25,000 troops to the Weser, found that they could do nothing there, and brought them back again. With them, however, came the officers and men of the Hanoverian Army, which entered the British service as the King's German Legion. Their cavalry was excellent, their infantry and artillery were very good, and altogether they were a welcome reinforcement of some 14,000 fine soldiers.

The Cape and Buenos Ayres

But in 1805 yet another British expedition of 6,000 men had been sent, under Sir David Baird, to recapture the Cape of Good Hope and secure the way to India. This Baird effected after a little action which cost him about 200 casualties, receiving the surrender of the Colony on 18th January, 1806. He was then persuaded by Sir Home Popham, the Commodore of the squadron which accompanied him, to spare his own regiment, the 1st Highland L.I., for a filibustering expedition against the Spanish Colony on Rio de la Plata. With these, a few dragoons and four guns, Popham sailed away, picked up a few troops at St. Helena, and landing them with a few seamen and marines—in all, 1,500 men—near Buenos Ayres, marched against the city, dispersed some raw levies which came out to meet him, received the surrender of the place, and left his one regiment there to hold it. As Buenos Ayres was already a thriving town of 70,000 inhabitants it was not likely to sit quiet for long under the domination of 800 British soldiers; and Popham was, in fact, guilty of a criminal imbecility which, as shall be seen, did infinite mischief.

Operations in the Mediterranean

In December, 1805, Napoleon utterly defeated the Russians at Austerlitz, and Austria made a separate peace, recognizing him as King of Italy. Napoleon then declared the Bourbon King of Naples to be dethroned, ordered one of his armies to enforce his decree, and appointed his brother Joseph his vice-regent in his Neapolitan dominions. Happily, Sir James Craig, with excellent judgment, withdrew his troops to Sicily and, when the French invaders came down to the Strait of Messina, with the Court of Naples flying before them, they found the access to Sicily barred. Two months later, at the beginning of April, Craig was compelled by ill-health to sail for England, and the command in the Mediterranean devolved upon Sir John Stuart, who was a very poor substitute for him. There was still a great opportunity for operations in Italy. One Neapolitan fortress, Gaeta, defied the French, and the Calabrese were ready to rise in insurrection against them at any moment. Joseph Bonaparte was, therefore, obliged to disperse his force to keep them in subjection; and small though Stuart's force was, he had transports and a squadron under Sir Sidney Smith, which would enable him to effect a landing anywhere. In June, 1806, accordingly, Stuart sailed with 5,400 men for the west coast of Calabria and, landing, encountered, on 4th July, a force of about 6,400 French under General Reynier at Maida. The fight took place on ground as level as a billiard-table, and the English simply blasted their enemies off the field by their musketry-fire. The French lost 1,500 killed and wounded and 1,000 prisoners, and the English no more than 327. In fact, it was a brilliant little affair, and, if properly followed up, might, and should, have caused the Peninsular War to be fought in Italy instead of in Spain. But Sidney Smith was an impostor who was always trying to carry out little military operations on his own account, and Stuart was not much better. Stuart did, indeed, capture a few outlying posts, taking another 2,000 prisoners; and he destroyed all the guns, stores and boats which the French had collected for the invasion of Sicily; but with a little more energy he might have made an end of Reynier's whole force. Yet Sidney Smith was the man who really deserved reprobation, for, in his anxiety to steal Stuart's laurels, he arrived too late to relieve Gaeta, the surrender of which liberated the whole of the French troops for service in the field.

Operations on the Rio de la Plata, 1806-1807

But the British Government had not yet learned to employ their whole force at any one point, and they were, through no fault of their own, distracted in September by the arrival of the news of the capture of Buenos Ayres. Baird had, meanwhile, sent there a reinforcement of 2,000 men from the Cape; but these arrived too late, for the Spaniards in August rose against the 1st Highland L.I., which after losing 165 casualties was obliged to surrender. Baird's reinforcement, therefore, occupied an island in the river and waited. The British Government, on hearing of Popham's escapade, was naturally at a loss what to do, but they decided first to send to Rio de la Plata 3,000 men under Sir Samuel Auchmuty and later nearly 5,000 more under General Whitelocke. Auchmuty reached his destination in January, 1807, and, finding himself too weak to attempt Buenos Ayres, decided to attack Monte Video on the other side of the river. Borrowing a few guns from the Navy he in a few days battered a practicable breach, and, on the 3rd February, carried the fortress by assault—a brilliant little piece of work, which cost him close upon 400 casualties, the enemy's loss being 1,300 killed and wounded and 2,000 prisoners.

In May Whitelocke arrived, and at the end of June he landed eight battalions and three regiments of dragoons on the south bank of the river, and marched upon Buenos Ayres. His conduct of the operations was not such as to inspire his troops with confidence; but on 4th July he came before the city, and on the 5th he launched his 4,500 bayonets upon it in twelve columns through as many parallel streets. The population barricaded their houses and assailed them with every kind of missile from the housetops; and, though some of the columns reached their objectives on the sea-shore after running the gauntlet of the population for a mile, more than one of them were there isolated and compelled to surrender. Whitelocke's casualties were 1,050 killed and wounded, and nearly 2,000 prisoners, many of them also wounded. The enemy on their side had lost 1,000 prisoners and 30 guns; but so anxious were they to be quit of Whitelocke that they gladly agreed to restore all prisoners and let him sail away in peace, which he did. On his return to England he was tried by court-martial and cashiered, though undoubtedly he had shown wisdom in abandoning the whole enterprise.

Operations in Egypt, 1807

This futile expedition occupied about 10,000 British troops for a year for no object whatever; and, unfortunately, it was not the only one of its kind. After much hesitation, Prussia had thrown in her lot against France, and high hopes were built upon her military strength. But it was shattered in a single day—the 14th October, 1806—by the French victories of Jena and Auerstadt; and England was again left with no ally of any power but Russia. Now Russia was at war with Turkey, and the British Government, having reinforced the garrison of Sicily to a strength of 19,000 men, resolved to make a diversion in Russia's favour by sending 6,000 of them to Egypt. It is difficult to conceive what so paltry a force could accomplish, and, in fact, it accomplished nothing. One column of about 1,700 men, on 31st March, 1807, attacked Rosetta, went through exactly the same experience as Whitelocke's troops at Buenos Ayres, and came out with 185 killed and 282 wounded. A second attempt upon Rosetta resulted in the overwhelming of a detached column of 800 men, of whom nearly 300 were killed outright and the remainder, most of them wounded, were captured. After that it was decided to withdraw the troops from Egypt; and it was high time.

The Treaty of Tilsit and the Berlin Decrees

For 1807 was for England the most critical year of the war. In November, 1806, Napoleon had launched the thunderbolt by which he hoped to shatter the power of England. "The British Isles," he declared in the Berlin decrees, "are declared to be in a state of blockade. All commerce or correspondence with them are forbidden." To enforce this measure it was necessary first for him to compel Russia to submission, and in December he entered upon his Polish campaign for this purpose. In February, 1807, he met with a check at Eylau which staggered him for the moment; but, recovering himself, he, in June, defeated the

Russians decisively at Friedland and gained the Tsar, by the treaty of Tilsit, as his ally against England.

Critical Situation of England

The moment was one of great peril for the British. News had just come in of a mutiny of the Native Army in India—generally known as the mutiny of Vellore—which, though crushed at the outset by the extraordinary courage and resource of Colonel Gillespie, was known to have wide ramifications. It was, therefore, imperative to send reinforcements to India. The expedition to Egypt had proved a costly failure. The treacherous Court of Naples was known to be seeking Napoleon's favour from Sicily. And now Russia—nearly half of Europe—had allied itself with France which, with her conquests, represented much of the other half, while England had not a friend left to her but the mad King of Sweden. The Ministry—a new Ministry which had just assumed office—acted with admirable promptness. The immediate danger was lest France should seize the Danish fleet and use the Danish ports for invasion of the British Isles. With all possible speed and secrecy a force of 18,000 men was dispatched to Copenhagen under Lord Cathcart; and after three days' bombardment the city, on the 7th September, was surrendered, and the Danish fleet was carried off. Thus baulked of gaining the Danish fleet, Napoleon tried to seize that of Portugal, and in October he ordered an army under General Junot to march to Lisbon and occupy the forts and harbour. But the British Minister succeeded at the last moment in persuading the King of Portugal to sail with his fleet for Brazil; and when Junot, on 29th November, marched into Lisbon, he could only see the sails disappearing over the horizon. However, he remained in occupation of Lisbon, and we shall very soon see him again.

Castlereagh's Military Measures

Meanwhile, Castlereagh, the best Secretary for War that we have ever had, took strong measures to create a real striking force. He transferred, by the offer of a bounty, 28,000 men from the Militia to the Army, and by a drastic use of the ballot raised 36,000 recruits to replenish the Militia. From thenceforth the Old Militia, as it was called at the time, was to serve as a recruiting depot for the Army. For Home Defence, therefore, he raised a new force of 300,000 Local Militia by enforcing compulsory personal service. Until these measures could be fulfilled he could count upon no stronger striking force than 12,000 men; but, to turn these to the best account, he took up copper-bottomed transports enough for the whole of them, so that they might keep the sea and proceed to any point at any time. Eight thousand of them, under General Brent Spencer, were sent to the Mediterranean early in 1808.

Napoleon's Invasion of Spain

In February of that year, Napoleon invaded Spain in great force, nominally as a friend, obtained possession through treachery of the principal frontier fortresses, occupied Madrid and proclaimed his brother Joseph to be King of Spain. On the 2nd of May—a very famous date in Spanish history—the population of Spain rose in fury against the invaders and invoked the help of England. Spencer, who was at Gibraltar, sailed round the coast, keeping the French in constant apprehension of a landing. The Spaniards succeeded in capturing one complete detachment of French, 18,000 strong, at Baylen, on 23rd July, and by August the French had been driven back to the line of the Ebro.

Meanwhile, in May the Government, mindful of England's one ally, Sweden, which was threatened by Russia, had dispatched to her

10,000 men under Sir John Moore. Since the King was mad, it was quite impossible to concert operations with him; and early in July Moore, on his own responsibility, brought his troops back to England. It is difficult, indeed, to say why he should have been sent away at all on so hopeless an errand; and, though Ministers were deeply offended at his action there can be no doubt that he saved them from a serious blunder.

The Peninsular War, Wellesley's Campaign of 1808

Happily, owing to the efforts of Castlereagh, there were other troops at disposal besides these 10,000; and, on receiving the appeal for help from Spain, the Government decided to send out an expedition at once under Sir Arthur Wellesley to recapture Lisbon and so to gain a base on the Peninsula. Wellesley sailed with 10,000 men in July, and in August disembarked on an open beach at the mouth of the Mondego, where Spencer joined him, raising his force to 15,000 men. He then advanced southward, drove back an advanced French detachment under General Delaborde after a brisk little action at Roliça (17th August) and, pursuing his way to the coast, took up a position at Vimeiro to cover the disembarkation of reinforcements which

CONVENTION OF CINTRA

were at sea waiting to join him. These raised his strength to 18,000 men; but, before he could advance, he was attacked on 21st August by Junot with 14,000 men. The French were utterly defeated; and, had Wellesley been left to himself, hardly a man of them would have escaped. But, unfortunately, at the critical moment, Sir Harry Burrard took over the command from Wellesley, and, before Burrard had held it twenty-four hours, he was in turn superseded by Sir Hew Dalrymple. The fact was that the Government had decided to send Moore and his 10,000 men to Portugal, but were so anxious that he should not be in chief command (for he was senior to Wellesley) that they had put two senior men over his head to keep him out. The result was that the French army, instead of being sent prisoners to England, was allowed to return to France under the Convention of Cintra. However, Lisbon had been recovered, and the Portuguese had joined the Spaniards in insurrection against the French, so that there was hope for the future.

Moore's Campaign of 1808-1809

Napoleon, meanwhile, had lost no time in assembling troops to repair his reverses in Spain. By the end of October there were in the country 150,000 French soldiers, of which he took personal command at Vitoria, on 6th November. The Spaniards were confident of success against him, and the British Government agreed that its own army should be reinforced by another 18,000 men under Sir David Baird, and that the whole, some 40,000 men, under the command of Sir John Moore, should co-operate with the Spanish armies. Baird landed at Coruña on 13th October, and Moore marched north-eastward from Portugal at the end of that month to join him. By the third week in November Moore learned that the Spanish armies had been scattered to the four winds by Napoleon, and that he stood alone. He gave the order to retreat; but, hearing of an isolated French corps within possible striking distance, he resolved to advance upon it and to threaten Napoleon's main line of communication with France. It was a most hazardous venture, but it was the only chance of obtaining breathing time for the Spaniards.

On 20th December, Moore and Baird joined hands, and on the first day of the advance the 15th Hussars fought at Sahagun a brilliant little action against the French cavalry; but on the 23rd, Moore received information that the French were in motion against him in force,

SIR JOHN MOORE'S RETREAT

and, in his own words, he prepared to run for it. Napoleon had, in fact, turned altogether some 100,000 troops against him, which he urged on with frantic haste to intercept him; but in vain. On 29th December, the British cavalry again met the pursuing French horse at Benavente with brilliant success; but the British were never very hard pressed. The troops, however, suffered much from the wintry weather, particularly during the passage of the Galician mountains, and in many regiments discipline broke down. However, despite the loss of thousands of stragglers, Moore brought the bulk of his army into Coruña on 11th January, 1809. He had expected to find his transports there; but, being detained by contrary winds, they did not come in until the 14th, when he at once embarked his horses and most of his artillery, expecting to get away on the 15th. Only one French corps, that of Marshal Soult, had pressed the pursuit to the end, and he seemed not very eager to interfere with Moore; but on the 15th he made a few menacing movements and on the 16th he attacked. Moore having detached one division to embark at Vigo, the numbers on both sides were about equal—16,000 men —but the French had 20 guns, half of them heavy pieces, and Moore only 8 light field-guns. The fight lasted for four hours and was broken off by darkness, when the French retired, having gained no advantage. But their heavy guns, which outranged Moore's, had punished one British brigade heavily, and had further mortally wounded Moore and disabled Baird. General Hope, therefore, embarked the army during the night and took it back to England where, having a strong gale astern, it arrived in four days. Men and officers alike were in rags, unshorn, filthy, and covered with vermin; and the sight of them shocked the British public into belief that they had suffered some great disaster. Indeed both the Army and the public were rather weary of expeditions which embarked, landed, re-embarked, and returned with nothing accomplished. The same story had been too often repeated since 1793; but this time, as shall be seen, some solid good had been done.

The Walcheren Expedition, 1809

At the end of 1808, Austria, realizing Napoleon's embarrassments in Spain, resolved to take up arms against him again, with financial assistance from England; and the question arose how England could best employ her military force to help her. In March, 1809,

THE WALCHEREN EXPEDITION

the Government determined that the defence of Portugal should be maintained with 30,000 men, but hesitated whether to employ every possible man there. At length they decided to send another force of 40,000 men, escorted by a powerful fleet, to the Scheldt to destroy the French ships that were built or building there, and if possible to capture Antwerp. The plan was not a bad one, provided that it were favoured by good fortune and that the operations were pressed with vigour and rapidity, Army and Navy working together in perfect concert. Unfortunately these conditions were not fulfilled. The information upon which the Government acted was vague and inaccurate. The expedition started late. The weather was unfavourable. The naval commander, Sir Richard Strahan, was not a first-rate man. The military commander, Lord Chatham, though not inactive nor incompetent, was not the man for the place. Flushing was taken and some advance was made up the Scheldt; but difficulties increased and, after a month's work, the campaign was practically ended by malarial fever. Of about 39,000 of all ranks embarked to the Scheldt over 4,000 died outright on the spot or after their return home; and, when the last of them were withdrawn in December, there were over 11,000 on the sick list. However, this Walcheren expedition gave Napoleon one of the worst frights of his life and, had it succeeded, would certainly have caused a revolt, and possibly the overthrow of his rule in Paris.

The Peninsular War. Wellington's Campaign of 1809

Let us now return to Portugal. Including the stragglers that had been gathered in from Moore's army there were some 16,000 British troops in the country. The French troops in the Peninsula numbered between 200,000 and 300,000. Moore had rightly pronounced the Portuguese frontier to be indefensible. Wellesley agreed; but he added that, if to 20,000 British troops there were joined 70,000 Portuguese regulars or militia, the French could not drive them from Portugal with fewer than 100,000 men, and that, if the Spaniards continued to resist, he doubted whether the 100,000 men could be spared.

There could be no question of the Spanish resistance. The Spanish generals and their raw troops were not yet worth much, but every Spaniard felt bitter hatred of the French. The country people cut the throat of every French straggler and annihilated every small party, while guerrilla-bands harassed their communications unceasingly. The French had tried reprisals, but in a very few weeks, after the French had burned peasants alive and Spaniards had sawn a captive French general asunder, reprisals had been found unprofitable. It must be remembered that it was a principle of the French armies of the Revolution and Empire to live on the country which they occupied, drawing from it not only their food but their pay, and frequently everything of value that they could lay their hands on. This did not make for content among the inhabitants. Moreover, since England had command of the sea, every French soldier had to march into Spain by land, often over mountain roads and through dangerous defiles, which gave many opportunities to the peasantry to inflict damage and loss. Certainly, with a little help, the Spanish resistance could be reckoned on.

The British Government, therefore, decided to give Wellesley a field force of 28,000 men, to reorganize the Portuguese army by the help of British officers and to take it into pay. The work of making the Portuguese army was entrusted to William Beresford, who had commanded the 1st Highland L.I. at Buenos Ayres. Very well he did it; but in 1809 he was only at the beginning of his task. However, on reaching Lisbon, Wellesley found that Moore's stroke at the French communications had had the effect of dispersing the French armies over a far wider area than they could safely control. Soult, after the action of Coruña, had moved south upon Portugal and lay at Oporto, with his force somewhat dispersed for the sake of subsistence. Victor, with another portion of the army that had pursued Moore, was two hundred miles to south and east of him, about fifty miles from the eastern frontier of Portugal. The two commanders were not in communication with each other, and each might, therefore, be dealt with in detail.

Leaving 12,000 of his British and Portuguese to watch Victor, Wellesley led the rest, about 30,000 men, upon Oporto. On the 12th he surprised Soult, after crossing the broad River Douro under his nose, and drove him north until the 18th, when he was forced to leave him owing to intelligence that Victor was in motion upon the Tagus. Soult's retreat had cost him the whole of his artillery, which he was obliged to destroy, and 6,000 men; and he was fortunate to escape capture with the whole of his army. Then, returning to deal with Victor, Wellesley joined his force to that of the Spanish General Cuesta, and advanced up the Tagus in pursuit of Victor, who had retired. The movement was a failure. Wellesley had imprudently trusted to the

CAMPAIGN OF TALAVERA

Spaniards for transport and supply, and found that nothing was ready. Cuesta, to say the least, was a difficult colleague; and, as Wellesley discovered just in time, King Joseph was ready to meet him with a superior force in front, while 50,000 French troops were, more by good luck than good management, ready to descend from the north into the valley of the Tagus upon his left flank. Ascertaining the strength of Joseph in front, the Allied Armies fell back to a position just north of Talavera and offered battle. The French attacked the key of the position on the night of the 28th July, but were repulsed. On the 29th they attacked again; and their first assault was beaten back with a loss to them of 1,200 and to the British of 400. A second onslaught on a larger scale led to severe fighting, but was equally repulsed, though some of the British suffered very heavily, having pushed a counter-attack too far. The French then drew off, having lost 7,000 men and 17 guns; but Wellesley was equally obliged to fall back to Portugal, owing to the menace against his flank. He had lost 5,000 men, and his victory was barren. In fact, the only excuse for his rash advance was that it was important to do as much as possible while a part of the French army was engaged in

Austria. He took the lesson to heart and resolved never to work with the Spaniards again. Meanwhile he was rewarded for his campaign with the title of Viscount Wellington.

Wellington's Military Policy

Unfortunately, Austria, defeated at the battle of Wagram, concluded peace with France in October. There could be no doubt that Napoleon would make every effort and employ every possible man to subdue Spain and drive the British from Portugal; and the question was whether Wellington could stand his ground. He decided that he could, and directed a chain of fortifications to be thrown up near Torres Vedras, about 30 miles north of Lisbon, on a line of about 25 miles from the sea eastward to the Tagus. He then argued thus: The French always live on the country. If they invade Portugal in superior force, I shall retreat before them, declining battle unless at great advantage, and denuding the country as far as I can, until I reach my fortified lines. If they attack me there, all the better, for I am sure to beat them. If they sit down outside, I shall wait until they move off; for, as they live on the country, they must move off sooner or later. I shall organize my service of transport and supply so that I can feed my army wherever I go, and, when they move, I shall follow them up. They cannot stop on their retreat, for they have eaten up the country as they advanced, but they must go back and back till they reach their food-depôts in Spain. The method is infallible. If I am driven out of Portugal, I shall land at Cadiz or some other place and play the same game there. Wherever I go, the French must collect a superior force to meet me, which means that they must weaken their garrisons in some part of Spain and give full play to Spanish insurgents. It is only a question of time. I must win in the end.

Curiously enough, before the year 1809 came to an end, the French commanders played into his hands. Having beaten a Spanish general who was rash enough to offer battle, King Joseph and Marshal Soult invaded Andalusia, the richest and most prosperous province in Spain. It was simple madness, for they had already occupied far more territory than they could safely hold, and moreover, they failed to take Cadiz which, once missed, was not to be mastered without a naval force. Andalusia without Cadiz was like Portugal without Lisbon. Napoleon was greatly annoyed when he heard what Joseph had done, and Wellington was correspondingly pleased. The more the French squandered their force upon hopeless enterprises, such as the siege of Cadiz, the better it suited him; and he gladly spared a battalion or two for the garrison of Cadiz, to which the British Government wisely added a few more.

Wellington's Campaign of 1810

As Wellington had expected, Napoleon, early in 1810, raised his troops in Spain to 300,000 men, and placed 65,000 of them under Marshal Massena for the invasion of Portugal. Leaving General Hill with about 18,000 British and Portuguese to watch the eastern frontier, Wellington led 32,000 up to the north-east to await Massena. In July Massena appeared and Wellington fell back slowly and steadily before him to a very strong position at Bussaco, where, having called Hill to him, he offered battle. Quite unnecessarily, for the position could (as Wellington knew) be turned, Massena attacked on the 27th September, and was repulsed with bloody losses, his casualties being 4,600, whereas Wellington's did not exceed 1,250. Massena then turned the position, and Wellington, quietly retreating as before, on 10th October entered the lines of Torres Vedras. Massena was abruptly checked. He saw that an attack on the lines was hopeless.

LINES OF TORRES VEDRAS

and he sat down before them. Wellington watched him and waited. On the 14th November, Massena, starved out, retired thirty miles and again sat down. Wellington followed him up cautiously, watched him and waited. In January, 1811, Soult, by Napoleon's order, moved 20,000 men up to the eastern frontier of Portugal. This was unpleasant for Wellington, for a combined attack from north and east might prove too much for him. However, he detached 10 battalions under Beresford to look after Soult, and waited. Massena would not move. He knew as well as Wellington that the existing British Government might fall on any day, and that the Opposition, if it came into power, would withdraw the British Army from the Peninsula. A reinforcement of 8,000 men widened Massena's provision ground for a time, and he held on. Wellington began to wonder if he would ever go.

Wellington's Campaign of 1811

At last, on the 3rd of March, Massena, under stress of starvation, began with admirable skill his retreat. Back and back he moved with Wellington always at his heels harassing and worrying, and with demoralization and mutiny steadily growing in his army. On the 3rd of April the accident of a fog alone saved one of his three corps from destruction; and on the 8th he recrossed the Portuguese frontier with his soldiers famished, barefooted and in rags. He had lost 25,000 men—2,000 killed in action, 8,000 prisoners and 15,000 dead of sickness or famine. Thus the French were finally driven from Portugal, and a gate was secured into the continent which could not be closed by Napoleon's Berlin decrees.

Meanwhile, in March the fortress of Badajoz, on the Spanish side of the Portuguese frontier, had been treacherously surrendered to Soult, and Wellington, in all the heat of pursuit, had been obliged to send 6,000 of his men to Beresford. But a few days later he heard that Soult had received alarming news from Cadiz, and had hurried back thither with most of his troops. The garrison of Cadiz had made a sortie with 5,000 British under Sir Thomas Graham and 14,000 Spanish; and, on the 5th March, the British with ten guns, engaged some 7,000 French with 12 guns, at Barrosa and drove them back with the loss of over 2,000 killed, wounded and prisoners, an eagle and six cannon. The British casualties numbered 1,238; the flank-companies of the Norfolks, 1st Gloucester, and 2nd South Lancs alone losing 236 out of 536 present. It was a great day for them, for the Brigade

BATTLE OF FUENTES DE OÑORO

of Guards, the 1st Royal Irish Fusiliers and the Rifle Brigade.

Wellington, therefore, directed Beresford to lay siege to Badajoz on the eastern frontier, reinforcing him strongly for the purpose, while he himself blockaded the fortress of Almeida in the north-east. He was pretty confident that Massena would presently advance to the relief of Almeida, and that Soult would do likewise to rescue Badajoz; and he was about to take the very great risk of fighting two general actions, one with his own main body and one with his flank-guard. Massena duly came forward, as soon as his army had been refitted and reinforced, with about 48,000 men, and Wellington met him with 25,000 British and 12,000 Portuguese on the frontier at Fuentes de Oñoro. In a preliminary attack, on the 3rd May, Massena was repulsed with 650 casualties against Wellington's 250; but in a general action on the 5th, Wellington, whose right flank was turned, was only saved by the extreme steadiness of the Light Division —the troops trained by Moore—and of his cavalry. After severe fighting, in which the 2nd Highland L.I. and Cameron Highlanders were greatly distinguished, Massena fell back, though his casualties numbered no more than 2,200 against Wellington's 1,530.

A few days later, on 16th May, Beresford, with 8,000 British and 21,000 Spaniards, fought a desperate action against Soult, with 24,000 French, at Albuera. Beresford occupied his position wrongly and fought his battle unskilfully and he had given it up for lost when one of his staff, Captain Hardinge (later Governor-General of India), on his own responsibility issued the orders which saved the day. Of the 8,000 British over 4,000 were killed and wounded. The two battalions of the Royal Fusiliers, the Royal Welch Fusiliers, the 1st Worcester, and the 1st Northampton each lost over 300 officers and men, the Buffs (who were caught and cut up by cavalry) over 600, and the 1st Middlesex, who here gained the name of Die-hards, over 400. Never have English soldiers—for no Scottish nor Irish regiment was present—shown their fighting qualities in greater excellence.

Massena, the French General whom Wellington most dreaded, was now recalled and replaced by Marmont, who joined his army to Soult's and advanced upon Portugal by way of Badajoz. Wellington could collect to meet them 37,000 British and 17,000 Portuguese; but the two Marshals did not venture to attack him. They presently fell at variance between themselves, and Soult returned with a great part of his force to Andalusia. Wellington then threatened Ciudad Rodrigo, on the Spanish frontier to the north-east, and Marmont collected 58,000 men to relieve it. There was one lively little combat between them at El Bodon; but Marmont was not inclined to risk a general action, and at the beginning of October both armies retired into cantonments.

Operations Outside the Peninsula. 1809-1811

During these first critical years of the Peninsular War, the Army had been by no means idle in other parts of the world. In 1807, after the rupture with Denmark, the three Danish islands in the West Indies had been captured without resistance by a small expedition from Barbados. But a more serious operation was undertaken when General Beckwith, the Commander-in-Chief to Windward, attacked Martinique with some 11,000 men, about half of them foreigners or negroes of the West India Regiments. Beckwith did his work skilfully and well, his casualties in action being little over 500, and through sickness—thanks to his care and good management—no more than 25 in two months. In April, he attacked and captured the French islands called the Saints; and in January, 1810, he sailed with 6,000 men for Guadeloupe. Once again Beckwith's skill was conspicuous, and within a month he was master of the island at a cost of 300 casualties. Two more islands, St. Eustatius and St. Martin, were then captured with little trouble, and practically the whole of the Windward Antilles were in British possession. This signified the locking-up of troops in no fewer than seventeen unhealthy islands; but it also saved the Navy from much hard work by depriving French privateers of any refuge in the West Indies, while it opened fresh markets for British trade in compensation for that lost in Europe through the Berlin decrees.

Operations in the East. Capture of Mauritius

But it was not in the West only that the flags of France and her allies or subjects were swept off the seas. In June, 1810, 3,500 soldiers—about half of them British—were embarked at Madras for an attack on Bourbon and Mauritius. Bourbon, after a short resistance, fell on the 10th July; and in October, the troops having been increased to about 10,000 men by reinforcements from Bombay, the expedition proceeded to Mauritius. The Commander-in-Chief was Sir John Abercromby, a son of Sir Ralph, and among the naval officers present was Captain Beaver, who had been in charge of the famous disembarkation

EXPEDITION TO JAVA

at Aboukir. The formalities of that landing were all religiously repeated, though there was no enemy to meet it, and after some slight skirmishes Mauritius surrendered on 2nd December, having held out for no more than three days. This deprived the French of any base for attack on India, and gave another little outlet for British trade.

The Expedition to Java

The East India Company then girded itself for a far more serious venture, the capture of Java, and to that end embarked in June, 1811, some 12,000 men, the bulk of them British regiments from Bengal and Madras, under Sir Samuel Auchmuty. In the first days of August they landed, and after some preliminary skirmishes came, on 14th August, before a great entrenched camp called the lines of Cornelis, which the French and Dutch had prepared for a prolonged resistance. Their numbers were unknown to Auchmuty, but seem to have been about 10,000—four-fifths of them trained and disciplined natives —and the guns mounted on the works numbered 280. It was imperative to break ground and raise batteries for a regular siege, and this operation was prolonged for eleven days, during which the men fell down fast from the heat, the unhealthiness of the climate and intense fatigue. Seeing that he must cut matters short Auchmuty, on 26th August, delivered his assault with brilliant success. The lines were carried; and practically the whole of the garrison was killed, wounded or taken, at a cost of 633 casualties. The hero of the day was General Gillespie who, though quaking with fever, guided his column on foot through very intricate ground to its appointed place and led it to the attack. He received so severe a contusion[1] in the course of the fight that, when the excitement was over, he fainted; but he had no sooner recovered than he took a gun-horse out of a gun, jumped on its back and led the pursuit. Following up his advantage, Auchmuty soon made an end of resistance in other quarters of the island, and on 16th September received its unconditional surrender. Thereby a valuable possession was wrested from Napoleon's subject, Holland, and yet another market was opened up for British trade.

The Peninsular War. The Campaign of 1812

Returning now to Wellington we may say that he had by this time made his Army. His

---

[1] A contusion signified a blow from a spent bullet. Generally it meant a bruise which turned half a man's body black and blue.

difficulties had been enormous, for he had never much money and, owing to the instability of the British Ministry, he was always apprehensive lest the Opposition should come into power and withdraw the Army from the Peninsula altogether. But he had trained his generals, he had trained his staff, he had organized a transport-service, chiefly of packmules, and he was getting his medical department into order. All of these things, which a general nowadays finds ready to his hand, a general in those days had to create for himself; and it was in these details that Wellington's Indian experience was of priceless value to him.

In 1812 his chance came at last. Napoleon, having quarrelled with Russia, was making great preparations for an invasion of that country, which involved the withdrawal of some of his troops from Spain. His orders, therefore, were that his armies in the peninsula should devote themselves to the subjugation of the east and south, and let Portugal wait for the present. The Spaniards, too, had substituted for their regular armies increased numbers of guerrilla-bands which, under very capable leaders, harassed the French continually and did them untold mischief. Wellington laid his plans for the capture of Ciudad Rodrigo, the Spanish fortress which guarded what may be termed the north-eastern gate of Portugal. Marmont, of course, was not far away; but his army, since it lived on the country, was necessarily dispersed and could not be readily assembled. Leaving General Hill, as a right-flank guard, to parry any possible thrust of Soult from Andalusia, Wellington on 8th January, 1812, suddenly invested Ciudad Rodrigo and, after a few days' cannonade, stormed it on the 19th, before Marmont could even collect his army to prevent him. This done, he invested Badajoz on 17th March and, after battering a breach, assaulted it on 5th April. The assault was repulsed with very heavy loss; but the place was carried by escalade, and Badajoz was his at the heavy cost of 5,000 casualties. A brilliant little stroke by General Hill destroyed the French bridge over the Tagus at Almaraz, which signified that the means of communication between Soult and Marmont was thrust back to the bridge of Toledo, a full hundred miles farther up the river and remoter from the Portuguese frontier.

Wellington then advanced eastward against Marmont with 50,000 men, 28,000 of them British. Marmont, who had 47,000, manœuvred skilfully against him, and Wellington, hearing

BATTLE OF SALAMANCA

that 14,000 more French were about to join Marmont, was contemplating retreat. In the nick of time Marmont, on the 22nd of July, when close to Salamanca, made a false movement. Wellington turned upon him instantly and routed him completely, inflicting a loss of 14,000 men and capturing 20 guns at a cost to himself of 5,000 killed and wounded. This was a great day for the British cavalry, which rode down and overwhelmed one French infantry division; yet greater for the Devons, the 2nd Shropshire L.I., and the 2nd Gloucesters which broke down the last of the French resistance and, out of 1,396 men of all ranks present, had 849 killed and wounded; the Devons losing 341 out of 509 and the 2nd Gloucesters 374 out of 536.

The French retreated north-eastward in discomfiture, and Wellington, having entered Madrid in triumph, moved also north-eastward and laid siege to Burgos. This operation he mismanaged badly; and late in October he was obliged, by the concentration of the French armies from all quarters against him,to raise the siege and retreat. On the 11th of November these armies, 90,000 strong, came up with him on the battle-field of Salamanca. Wellington, having gathered in every man, British, Spanish and Portuguese—in all, 68,000 men—turned and offered them battle. They declined it; and he pursued his retreat, not much molested by the enemy, to Portugal. Of all his achievements some foreign critics account this retreat the greatest.

Altogether it was a grand campaign. He had worked his troops very hard, and they had served him well. He had lost 20,000 men—British, Spaniards and Portuguese—but he had stormed two fortresses, won one great general action, compelled the French to evacuate the southern half of Spain and, by forcing the French to concentrate against himself, had given opportunities to the Spanish guerrilla-bands which they did not neglect. The French lost 20,000 prisoners alone, and at least as many again killed and wounded, besides hundreds of guns taken at Madrid and outside Cadiz. Wellington was rewarded first with an earldom, and next with a marquisate.

Campaign of 1813

In the spring of 1813 came the news that Napoleon's invasion of Russia had ended in disaster, and that he was withdrawing many troops from the Peninsula. In 1812 a small British force from Sicily had already landed on the east coast of Spain, which was to all

BATTLE OF VITORIA

intent a separate sphere of action from the rest, and in 1813 these were to be reinforced. Wellington himself also had been reinforced from England, and by the spring had 100,000 men, half of them British, the remainder Spanish and Portuguese; whereas the French were diminished, and, as in 1808, had shrunk behind the line of the Ebro. In May, 1813, Wellington advanced in force and the French retired before him to Vitoria where, on the 21st of June, they stood and fought a delaying action which, if Wellington's plans had been executed aright, would have been fatal to them. They escaped, however, with the loss of 7,000 men, 150 guns and every scrap of baggage that they possessed; and Wellington, following them up, drove them over the frontier into France. He himself halted in the Pyrenees until he could reduce the frontier fortresses of Pamplona and San Sebastian, the latter of which repelled an assault on the 25th of July. But meanwhile, Soult, to whom Napoleon now entrusted the command of the Army of Spain, had scraped together 70,000 men, with which, on the 20th July, he essayed a counter-attack to drive the British out of the Pyrenees. He succeeded in pushing them back some little way, but on the 28th he, with 30,000 men failed to dislodge 16,000 British at Sorauren;

and Wellington, resuming the offensive two days later, drove the French back headlong to their former position. Soult admitted a loss of 13,000 men. Wellington's casualties little exceeded 7,000.

On the 31st August San Sebastian was taken by storm, and on the 7th October Wellington crossed the Bidassoa into France and drove Soult from his defensive position on the French frontier. Pamplona, after a blockade of three months, surrendered; and Wellington, again advancing on the 10th November, drove Soult from another fortified position on the river Nivelle, capturing 69 guns. Soult retired to yet another position on the river Nive, from which Wellington drove him on the 9th December, repelling sharp counter-attacks on the 10th and 11th. The operations were rendered difficult by the rivers running down from the Pyrenees, which were liable to sudden and rapid floods; and, owing to one such flood, General Hill was left, on 13th December, in isolation at St. Pierre, with 14,000 men and 14 guns. Soult attacked him with 20,000 men and 30 guns, but after a very severe action was repulsed with a loss of 3,000 killed and wounded, Hill's casualties being about 1,700. The 2nd Gordon Highlanders—which in one of the combats in the Pyrenees on 25th July had done great service, losing 350 out of 850 men—were again conspicuous at St. Pierre. In the five days of fighting Soult and Wellington, each of them, lost over 5,000 men.

Campaign of 1814

Meanwhile, there had arrived, on 8th December, the great news of the total defeat of Napoleon at Leipzig—"The Battle of the Nations," at which England was represented by a rocket-battery—on the 16th–19th October; and it remained to be seen what advantage would be taken of it. Wellington's advance during 1813 had been one long series of victories, only here and there chequered by some slight mishap. His coadjutor on the east coast of Spain, General Murray, had done badly; for though he had accidentally won a little victory at Castalla, he had failed disgracefully in an attack upon Tarragona and had deservedly been recalled for trial by court-martial. In February, 1814, Wellington again advanced, crossed the Adour, manœuvred Soult out of his entrenched camp at Bayonne and leaving a force to invest that fortress, pursued Soult, who had retreated eastward, with 33,000 men. On the 27th he overtook him at Orthez in a strong position, and attacking with inferior numbers drove him on with a loss of 4,000 men, his own casualties not exceeding 2,000. Following Soult up Wellington engaged him for the last time, on the 10th April, at Toulouse, taking such liberties as can only be hazarded in the presence of a beaten enemy, and again drove him on, though his casualties—4,000— were double the number of Soult's. Soult was in full retreat when news came, on the 12th, of the fall of Napoleon; and Wellington at once proposed a suspension of arms. A sortie of the garrison of Bayonne brought on a sharp little action on the 14th; but on the 18th the Peninsular War came to an end.

The American War

For the sake of convenience the narrative of the Peninsular War has been continued without interruption since 1810; but between 1812 and 1814 the Army was employed also in other spheres, which must be briefly noticed. The first of these was North America. In any war the relations between belligerents and neutrals are subject to strain, and the United States particularly resented England's claim to impress British sailors serving on foreign ships on the high seas—a right which England could not forgo unless she was content to surrender to Napoleon. Trouble arose also out of the blockade proclaimed by the Berlin decrees,

AMERICAN AGGRESSION

and out of the Orders-in-Council which were England's counterblast thereto. The differences might have been adjusted amicably had not Napoleon done, as was natural, his utmost to aggravate them, less by humouring the Americans than by bullying and frightening them by acts of downright violence. Unfortunately two successive Presidents, Jefferson and Madison, wished to make capital with the American electors out of unfriendliness to England —the familiar process of "twisting the British Lion's tail." There was a party in America, too, which clamoured for the conquest of Canada; and though the New England States, which had been foremost in the struggle for independence, were strongly opposed to hostilities, the faction of violence gained the upper hand. On the 17th June the British Government made a concession which should have averted an open breach; but on that very day the American Government declared war, and, having done so, would listen to no conciliation.

To all appearance Canada was doomed. The regular troops in it, including four battalions of the British Line, numbered fewer than 7,000 and were widely scattered. The Americans had enormous numerical superiority in population, and far greater facilities for building and manning fleets on the Great Lakes, which were the principal means of communication. The British Navy, even if it had not had its hands already full, could not enter these lakes owing to the rapids of the St. Lawrence and the Falls of Niagara. The British Army likewise had its hands full and could spare few, if any, reinforcements. The game was in the hands of the Americans, if they knew how to play it.

They began by marching 2,500 men to Detroit—the strait between Lakes Erie and Huron—under a miserable commander, who no sooner found an enemy opposed to him than he surrendered (16th August, 1812). They then assembled about 10,000 men about the Strait of Niagara and attacked the Canadian shore, but were completely defeated by Colonel Isaac Brock of the 1st Berkshire, with a force of 800 regulars and 400 militia. The Americans retired with a loss of 1,200 men, 900 of them prisoners, whereas the British casualties did not exceed 94. Unfortunately Brock was killed in this fight, otherwise the subsequent story of the war would have been very different. A second American expedition to Detroit was likewise defeated with heavy loss, though, owing to the tactical blunders of the British commander, his casualties numbered over 180. However, those of the Americans were four

CAMPAIGNS IN AMERICA

times as great; and this was all that they accomplished in the campaign of 1812.

The campaign of 1813 was taken up by a number of petty little affairs on the shores of Lakes Ontario and Erie with varying fortune, but no substantial gain to the Americans except the establishment of naval supremacy on Lake Erie.[1] Had Brock been alive to lead the British, the balance of advantage would certainly have been on the British side on land.

In 1814 the contest on the Lakes was renewed; but the Americans by this time had learned wisdom, and both their troops and commanders were much improved. The British sustained a reverse at Chippewa on the Niagara Strait on 5th July, and this was not made good by a very bloody, though indecisive, little action at Lundy's Lane on 25th July. The British engaged were about 2,800, the Americans rather more—probably about 4,000—and the British and Americans each lost exactly 643 killed and wounded. Of 400 men of the 2nd Royal Irish Fusiliers present at this action there fell 217. A British assault on the American Fort Erie on 15th

---

[1] The Royal Navy had no share in these engagements on the Lakes, beyond furnishing a very few officers. The ships were built on the Lakes and manned by any crews that could be scraped together—landsmen of miserable quality. The Americans had more and better shipwrights and could command plenty of skilled seamen.

August failed, chiefly owing to an accidental explosion, and cost the assailants 900 casualties; after which a formidable sortie by the garrison on 17th September compelled the assailants to retreat. But these petty incidents left the general situation unchanged.

Meanwhile, reinforcements from Wellington's army in France, to the number of 7,000 men, had arrived; but the plans of the Commander-in-Chief in Canada—Sir George Prevost—for turning them to account were wrecked by an overwhelming defeat of the English fleet on Lake Champlain, on 11th September. However, another expedition was already on the American coast, with about 4,000 men from Wellington's army, which under escort of a squadron of the Navy sailed up the Patuxent River, landed, brushed away an American force of about 6,000 militia at Bladensburg and entered Washington. The General and his Staff supped off a meal which had been prepared by President Madison for his victorious officers; and then every public building was burnt down. The Americans had burned not only the public but the private buildings of the capital of Canada as well as of many villages, and had only themselves to thank for these reprisals, which were executed by order of the British Government.

THE DEFEAT OF NEW ORLEANS

Then, in an evil hour, this force, increased to a strength of 6,000, was turned against New Orleans, through the influence of an admiral, greedy for prize-money. General Pakenham, who had commanded a division under Wellington, joined the force after its disembarkation in the Mississippi, and was furious when he discovered the very dangerous situation into which it had been decoyed by the admiral; but there was no help for it. On the 8th January, 1815, he attacked the Americans, who were equal to him in strength and strongly entrenched, and was disastrously repulsed. He was killed, his second and third in command were disabled, and the casualties amounted to 2,000. With great difficulty and danger the troops were withdrawn and re-embarked; and, before any further operations could be undertaken, it was learned that peace had been concluded between England and the United States on the 14th December, 1814. Therefore all the blood shed at New Orleans was unnecessary. In fact, the whole war was unnecessary; but it was none of England's making. Neither side gained anything by it, nor by the treaty which followed it. In the matter of injury inflicted, the Americans, owing to the English naval blockade, suffered far more than their enemies; but the New Englanders at least made a handsome profit by feeding the British. Wellington pronounced the war to have been successful and highly honourable to the British arms; but it would be truer to say that the Americans made a wretched failure of it, and that it was highly dishonourable to the American arms.

Operations in Italy and Holland

Two more subordinate spheres of operations must also be mentioned. A force of some 6,000 men from Sicily was landed in March, 1814, at Leghorn under Lord William Bentinck, which after a few insignificant skirmishes with small parties of French, occupied Genoa. Another detachment of about 5,000 men, composed of such soldiers—mostly very raw—as could be scraped together in England, was sent to Holland under command of Sir Thomas Graham, there to co-operate with about 30,000 Russians and Prussians in upholding a Dutch counter-revolution. After some trifling and feeble operations in concert with his allies, Graham conceived the audacious idea of surprising Bergen-op-Zoom with his own troops only. On 8th March he made the attack with, as it seemed, perfect success; but, by an extraordinary series of accidents and through bad management on the part of some of Graham's subordinates, the assailants, after five or six hours of possession, were driven out with a loss of about 2,500, of whom 1,600 were prisoners. These last were speedily liberated, and Graham's little detachment became the nucleus of the Army of Waterloo.

The Waterloo Campaign

Napoleon, after his overthrow, was consigned on 2nd April, 1814, to Elba. The representatives of the Allies, Wellington among them, were busy settling the affairs of Europe at Vienna when, on 26th February, 1815, Napoleon escaped from Elba and, being received with wild enthusiasm by the French Army, entered Paris in triumph on 20th March. The Allied Powers promptly formed a League to drive him out, and the British, Dutch and Prussians, being nearest to the spot, occupied Belgium, together nearly 250,000 strong. The British contingent was weak and of poor quality, Wellington's veterans, excepting 6 battalions, being in America or disbanded. Indeed, the Government had been in such a hurry to disband them that it could not provide gunners for more than 42 guns, nor drivers even for so many. The remainder of Wellington's own troops, Dutch, Belgian and German, were of exceedingly varied quality.

THE EMPIRE AND THE ARMY

Quatre Bras and Ligny

He, and the Prussian commander Blücher, had their troops still dispersed over a very wide area when, on 15th June, Napoleon suddenly advanced upon them before they were aware of him. His design was to strike in between Blücher and Wellington, separate them and beat each of them in detail. His operations on the 15th promised success, but on the 16th he found himself fighting both Blücher with 80,000 Prussians at Ligny, and Wellington at Quatre Bras, not more than six miles away, which was not at all what he had intended. He beat Blücher; but Wellington, who began the action at Quatre Bras with only about 7,000 men against 19,000, contrived to hold his own until gradually 22,000 men joined him, when the French drew off discomfited. On the 17th, Wellington fell back to Waterloo and Blücher to Wavre, 12 miles to east of Waterloo; and it was arranged that Wellington should accept battle on the 18th and that Blücher should hasten to his assistance.

Waterloo

The battle began at 11 a.m., Napoleon had about 70,000 men of one nation, and 224 guns, against Wellington's 63,000 of four nations, and 156 guns. With his vast superiority, not only in numbers but in calibre and range of cannon, Napoleon sought to tear the Allied array to pieces and to sweep it away by successive attacks of infantry, cavalry, mixed infantry and cavalry, and finally of the infantry of the Imperial Guard. Blücher was late in arriving on the field, but Wellington contrived to make most of his troops endure this terrible trial until the Prussians came up in force and attacked in earnest. Then his whole line advanced to the counter-attack; the French gave way, and the Prussians pursued with such ardour that in 36 hours the French army had ceased to exist. Never have the British given a finer example of their powers of endurance, and this quality was especially shown by the regiments that had fought already at Quatre Bras. In the two actions the First Guards lost 1,100 rank and file out of 2,000 present; the 1st Gloucester lost two-fifths of their numbers, the Royal Scots and the 1st Cornwalls one-half, the 1st Black Watch, the Cameron Highlanders and 2nd Gordon Highlanders considerably more than one-half. Lastly, the 1st Inniskilling Fusiliers, which had remained firm in square under artillery fire all day, "never moved a step and never fired a shot," and lost 446 rank and file killed and wounded out of 700 present.

Survey of the Empire and the Army. The Duke of York's Reforms

Real peace came at last in Europe; and the changes in the Army during this momentous period 1793–1815 must be briefly summed up. The first great reform was the appointment, already mentioned in passing, of the Duke of York to be Commander-in-Chief. He gathered good men round him and created the Head-quarters Staff, with gradual but astonishing improvement to the organization and discipline of the Army at large, and to the discipline of the officers in particular. In 1799 he founded the Staff College and the Royal Military College for the better education of officers and their sons. As regards the men, the first great changes came in 1797 when, in consequence of the mutiny in the Navy, the increase of pay (long besought by the military authorities) was suddenly granted in a moment of panic.

Barracks

The second great reform, begun in 1793 and extended over many years, was the building of barracks all over Great Britain and the gradual transfer of all soldiers to them from their old billets in ale-houses. The barracks, according to modern standards were bad, and they were distributed—though with good reason, for there

STATE OF THE SOLDIER, 1816

were as yet no police—far too much like little police-stations all over the manufacturing districts. But they kept the men more or less together, which was to the advantage of discipline. The barracks had canteens in which spirits—and very bad spirits—were sold, it being thought better to permit the sale owing to the difficulty of preventing men from smuggling spirits into barracks. These canteens were a fertile source of crime. The men were badly overcrowded, sleeping four in a crib, and if they felt ill (as they very well might), or thought themselves aggrieved, they resorted to drink at once. Discipline was still maintained wholly by the lash. There were no good-conduct badges nor good-conduct pay given by the country; but in many regiments the officers made good this defect at their own cost by regimental badges, medals and allowances, so matters were not so bad as they seemed. Moreover, on Wellington's recommendation, a higher grade of non-commissioned officer was introduced for the encouragement of good men, and thus came into being troop-serjeants-major of cavalry and colour-serjeants of infantry.

Recruiting

An experiment was made in 1806 of enlisting men for short service, but it was not a success, and the old long-service system was perforce restored. The greatest damage done to recruiting was by Pitt's system of making the West Indies the principal seat of war. Men would not enlist to meet with certain death by yellow fever. The raising of negro West India regiments (there were at one time twelve), the enlisting of foreigners, and the relegation of bad characters to the West Indies in penal battalions to some extent solved the problem of tropical garrisons; and then the difficulty of obtaining recruits, especially after the old Militia had been turned into a recruiting ground, was lessened. It was the Duke of York's object to maintain 100 regiments of infantry of the line, each of two battalions, of which one battalion to be on foreign service and the other at home; and to all practical purposes he carried it out. He wished, at the same time, to affiliate the Militia as third and fourth battalions to these regiments; but this was not done until many years later, when the credit for the idea was given to another. In general, the great mistake made by the Government, until it was corrected by Castlereagh, was the neglect to enforce compulsory personal service for home defence. After that great step had been taken, the proportion of the population under arms in Navy and Army was fully as great as in the late German war.

The Cavalry

A word must be added about the different arms and departments of the service. In the cavalry the old war-horse (he seems to have been rather like a hearse-horse), disappeared and ordinary horses were adopted. A new drill, in which the men were told off by threes, and a code of trumpet-calls were introduced in 1795. Veterinary surgeons were appointed in 1796, and saddlers, armourers and armourer-serjeants were added between that year and 1802. In 1812 the Heavy Dragoons discarded the old cocked hat, long-skirted coat and boots in favour of a metal helmet, shorter jacket and overalls. The Light Dragoons likewise, after 1812, wore overalls and a shako; and only a few of them, which had been turned into Hussars, kept the old white leather breeches and Hessian boots.

The Artillery

In the Artillery a great advance was made by the formation, in 1794, of a corps of drivers for the field artillery, the organization of which was slightly changed in 1801. Its defect was that the officers could not rise above the rank of captain; but it was a great improvement on the old system of hired teams. Only in the Horse Artillery did the drivers form part and parcel of the troop. A far more important change was the introduction, in 1802, of a new shell invented by Major Shrapnel, of which a word more shall be said presently. There is not much to tell about the Engineers. So greatly was the inconvenience felt through the subordination of the Engineers to the Board of Ordnance instead of to the Commander-in-Chief, that the latter created some Engineers of his own called the Royal Staff Corps. It was this corps that accomplished remarkable feats of bridging rivers in the Peninsula, and did all the work of surveying for Wellington.

The Infantry

In the Infantry the most important changes were those wrought by Sir John Moore in the regiments which he trained at Shorncliffe, and which made Wellington's Light Division about the finest troops in the world. But this improvement did not extend to other battalions. The dress was changed after 1800 by the gradual substitution of a shako for the cocked hat, a coatee for the long-skirted coat, and trousers for breeches and gaiters. The truth is, that civilians had begun to wear tall hats, tail-coats and trousers, and that the army could not be behind the fashion. In hot climates (e.g., at Maida and in Egypt), the troops actually wore something very like a tall hat; and the shako was simply a modification of it, with a peak instead of a brim all round.

Transport and Supply

The Transport remained a matter for the Treasury and its commissaries, who had to learn their business in the field. Wellington created his mule-transport service in the Peninsula. The Wagon-train did exist, but was so weak in numbers that the wagons in the Peninsula were used chiefly as ambulances.

For the first time in an European war the Commissariat itself did all the work of Transport and Supply in the Peninsula, being unable to find contractors to do it for them. When once they had, with Wellington's help, learned their business, the Commissaries were admirably efficient.

The Medical Department

The Medical Department, having been found wanting in 1793, was reformed in 1798 and made still worse. The Medical Staff, as a central establishment, was hopeless. On the other hand, many of the regimental doctors were excellent, and one of them, Dr. McGrigor, not only organized the whole department for Wellington's army on a serviceable basis, but became the father of British military hygiene. There was, of course, much unavoidable suffering in the days before anæsthetics were known, but it was a point of honour with all ranks to endure pain with fortitude, and many fine examples of it are recorded both among officers and men.

The Chaplains' Department

Chaplains were little seen or heard of at the beginning of the war. There was only one chaplain with the Duke of York's army in 1794, and later many expeditions left England without any chaplain whatever. The Duke of York, in 1796, therefore, gradually substituted a Chaplain-General's department for the regimental chaplains; but even so, there was only one chaplain to the whole of Wellington's army in 1811. The result was that officers and men began to preach to each other, whereupon Wellington sent home for a batch of chaplains. They were not a great success; but there was one of them who insisted upon going into the firing line with the men; and he has had hundreds of successors since.

WELLINGTON AS TACTICIAN

Wellington's Tactics

A last word must be said of the secret of Wellington's victories. In the matter of tactics, when taking up a position on a hill, he always hid his troops away on the reverse slope, and he met the shock attack of French column with the missile action of British line. From Fontenoy in 1745, and Minden in 1759, down to Maida in 1806 and Waterloo in 1815, the British musketry-fire proved itself the deadliest in the world. In the matter of artillery Wellington was at a disadvantage, because the French had many guns[1] of greater calibre and range than his own; but against these he could pit the shrapnel-shell. The equivalent for the modern machine-gun in his day was grape-shot—a bag of bullets fired from a field-gun—which was very effective and demoralizing up to 200 yards. But the shrapnel-shell, a spherical iron case filled with bullets and fired by a time-fuse, produced the effect of grape-shot at a range of 800, 1,000 and even 1,200 yards; and the French did not relish it at all. We owed more to Major Shrapnel during this war than we acknowledge.

But Wellington's great effort was to im-

---

[1] The heaviest British field-guns were 9-pounders. Napoleon had given the French army a number of 12-pounders, which he called his "pretty girls."

prove the discipline of his Army, and the first step was to feed it regularly, so that the men might have no excuse for misconduct. Even when this had been accomplished, he found difficulty in maintaining order, and more than once his men were completely out of hand for two or three days. But by the time that he had crossed the French frontier all was well. The French inhabitants were more ready to supply him than their own countrymen with what they needed; and, at the end of the war, one English division marched almost the whole length of France to its port of embarkation not only without a single crime, but without a single complaint from the inhabitants.

It is difficult in a small space to give any just notion of the desperate nature of this long struggle against France, particularly after Napoleon, hopeless of reducing England by other means, tried to ruin her financially by the exclusion of her trade from Europe. He very nearly succeeded, though the effort involved him in wars which brought about his own downfall.

Let us now turn to the additions made by the war to the Empire. These were the spit of sand called Heligoland in the North Sea, which had been occupied since 1807 as a depôt for goods to be smuggled up the Elbe in defiance

THE NEW EMPIRE

of Napoleon's decrees; Malta, in the Mediterranean; Tobago, St. Lucia and Trinidad in the West Indies; British Guiana on the mainland of South America; Cape Colony; Mauritius and Ceylon; besides a vast addition to the territory under British protection in India. Apart from these, there was Australia, first settled as a penal colony in 1788, and needing first a few companies and later a complete battalion for the preservation of order. There was still need for a considerable Army.

CHAPTER X

THE CONSOLIDATION OF THE EMPIRE

EVERY one of the newly acquired places, besides Gibraltar, Canada and all the old possessions in the West Indies, required garrisons; while India also demanded a larger British force than ever before. But the National Debt was enormous; trade was bad; and the House of Commons, wild to reduce expenditure, abolished all auxiliary departments, and would not permit a sufficient force to be kept for the needs of the Empire. For, apart from numerous garrisons in unhealthy climates where the mortality was frightful, the Empire required police for the maintenance of order and security. The military history of the Empire in the 19th century is the history of its consolidation. The work, as shall be seen, was very arduous and kept three-quarters of the Infantry of the Line on foreign service. The result was that both soldiers and officers had very hard times; but they did their work well; and we must now see what that work was.

The Nipal War of 1814-1816

War with Nipal was brought about in 1814 by the encroachment of the Gurkhas on the northern frontier of India, which could not be permitted by the paramount power in the Indian Peninsula. Being the first serious mountain-campaign conducted by the Indian Army, it puzzled the generals a good deal. The Gurkhas were one of the many communities which had imitated the British military models, and, being brave men, they gave a great deal of trouble. The war resolved itself into a campaign of tactical positions, which the Gurkhas had the gift of choosing and of fortifying with stockades. After many petty reverses the British learned their trade from their enemies, and successfully turned their own methods against them. The man who brought the operations to a successful end was Major-general David Ochterlony, for whom the troops willingly endured extreme hardship and fatigue.

The Pindari War. 1817-1819

The next trouble also came in India. Central India, ever since the fall of the Moguls, had been in a state of anarchy and was full of huge groups or armies of banditti, known as Pindaris, which raided in all directions and were countenanced by some of the Mahratta Chiefs. No stable government can suffer anarchy on its borders, nor raids across them. To put an end to an insufferable nuisance and danger, the Governor-General, Lord Moira, set in motion some 120,000 troops, half moving southward, half northward, so as to pen in these Pindaris and make an end of them. The only pitched battle of any scale was that of Mehidpur, on 21st December, 1817, fought by General Hislop with 6,000 regular troops, nearly all Sepoys, 3,000 irregulars and 18 light guns, against Holkar with about 5,000 trained infantry, 20,000 irregular horse and over 60 guns. Hislop delivered a frontal attack in the face of Holkar's massed batteries, and lost 778 killed and wounded, but defeated Holkar completely and captured 63 guns. The war ended in a long and arduous task of hunting down fugitive parties, with great hardship and fatigue to the troops, until by February, 1819, the last gang had been exterminated and quiet was restored in Central India. Cholera, for the first time, attacked India and a British Army in the field in this war.

The Kandyan War. 1818

Meanwhile, in 1818, there was undertaken a small expedition for the final subjugation of the mountainous portion of Ceylon, the

Kandyans making constant intrusions upon the plain. They were a contemptible enemy, but the difficulties of the country and the unhealthiness of the climate were appalling obstacles. Of 5,000 men, 2,000 were at one period sent to hospital within three weeks. The operations, after six months of most trying work, were successful; but they were so arduous that the three British battalions engaged (Green Howards, 2nd Black Watch, and 1st Ulster Rifles), were quite broken down at their close.

The Burmese War. 1824-1826

A few years later trouble arose in a new quarter. The Burmese had for some time past been encroaching on the north-eastern territory of British India, within 150 miles of Calcutta Such was the alarm created by their raids that on one occasion the native merchants of Calcutta left their homes and encamped under the guns of the fort. The Burmese were warned more than once; and, since they refused to desist, an expedition of 11,000 men under General Sir Archibald Campbell was sent, with a naval force, to Rangoon. His instructions were to ascend from 400 to 500 miles of the river Irrawaddy to the Burmese capita' at Ava, and there to dictate terms. The troops landed at Rangoon practically unopposed in May, 1824, and found there literally nothing—not a bullock, not a boat, not a fowl, not a vegetable, not so much as an egg. This was done of set purpose, the Burmese plans being contrived to remove all the inhabitants and lay the country waste as the British advanced. With no means of land-transport, the force was obliged to sit still and live on ship's provisions; and the troops suffered terrible mortality from fever and scurvy. With the aid of the fleet's boats Campbell made little raids upon the Burmese, and after a little failure or two learned how to deal with them.

Their practice was to build elaborate stockades, too solid to be breached by round shot, and to arm them with scores of swivel-pieces and cannon; but, if they were attacked by escalade, they resisted very feebly and ran away. In October a Burmese army, 30,000 strong, advanced against Campbell's entrenched position before Rangoon, took up its ground with a precision which no European army could have excelled, and in two hours was invisible, having dug itself and begun to sap forward.[1] Though Campbell had little more than 1,300 men fit for duty,

[1] This was the first enemy encountered by the British which consistently "dug themselves in." The British troops were rather uneasy when they saw 30,000 men vanish underground in two hours.

he repelled the attack with little trouble and forced the Burmese to retire 50 miles up the river. Then the population returned to Rangoon with its bullocks, boats and produce, and matters became easier. Reinforcements arrived from India, and in 1825, after many little actions, Campbell made his way to Prome, 120 miles above Rangoon, and halting there during the rainy season (May-October) continued to advance northward in November. It was a terrible experience. Cholera was raging both among the troops and among the Burmese; and for days he marched through heavy jungle, seeing no living thing except the dying inhabitants, who had not strength to obey the order to desert the country, and often unable to find any camping ground clear of corpses. A last action, fought within 45 miles of Ava, in February, 1826, brought the King to reason.

In 1825 another column of about 11,000 men had been sent to try and reach the Irrawaddy by way of Arakan. It failed, owing to difficulties of transport and the deadly unhealthiness of the climate, the mortality among the troops being appalling. Of the British battalions, whether of the King's or the East India Company's Army, which went through the war from beginning to end, six out of every seven men perished.

The provinces of Arakan and Tennasserim were ceded to the Empire by Burma under the conditions of peace.

Siege of Bhurtpore

Simultaneously with the operations in Burma there arose, in 1824, another little war against the Jâts in India, which led to the second siege of Bhurtpore. The troops assembled for the operation were two regiments of British and six of native cavalry, 18 battalions of infantry—of which two only were British—with 50 light guns and 112 siege-pieces, the whole under the command of Lord Combermere. The first batteries were erected on 22nd December, and on 18th January, 1825, the great fortress was successfully stormed at a cost of 569 casualties, of which fully half fell on the West Yorks and the 2nd East Lancs.

The Ashanti War

A third little war was going on during these same years on the West Coast of Africa. There the Ashantis had copied the British discipline and, after some years of arrogant bearing, threatened to drive the British into the sea. The Governor, Sir Charles Macarthy, a good and experienced soldier, made his dispositions to meet them with a handful of white

FIRST ASHANTI WAR

troops—a British penal battalion called the Royal African Corps—and a multitude of timid native levies. The Ashantis, feinting to advance in several columns over a wide front, suddenly concentrated and came down upon Macarthy in overwhelming strength. Macarthy was killed, and his force for the most part destroyed. The Ashantis then attacked Cape Coast Castle, whither the remnant of the defeated army had retired. The condition of the garrison was so terrible from filth, overcrowding and bad water that every man would probably have perished had not reinforcements turned up in the nick of time. The war was prolonged until 1826, when on the 7th August a savage and terrible battle was fought, in which 5,000 Ashantis on one side and over 1,800 whites and native levies on the other, were killed and wounded. The penal battalion saved the situation from the beginning to the end of the war, and though they were, according to their record, the refuse of the British Army, they behaved like heroes. In those days the average annual mortality of white troops in time of peace on the West Coast of Africa was from 75 to 80 per cent. Yet even so, there were found there skilful and devoted officers, and brave and steady men.

THE EMPIRE AND THE ARMY

The South African War. 1834

The next scene of warfare was the Cape Colony.

From the first occupation of South Africa by Europeans there had been, of necessity, encroachment upon the lands of the Kafir tribes, with natural reprisals by those tribes upon the flocks and herds of the settlers. The chief value of the Cape Colony to England, in those days before the Suez Canal, was as a half-way house to India; and, had Simonstown been a Gibraltar she might have held no more than that harbour. But, as things were, she had to take over the butt-end of a huge continent, full of warlike natives; and it was inevitable that she should come into collision with more and more of them. At the end of 1834 there was, from a conjunction of various causes, a general invasion of the European settlements by the Kafirs along a hundred miles of the eastern frontier, for the defence of which there were on the spot no more than 800 men. The Dutch farmers were called out; the inroad was checked; and under the leadership of Colonel Harry Smith some 3,000 men of all kinds invaded the Kafir territory to inflict the only possible punishment, namely, to carry off the cattle which was the Kafirs' only wealth.

KAFIR WAR OF 1834

The operations involved bush-fighting against a wary and cunning enemy, who never overlooked a tactical blunder, with untold fatigue and hardship to the troops and desperate difficulties of transport and supply. But the British soldier quickly adapted himself to this strange warfare; and, under the energetic impulse of Harry Smith, the Kafirs were brought to submission within six months. Harry Smith had already served in South America, in the Peninsular War from beginning to end, in North America and at Waterloo; and he was still to share in two campaigns in India and another war in South Africa. Yet, though all his training had been in regular and orthodox operations, he seized at once the essential principles of savage warfare; and his men, soldiers or civilians, would do anything for him. The absurd clothing of the British regiments being utterly unfitted for such rough work, the soldiers were soon more suitably, though most disreputably, dressed; and it is worth mentioning that some of the 1st Gordon Highlanders made extremely efficient mounted infantry.

Improvements in the Treatment of the Soldier

Throughout the twenty years since Waterloo, the Army had been overworked and very shabbily treated. The soldier was expected to live on beef-broth every day from the beginning to the end of his service; he was overcrowded in barracks; he was so housed and fed in the tropics as if it were an object to kill him rather than to keep him alive; and he was kept to his duty by the fear of the lash. If it had not been for the care and initiative of the regimental officers, who worked untiringly to mitigate the hardship of his lot, the Army might have been dissolved by mutinies. But in 1837 a new era began. Flogging, though still maintained as the ultimate punishment, was inflicted as little as possible and with far less severity. Good conduct pay and good conduct badges were introduced for the encouragement of deserving soldiers, and the diet and quarters in the tropics were improved. An effort was also made to ensure the more regular relief of regiments abroad, which was not easy, seeing that since 1815 the average number of line battalions on service beyond sea had been four out of five.

The Australasian Colonies and Canada

In the Empire the transportation of convicts to New South Wales ceased in 1838, and though it was continued for another thirty years to Tasmania and elsewhere, the system was from 1838 doomed to extinction. So Australia began to assume her rightful place; and in the year 1839 the formation of a company to colonize New Zealand practically forced the British Government to take that country under its sovereignty. Meanwhile, a petty rebellion in Canada, easily and with little bloodshed repressed by the Governor —Sir John Colborne, a veteran officer of the Peninsula—in 1837 and 1838, resulted presently, through excellent constitutional reforms, in the transformation of the colonists into a loyal and prosperous community.

The Percussion-Cap

One small but momentous detail of armament must also be mentioned. In 1839 was introduced into the Army the percussion-cap, which has brought about nothing less than a revolution in small arms. By the substitution of the percussion-cap for the flintlock in the musket, missfires were reduced from 411 per 1,000 shots to 45. As a further improvement the calibre of all small arms was, for the first time in the Army's history, made uniform, so that one pattern of ammunition served for the whole.

The First Afghan War, 1839-1842

We now approach a sad story of mismanagement in the East.

Ever since Waterloo Russia had been extending her borders steadily eastward; and the Government of India took reasonable alarm. It was their idea to gain the friendship of Afghanistan to west of the Indus, of the Sikhs in the Punjab—which under the leadership of Ranjit Singh had become a very formidable military power—and of the Amirs of Sind, to east of the Indus, and to unite them into a buffer against Russian invasion. The only difficulty was that the ruler of Afghanistan, Dost Mohamed, and Ranjit Singh were deadly enemies; and the Indian Government in an evil hour decided to invade Afghanistan and replace Dost Mohamed by a prince, Shah Shuja, who had been expelled from the throne by the Afghans. It was the maddest project ever conceived, for between the British frontier of India and the passes into Afghanistan there lay a margin of 400 to 500 miles in the hands of the Amirs of Sind and of Ranjit Singh, both of them uncertain friends, who might turn upon the British at any moment. However, about 5,000 men were sent from Bombay to land at the mouth of the Indus, and about 10,000 men moved from the Bengal frontier

THE FIRST AFGHAN WAR

to join them. Little was known of the country to be invaded, and the experience of mountain-campaigns was small; but it was supposed that the march was simply to be a military promenade, and therefore the military commanders were subordinated to the political.

With great difficulty, with terrific loss of transport, and in constant peril of starvation, the force reached the Bolan Pass, and threaded it to Kandahar, where Shah Shuja was installed as King without resistance. After a long halt Sir John Keane, the Commander-in-Chief, marched on Kabul, stormed the fortress of Ghazni, which barred his way (23rd July, 1839), and entered Kabul with Shah Shuja unopposed on 7th August. The Bengal portion of his Army had by that time marched 1,500 miles. Leaving most of his infantry behind him, Keane then returned with the cavalry through the Khyber Pass, and his work was supposed to be done.

But, in fact, it was only begun. The British troops were widely scattered in many posts and garrisons, and they were incessantly attacked on their lines of communication throughout 1840. In 1841 matters became even more menacing, and at the end of the year there was a general rising which practically confined all British garrisons to their posts. At Kabul, General Elphinstone, a dying man, made a feeble resistance and at last negotiated for the retreat of his force, about 5,000 strong,[1] under Afghan escort, through the Khyber Pass. The Afghans delayed his departure on various pretexts until December, when the snow was thick, attacked his column continually on the march and destroyed it almost to a man.

Such a disaster shook the nerve of the Indian Government. With great difficulty transport was secured for a new force under General Pollock, who forced the Khyber Pass with little difficulty in April, 1842, and in September captured Kabul; after which the country was evacuated. The entire expedition was a hideous mistake; it was misconducted owing to the incessant interference of the political officers; and its failure injured the prestige of the British in India. The Governor-General, to make the best of a bad business, gave medals to all ranks for this war. This roused a clamour of Peninsula veterans in England who had done much better work and received no medal. A medal for the great war against France was granted in 1847; and it then became the rule to give medals to all ranks for all campaigns.

[1] The only British troops were a few gunners and the 1st Essex.

The Conquest of Sind

The withdrawal of the British from Afghanistan necessitated careful watching of Sind, where at the end of 1841 Major-General Sir Charles Napier assumed command. By January, 1843, the Amirs had satisfied Napier of their hostility; and he advanced against them with a little column of about 3,000 men, of which the Cheshire was the only British battalion. On 16th February he attacked and beat them at Miani, and on 24th March, with a rather larger force, he again beat them at Dabo. There remained the task of hunting down the last of the hostile chiefs with small columns—most arduous work owing to the frightful heat—but by the middle of June the work was done and the conquest of Sind was accomplished. This was a smart little campaign, well carried out against greatly superior numbers. But less might have been heard of it had not Napier's two victories come timely to restore British military reputation in India, and had not his brother William written the history of the operations with the vivid vehemence of which he was master.

The China War. 1841-1842

Meantime there had broken out a quarrel with China. This arose chiefly from the abolition of the East India Company's monopoly of the China trade, and from the arrogant insolence of the Chinese Government towards traders who carried on commerce under the British flag. A joint naval and military expedition was, therefore, sent to China in January, 1841, the troops being under the command of Sir Hugh Gough. After a year spent, against Gough's judgment, in successful but futile operations on the Yang-tse-kiang, he in 1842 transferred the force to the Pei-ho and moved against Peking. In August the Chinese came to terms, ceding Hong Kong to the British, and opening five ports to their traders. The campaign is not worth detailed narration, for the Chinese always prepared to receive attack in front, and always ran away when Gough assailed them in flank. There were few casualties among the British in action; but the losses from sickness were terrible. As a example of excellent co-operation between Army and Navy it is worth study; but the hardest of the work fell on the navigating officers of the Navy, who took the Army over many uncharted seas and into many uncharted ports with perfect safety.

The Gwalior War of 1843

Next a little squabble arose out of a disputed succession to the sovereignty of Gwalior,

THE "ONE DAY" WAR

when the British sent two columns, one of about 6,500 men under Sir Hugh Gough and one of about 6,000 men under Sir John Grey, from opposite directions to uphold their favoured representative. A peaceful settlement seemed so certain that the Governor-General and half a dozen ladies[1] were with Gough when, on 29th December, 1843, he found himself obliged to attack the Mahrattas, about 10,000 strong, in a strong position at Maharajpur. The fight was stubborn, for the Mahratta artillery far outmatched Gough's both in number of pieces and weight of metal; the Mahratta gunners were brave and skilful men; and their batteries could not be silenced until they had been stormed by the British infantry. The 1st Dorsets and 1st South Lancs —Gough's only white regiments—did the brunt of the work, claiming between them nearly 400 out of the 800 casualties for the day. Simultaneously Sir John Grey had a successful running fight with another Mahratta force at Panniar, some 25 miles south of Maharajpur, and thus the issue of the campaign was decided in one day. It is therefore known as the "One day war."

---

[1] Mrs. Harry Smith, who was an old soldier, having gone through the Peninsular campaigns of 1812–14 with her husband, took charge of the ladies. She reported unfavourably of every unit of her command.

The First Sikh War. 1845-1846

Within little more than twelve months, it was necessary to meet a still more formidable enemy. Ranjit Singh, who had made the Sikhs into a disciplined military people, died in 1839; and after his death came anarchy. The Sikh army, trained by Europeans and reckoned at from 40,000 to 100,000 men with 200 guns, was masterless and disposed to sally out against any neighbour to plunder and despoil. The Governor-General, Sir Henry Hardinge, who was also a distinguished soldier, assembled 30,000 men at wide intervals on the frontier, unwilling to concentrate them more closely lest he should give provocation. But on the 11th December, 1845, the Sikhs crossed the Sutlej into British territory, and Sir Hugh Gough hastily collected from 11,000 to 12,000 men to meet them. He was not in a pleasant position. His Bengal Sepoys were in a very bad state of discipline and were mortally afraid of the Sikhs; and his field-guns were far too light and too few to cope with the Sikh artillery. The Sikh batteries must therefore be stormed by infantry, and he could count upon none but his white battalions, of which he had four, and one regiment of British cavalry.

On the 18th December he attacked the Sikhs in a position screened by jungle at Mudki,

THE FIRST SIKH WAR

and after a blind engagement drove them off, his casualties numbering 872, of which 506 were Europeans. Reinforced by four battalions, of which two were British, and by two heavy howitzers, which gave him in all about 16,000 men and 63 guns, he on the 21st once more engaged the Sikhs at Ferozeshah. Once again he carried most of the enemy's position after a very severe fight, which lasted far into the dark hours, and continuing his attack next day captured 70 guns. But presently he found himself confronted by a fresh Sikh force, and was obliged for some hours to endure their cannonade without retort, for he had no ammunition left. At last the enemy drew off after a very critical interval, during which the fate of India trembled in the balance. In the two days Gough's casualties were 2,400, of which just half fell on the Europeans, though the native troops present outnumbered the Europeans by three to one. The heroes of both actions were the 3rd Light Dragoons (Hussars), who at Mudki had lost 250 men, but charged with their remnant and drove off the Sikh cavalry at Ferozeshah. Among the infantry the 1st East Surrey and the Norfolks both had over 300 casualties.

The Sikhs now threatened Gough's communications, so he detached Harry Smith with 12,000 men and 32 guns to clear them. On 29th January, 1846, Smith routed and destroyed a strong Sikh force at Aliwal, capturing everything that they had, including 67 guns. The 1st East Surrey were in this action, too and the 1st West Kent, which had lost 233 men and officers at Mudki and Ferozeshah, lost 73 more at Aliwal. But the heroes of the fight were the 16th Lancers, who rode down Sikh squares and Sikh batteries irresistibly, though at the cost of 144 officers and men. The decisive battle of the war was fought on 10th February at Sobraon, when the contest of infantry against artillery was as stubborn as ever, though the Indian infantry this time took a fair share in it. Gough's casualties were nearly 2,300, and once again the 3rd Hussars, the 1st East Surrey, and the 1st West Kent were prominent—the East Surrey losing 154 out of 400 present, and the West Kent 239. But the Sikhs had accepted battle with their backs to an impassable river; and from 8,000 to 10,000 of them perished. As the price of peace the Sikhs ceded the territory which lies between the Sutlej and the Beas.

Second Sikh War. 1848-1849

Few expected that the Sikhs would be permanently curbed by Gough's campaign.

THE SECOND SIKH WAR

In 1848 they again took up arms; but little was effected during the year because the British troops were divided between operations in the field and the siege of Multan, for both of which purposes simultaneously they were insufficient. Multan fell on 3rd January, 1849, and Gough advancing engaged the enemy in a position at Chilianwala on 13th January. Matters went ill. The South Wales Borderers, after gallantly storming a Sikh battery, were counter-attacked and driven back with 600 casualties. In another part of the field there was a panic, owing to bad leadership, among some of the cavalry, and, at the end of the day, Gough had little to show for 2,300 killed and wounded. He then stood fast until reinforcements reached him from Multan, when by masterly manœuvring he fairly forced the Sikhs to come out and fight him on the ground of his choice. He had now at last a sufficiency of heavy artillery, and, attacking the Sikhs on 21st February at Gujarat, he defeated them utterly and finally. A rapid pursuit completed the victory; the power of the Sikhs was broken; and the Punjab was annexed to the British Empire after the hardest fighting ever known to the British in India. Other Indian soldiers had run away when their positions and batteries were captured, but the Sikhs counter-attacked, which was a new experience.

The New Zealand War of 1845

Meanwhile there had been, in 1845 and 1846, a little brush with the native inhabitants of New Zealand, who resented the encroachment of white men on their lands. The Maoris were very fine fighting men, who threw up almost impregnable stockaded fortifications and defended them gallantly with American rifles. The country being then roadless and practically devoid of transport, it was extremely difficult to get near these enemies, and not much easier to know what to do when they were reached, for the stockades could not be breached except by heavy cannon. The forces engaged at no time numbered 1,000, but they were repulsed more than once with relatively heavy loss in the country north of Auckland, before they brought the Maoris to reason; while other tribes gave much trouble in the vicinity of Wellington before they would agree to live in peace.

The Burmese War of 1852

Quiet had not yet settled down upon the Punjab, when maltreatment of British mer-

BURMA AND KAFIRLAND AGAIN

chants at Rangoon by the Burmese, in defiance of treaty agreements, compelled the dispatch of another expedition to the Irrawaddy. The experience of 1826 was remembered, and the troops—about 6,000 strong—disembarked practically unresisted at Rangoon in April, 1852. They were presently joined by 14,000 more, and after very little fighting, though with heavy loss to the British from cholera and other sickness, the Court of Ava purchased peace by the cession of Pegu.

The Cape War. 1850-1852

Meanwhile the embers of rebellion had flamed up afresh in South Africa.

At the close of the Cape War of 1836 the English Government had upset all the arrangements made by the Governor, with the result that many of the Dutch Boers had trekked away, so as to be out of reach of the British Government, and that the Kafirs were incessantly stealing cattle. Little military operations were constantly necessary to restrain them, and they remained in a dangerous state of unrest. There was trouble also with the Boers, one result of which was the annexation of Natal in 1843. At last, in December, 1850, the Kafirs burst across the frontier with fire and sword, sweeping off cattle and murdering settlers, while many of the natives within the Colony also rose, and murdered and plundered wholesale. Sir Harry Smith, the Governor, at once hastened to the frontier and, regardless of the danger in his rear, resolved to hold the frontier-posts at all hazards. He had only four weak regular battalions, for such of the Boers as remained in the Colony refused to come to his aid; but with extraordinary nerve he stood fast until native and other levies reached him from Capetown. Then, taking the field himself, he followed the Kafirs into their strongest fastnesses of precipice, forest and crag, and fairly beat them into subjection. The sufferings of the troops from hardship, privation and fatigue were very great. Frequently after hours of hard work in heavy rain they returned to bivouac in a sea of mud. Sometimes the rain turned to snow and the cold was intolerable. Then the sun would come out, and they fled to the shade to escape from unbearable heat. Their clothes were torn off their backs in the forest, and the boots worn off their feet by scrambling among rocks; but still they worked on, against a very wily and dangerous enemy; and by extraordinary exertions Harry Smith kept them fed. By the beginning of April, 1852, he had finished his work, and for his reward was recalled in disgrace. But, excepting a little march against the Basutos, there remained nothing for his successor to do; and the Cape Colony was left for the present at peace, by extension of the eastward boundary to the very frontier recommended by the military commander in 1835.

In this campaign the first trial was made of a new muzzle-loading rifle, the Minie, six of these weapons being issued to the six best shots in each company. It threw a conical bullet fairly accurately up to 500 yards, and was not ineffective at 900 yards. Nearly every officer in this campaign carried a sporting rifle, and one of them told the present writer that he saw a Kafir on the skyline shot dead at a range of 1,000 yards. So the era of the rifle was opening in earnest.

Neglect of the Army. 1815-1854

The reader will now have gathered some idea of the burden that was cast upon the Army, in the years that followed upon Waterloo, for the consolidation of the Empire. It is true that under the administration of the Duke of Wellington in 1829 and 1830, the establishment of the Metropolitan Police—most of them old soldiers—and of the Irish Constabulary had saved the Army from much unpleasant and difficult duty; but, without this help, it could not possibly have attended to the policing of the Empire. "You have been carrying on war," said the Duke of Wellington in one of his last speeches in Parliament, "by means of your peace-establishment, yet on that establishment you have never had more men than are necessary to relieve the sentries and regiments on foreign service, some of which have been 25 years abroad." The niggardliness of Parliament towards both services had been invincible. The Navy was dangerously weak. The Militia had been allowed to perish, and was only revived on a basis of voluntary enlistment in 1852. The regiments of the Army had been grudgingly maintained; and only after 1852 were there signs that better treatment was in store for them. In that year there were peace-manœuvres at Chobham, and in 1853 Aldershot was purchased as a manœuvring ground. But the other military services, such as the Staff Corps and the Wagon-train, had been abolished; and now the consequences of these economies were to make themselves felt.

The Crimean War. 1854-1856

In 1854 England found herself at war with Russia; though for what reason it is hard to say. Russia had opened hostilities against Turkey, as she did periodically in the hope of gaining an outlet to the Mediterranean; and English policy had for some time past favoured the maintenance of Turkey as a menace to Russia's flank, during her steady advance eastward towards the frontier of India. By committing herself more and more deeply to the support of Turkey, England at last drifted into war. France joined her; and the two Governments agreed to conduct operations together, France furnishing at the outset about 25,000 troops and England 26,000. The armies were landed first in Bulgaria to meet a Russian advance on Constantinople; but, since that peril was averted by the exertions of the Turks alone, France and England between them concocted one of the maddest schemes of operations that ever was projected. The troops were to land on the Crimea, where they had no naval base and where bad weather might cut them off at any moment from their ships, and attack Sebastopol. Nothing certain was known about the defences of that fortress, except that they were very strong to seaward, and nothing as to the strength of the Russians in the Crimean peninsula; but it was assumed that the place could not be taken without a siege. So it was boldly proposed that some

50,000 troops should land on an open beach, march without any land-transport overland upon Sebastopol and lay siege to it, with their rear exposed to attack by all the strength of Russia.

Alma, Balaclava, Inkerman

Moreover, this was actually done. The disembarkation was not opposed; but the Russians took up a position on the river Alma to resist the Allied advance. They were attacked and driven back in disorder; the British, who bore the brunt of the action, having 2,000 casualties. Lord Raglan, the British commander, wished to follow up this success at once and, had the French commander consented, the Allied armies would probably have marched straight into Sebastopol. As things were, they made a flank march round to the south side of the fortress and regained communication with their fleets; the British taking, on the advice of their naval officers, the port of Balaclava, which was eight miles from their camp on the bleak plateau above Sebastopol. Heavy guns were brought up, and after a bombardment Raglan wished to assault, but the French would not agree; and a great opportunity seems to have been lost. On 25th October the Russians came down in

BATTLE OF INKERMAN

force to threaten the British communications with Balaclava, but were easily repulsed, the Heavy Cavalry delivering a brilliant charge against thrice their number. But the Light Brigade of cavalry, through a staff officer's mistake, attacked some batteries in front, with more batteries playing upon their flank, and lost half of their strength. On 5th November the Russians made a great attack from within and without Sebastopol, which should have made an end of the Allies; but they were repulsed with great loss by the British after a very fine fight, and they never really developed their assault upon the French. The British troops engaged at the battle of Inkerman numbered about 8,000, and their casualties were nearly 2,600. They had had cholera among them for months, and were already so much weakened by sickness that this action very seriously reduced their strength.

The Siege of Sebastopol

In the middle of November a great storm flattened out the camp, wrecked several ships, and reduced the track from Balaclava to the camp to a sea of mud. It became almost impossible to bring even food, much more fuel and clothing, to the British Army, and the men and officers died like flies of fatigue and exposure. Raglan had begged for a Land-transport Corps months before he landed, but nothing was done until March, 1855. He sent urgent entreaties for forage, without which he could not keep transport-animals alive; but months passed before an adequate supply arrived. Ministers did not lack good will, but they had not the slightest idea of the meaning of war.

Somehow, though with terrible losses from starvation and exposure, the British got through the winter; but the Allies were really the besieged rather than the besiegers throughout, for the Russians could always reinforce Sebastopol on one side and threaten their rear on the other. The French, understanding war better and being strongly reinforced, now took the greater share in the operations. A railway from Balaclava improved communication with the British camp. A Land-transport Corps was formed. The operations were pushed on during the summer, and on 18th June, 1855, British and French unsuccessfully assaulted the keys of the Russian position. After further bombardment the assault was repeated on 8th September. The British were again repelled with heavy loss, but the French carried the Malakoff Tower; and the Russians thereupon evacuated Sebastopol. By the end of the year the British had a properly organized army of 50,000 men in the Crimea; but no further operations were undertaken, and in March, 1856, peace was concluded with Russia.

Reforms during the Crimean War

This was the first war in which, owing to the presence of a war-correspondent, the newspapers admitted the British public behind the scenes. There were exhaustive inquiries as to who was to blame for the sufferings and failures of the Army, which resulted in very little. The Ministers were responsible for fastening a mad plan of operations on the military commander; and the British public was responsible for persistent starving of the Army during forty years. The greatest permanent advantage that came out of the Crimean War was the placing of the Engineers, Artillery and Commissariat under the War Office, the transfer of clothing from the Colonels to an Army Clothing department; the founding of the Small Arms Factory at Enfield; the improvement of Army hospitals, and the training of expert nurses by Miss Nightingale—the mother of skilled nursing in all hospitals. From the Crimean War also dates the institution of the Victoria Cross.

The Persian War of 1856-1857

The Crimean War was hardly over before trouble showed itself in the further East.

This arose out of the occupation of Herat by Persia, contrary to treaty, which led to the dispatch of a joint expedition to the Persian Gulf from India. The military force, about 7,000 strong, included two battalions of the Queen's Army and was under the command of Sir James Outram. It landed at Bushire, fought a little action, and proceeded to the mouth of the Euphrates, where some further operations constrained Persia, in April, 1857, to renounce further claims over Herat or interference with the internal affairs of Afghanistan.

Second China War. 1856-1857

Then came a second quarrel with China. The treaty of Nankin at the close of the war of 1842 had not been observed by the Chinese; and an attack on a British ship in October, 1856, brought differences between the two nations to a crisis. The French, being also aggrieved, joined forces with the British; but, owing to the Indian mutiny, operations were delayed until the end of 1857. Canton was stormed by the Allied troops on 29th December, and in May the Taku forts were taken, whereupon new treaties were accepted by the Chinese and the war came to an end. The British troops engaged were few and chiefly marines.

We must now turn to more serious events in India.

The Indian Mutiny. 1857-1859

The discipline of the Bengal Native Army had long been going from bad to worse; and the issue of a new cartridge, which was said to be greased with a mixture of beef-fat and hog's lard—an abomination to both Hindus and Mohammedans—brought matters to a crisis. On the 10th May, 1857, the native garrison at Meerut mutinied, massacred many Europeans, and marched to Delhi, the ancient capital of the Mogul Empire, which they occupied. Many other outbreaks followed in quick succession, and the discontented, the disreputable, and the adventurous sprang quickly into rebellion. The British troops, 38,000 in all, were widely scattered from Persia to Burma. Very soon the chief centres of operation declared themselves to be three: Cawnpore, Lucknow and Delhi itself. At Cawnpore a tiny British garrison was defending itself behind weak entrenchments in desperate straits. At Lucknow the garrison, after an unsuccessful sortie, was closely beleaguered but held its own. Delhi, as the centre of rebellion, was the most important point of all; and, the Punjab being kept quiet under the masterful rule of John Lawrence, a British force of about 4,000 men fought its way with little difficulty from Ambala to Delhi and on 8th June took up a position before it. Reinforcements from time to time reached them, and the erection of batteries was begun; but the work was most arduous owing to constant harassing attacks from the enemy and, above all, to the intense heat. As before Sebastopol, the besiegers were for long really the besieged. In August the force was nearly doubled in strength by the arrival of a column from the Punjab, under General John Nicholson. Delhi was stormed on 14th September and finally mastered on the 20th, the casualties in the assault amounting to 1,170.

Meanwhile, another column about 1,500 strong—including two battalions just returned from Persia—had left Allahabad on 30th June under General Havelock to relieve Cawnpore. Havelock came too late, for the garrison had already surrendered and had been treacherously massacred; but he fought his way there, recovered it and marched for Lucknow which, after many unavoidable delays and innumerable little actions, he successfully reinforced with 3,000 men on 25th September, his casualties in the final capture of Lucknow exceeding 500. His column then occupied Lucknow, where it was besieged in turn by 60,000 rebels. Meanwhile, reinforcements had arrived from England, and Sir Colin Campbell, assuming the chief command, led about 5,000 of them from Cawnpore, forced his way into Lucknow after hard fighting on 17th November, brought off the garrison, returned to Cawnpore, which was hard beset by 25,000 rebels, and dispersed them. The bulk of the enemy, some 120,000 strong, then assembled at Lucknow, where Campbell attacked and defeated them on 11th March, 1858, but failed to deal them a decisive blow. In Central India Sir Hugh Rose, with a very small force, stormed Jhansi and struck the rebels hard again at Gwalior. By June all organized resistance came to an end; but for another twelve months and more small columns hunted down bands of rebels until the last embers of rebellion had been trodden down.

Before the operations were concluded Sir Colin Campbell had under his command some 120,000 men of one kind and another; but the brunt of the hard work was borne by a handful at the beginning. Among these the Gurkha regiments were conspicuous. The steadfastness and endurance shown by the British soldier whether before Delhi, in Oude or in

Central India, amid the appalling heat of the Indian summer, are perhaps the most remarkable things in the story of the Mutiny. The longing to avenge the murder of white men, women and children kindled a wonderful spirit in the men. But the demon of plunder was also abroad, and more than once relatively large bodies of soldiers passed for a time beyond control. Many deeds of heroism were done by individuals during these campaigns. It is more instructive, however, to look also to the weakness and incompetence shown by many in high places, both military and civil, and to the reaction of these upon the headway made by the Mutiny, and upon the delay in its final suppression. The principal result of the Mutiny was that the Government of India was transferred from the East India Company to the Crown, and the 24,000 British troops in the Company's service to the Queen's Army.

The Third China War. 1860

A third China war followed quickly upon the Indian Mutiny, having its origin in the refusal of the Chinese Government to admit the British and French envoys, who came to ratify the treaty of 1858, to enter the mouth of the Pei-ho. The British naval

THIRD CHINA WAR

squadron, attempting to force the passage, was repulsed with heavy loss; and a body of 11,000 British and 7,000 French was sent out to obtain satisfaction. The British detachment, under the command of Sir Hope Grant, included 6 British battalions and one regiment of British cavalry. The troops landed at Peh-tang at the mouth of the Pei-ho on 30th July; the Taku forts were stormed on 21st August; Tientsin was occupied two days later; a Chinese force was easily beaten in the field on the 18th and 21st September; and on the 13th October the Allies entered Pekin. On 24th October a treaty was signed whereby China reaffirmed the treaty of 1858, opened Tientsin as a treaty-port, and ceded Kaolun to England.

The Umbeyla Expedition. 1863

We must next turn to an early example of the punitive expeditions—too frequent even to be enumerated—against the mountain tribes of the north-west of India, which were an inevitable result of the extension of the British frontier beyond the Indus. It is a general rule in history that where barren mountains adjoin rich plains, the poor but hardy mountaineers descend from time to time to plunder their soft and wealthy neighbours on the flat land. In this case the force employed numbered between 5,000 and 6,000 men, one-fourth of them Europeans, under the command of General Neville Chamberlain. It began operations in October, and by the end of November had lost nearly 1,000 killed and wounded, among the latter being Chamberlain and his second-in-command, with little advantage to show in return. The column was then reinforced to a strength of 9,000, including two more battalions of the Queen's Army, when two days more of sharp fighting —which cost 172 more casualties—brought the offending tribes to submission before the end of the year.

The Second New Zealand War. 1860-1869

Meanwhile for the second time a quarrel had arisen with certain Maori chiefs, which was composed after some fighting in 1861, but broke out again in 1863 and continued until 1866, not without reverses to the British. The difficulties of transport and supply were most formidable. The Maori fortresses, or *pas*, were very strong, and only to be reached through forests, where the work of bringing up guns was most arduous. Moreover, assaults upon these *pas* were always costly—we suffered more than one ignominious repulse—and the Maoris always contrived to slip away before they were carried. At last the British took to marching up to a *pa*, entrenching themselves before it, and provoking the Maoris to attack, which, when feasible, produced good results. At one time there were 6,000 or 7,000 British troops in the Colony, to the great satisfaction of the local traders; but, when all of them were withdrawn in 1866, the Colonists, being left to themselves, did not take very long to put a final stop to Maori wars.

The Abyssinian Expedition. 1868

The year 1868 found us engaged with a new enemy.

King Theodore of Abyssinia brought war upon himself by imprisoning and torturing British subjects, the British consul among them, in 1863, and refusing, after years of negotiation, to release them. An expedition of 13,500 men, nearly one-fourth of them Europeans, was therefore dispatched from Bombay under the command of Sir Robert Napier, which landed at Annesley Bay and marched upon Magdala, some 380 miles distant. The difficulties of transport and supply were very great, but the resistance of the enemy was not serious, and Magdala was stormed

THE EMPIRE AND THE ARMY

with little loss on 13th April, when King Theodore shot himself. All trouble then came to an end; the prisoners were released; and the expedition returned to India.

The story of little campaigns must now be interrupted for a space. Most of our little wars since 1815, as the reader will have noticed, were concerned with India, and with the Cape Colony on the way to India. Let him now note that a new route to India was opened in 1869 by the completion of the Suez Canal, an important fact which greatly influenced British policy.

CHAPTER XI

THE ARMY REFORMS OF 1870-1899

THE incessant calls upon the Army for the consolidation of the Empire, the breakdown of all administrative services in the Crimea, the long neglect of the Militia, and an uneasy feeling that there was no reserve behind the troops of the line, had for some years impressed successive Governments with the military insecurity of England. Sundry remedies had been suggested with no great result. Alarm at some bellicose utterances of France had, in 1859, called into existence many tens of thousands of Rifle Volunteers—an old expedient which had been tried and found wanting between 1793 and 1807, and had been abandoned by Castlereagh. By a curious coincidence in the year 1870 was passed the Act which provided for the compulsory education of all children at the expense of the State; but it occurred to no one to insist that, as in other countries, the youth of the country should pass through some military training in return for this free education. There was little idea, in fact, of any military force apart from the regular army; and the difficulty was to devise a scheme under which at one and the same time that army should be able to do the police-work of the Empire in all climates from the Equator almost to the Arctic Circle, and build up a reserve to meet more serious dangers. Young soldiers could not stand such arduous work; but without young soldiers there could be no reserve. There must evidently be a transition-period of extreme danger while the reserve was accumulating; but the Government in 1870 resolved to take the risk, and began its reforms by enlisting private soldiers for 6 years with the colours and 6 in the reserve. In 1871, further, the purchase of commissions by officers of cavalry and infantry was abolished.

The Abolition of Purchase

The abolition of purchase at once stopped the free flow of promotion which had gone on automatically for 200 years, and gave rise to endless difficulties which took years to set right. It was ordained that officers who did not reach the rank of major by a certain age must retire; but this rule would have caused such hardship that it was evaded by increasing the establishment of majors in each regiment. The period during which an officer could com-

SHORT SERVICE INTRODUCED

mand a regiment was also limited; and at one moment the rank of Major-General was so freely offered to field-officers, to tempt them to retire, that the country was flooded with Major-Generals. Some thirty years were needed before the new arrangements, complicated as they were by a steady demand for a higher standard of education and efficiency among officers, could be brought to work smoothly and kindly.

Enlistment for Short Service

Short service, though tried as temporary expedient in the wars both of Marlborough and of Wellington, also took long to accommodate itself to the ways both of the Army and of the nation. The profession of a soldier, ever since the disbandment of the New Model Army in 1661, had been in bad odour. Both parties in Parliament loathed the name of the Standing Army. Even poor families of villagers or townsmen thought it a disgrace for one of their sons to enlist. The soldier was supposed to be a drunken ne'er-do-well, and fit for nothing but fighting. Hence, when the first batch of reservists was turned loose upon the country, they were not well received nor readily employed. The present writer can well remember swarms of them begging in the streets of London.

The dearth of old soldiers became a far more serious matter. England was prosperous in the 'seventies and 'eighties; and recruits were, therefore, difficult to find. The majority of recruits enlisted were boys, who needed some years of training and feeding before they were fit to work; and, as fast as they matured, they were drafted off to India. For many years, if anyone wished to see a real battalion of British soldiers, he had to travel to India to find it. As shall presently be told, a few battalions of boys were sent abroad on active service, but were naturally found wanting. The matter became so urgent that very soon the 6 years with the colours and 6 with the reserve were changed to 7, or even 8, with the colours, and 5, or even 4, with the reserve; while, after a time, in the Guards, it became 3 with the colours and 9 with the reserve. The great source of recruiting was the Militia, with its annual training of two months for recruits and one month for other men; and, in fact, the Militia tended to become more and more a mere recruiting depôt for the Army, instead of the second line.

The Territorial System

The next important change was one of organization. In 1870, a most fateful year,

THE TERRITORIAL SYSTEM

France declared war against Prussia. Within a few months France was beaten to her knees, and the German Empire came into being. A pamphlet entitled *The Battle of Dorking*,[1] which had an enormous circulation, set forth the certain fate of England if invaded by Prussia, and stimulated the general impulse towards military reform. A second battalion had been added in 1857–1859 to the first 25[2] regiments of the infantry of the line; and a few years later the remaining regiments were linked together in pairs. In 1881 these pairs were made permanent under territorial designations. The old numbers and the old facings (except in the case of the Buffs) were swept away; all Royal regiments retaining their blue facings, and the remainder adopting uniformly white for English regiments, yellow for Scottish, and green for Irish. To these pairs of battalions their county militia and their county volunteers were affiliated as additional battalions, the distinction in dress being that the officers of the regulars and militia wore gold lace, and the volunteers silver, the men having respectively yellow and white lace.

The change was not so new as it seemed.

[1] It was written by Colonel Chesney, one of two brothers who were both very able officers.

[2] In reality 24 regiments, for the Royals have always had 2 battalions.

THE EMPIRE AND THE ARMY

Territorial designations [1] dated from 1782, and the proposed reforms of the Duke of York, nearly identical with those of 1870, have already been mentioned (*see* page 224). The British, however, know little of their military history. The abolition of the old numbers and facings raised a violent outcry, the sentimental attachment to them being extremely strong both among officers and men. Old nicknames such as the Slashers, the Springers and the Pompadours, seemed to become meaningless when the battalion that claimed them no longer stood alone; and many old battalions strongly resented their enforced union with younger yoke-fellows. The present writer, who has a vivid recollection of all these things, has, however, lived to see the old numbers (with the possible exception of the 60th), die a peaceful death; the territorial designations, however cumbrous, joyfully and even proudly accepted; some of the old titles (such as the Green Howards), which existed before numbers, and even some of the old facings restored; and the existence of single-battalioned regiments nearly forgotten.

[1] But many of these were changed owing to the shifting of populous centres from the South to the North. Devonshire used to have 3 regiments. She has now only one. Yorkshire and Lancashire have now the great preponderance.

The Army Service Corps

A most important reform belonging to this same period was the establishment of the Army Service Corps. Brief notice has been taken of the efforts at sundry times to give military organization to the transport-service. There was in the Crimea a belated Land-transport Corps, and after it a Military Train, which during the Indian Mutiny were turned into Dragoons, and in China in 1860 were indisposed to do any but combatant work. More than one experiment was tried in 1870 and in the following years to put Transport and Supply under the control of a single department, but there was reluctance to give the officers combatant rank or to recognize it as a military organization, until in 1888 Sir Redvers Buller called into being the Army Service Corps.

Training and Armament

The changes in the training of the Army, in consequence of the improvement of missile weapons, are too many to be even glanced at. It may, however, be mentioned that Salisbury Plain was purchased as a new manœuvring ground at the close of the 19th century.

In the matter of armament, the Minie rifle during the Crimean War gave place to an improved muzzle-loader, called the Enfield rifle, and that in turn in 1866 to the first breech-loading rifle, the Snider.[1] But this was little used on active service, except by Indian troops, for the Snider was superseded before the South African and Afghan wars of 1878 by the Martini-Henry, the first hammerless rifle. Smokeless powder and the magazine rifle, of much longer range and greater accuracy than the Martini, were introduced in 1889.

The first machine-guns, called *mitrailleuses*, were used by the French in the war of 1870. In the British service a machine-gun, known as the Gatling, was used both in Afghanistan and in South Africa in 1878-1880. Both weapons had many barrels, and were untrustworthy owing to frequent jams. In fact, the Maxim was the first efficient machine-gun. The British encountered it for the first time against the Boers in 1899.

Breech-loading rifled field-guns were first used in the China War of 1860. The projectiles were, at first, coated with lead to fit the grooves, and were accurate up to 1,800 yards; but they were objected to because the lead casing, being stripped off in their flight, fell among the infantry over whose

---

[1] The Snider was converted from the muzzle-loading Enfield. To make the bullet take the grooves it had a hollow base filled with clay, which practically made it an expanding bullet. The Martini-Henry threw a heavy but solid bullet.

heads the guns were firing. The artillery continued to use muzzle-loaders until 1886.

Clothing

As to clothing, the troops, until 1882, took the field in the absurd uniforms which they wore at home, no matter where they were serving. In Burma, in 1826, the men had no protection from the sun but their shakos; but in the Sikh wars and the Mutiny they wore their forage caps with a white curtain round them. The result was that in rough campaigns, as in the South African bush, officers and men wore very much what they pleased or indeed what they could get, and presented a most ruffianly appearance. When the Crimean army was in Bulgaria there was much complaint because officers changed into plain clothes as soon as they came off duty; but the reason was simply because the uniform was so inconvenient, unpractical and costly that no man would wear it longer than he could help. After the Crimea the tunic—an imitation of the French—was substituted for the coatee; but shortly after the triumph of the Germans over the French in 1870-1871, German military fashions rose in the ascendant and the spiked helmet superseded the shako. Amid all these absurdities common sense began slowly to prevail. Some at least of the men had sun-helmets during the Indian Mutiny, and by 1879 no soldier went to a hot climate without a sun-helmet. Khaki came into use first during the Indian Mutiny, being then apparently of a greyish hue. At least one British regiment wore khaki during the Afghan war of 1879. The troops sent to Egypt in 1882 wore Norfolk jackets of scarlet serge with a sun-helmet; and after this the parade-uniform appeared less and less on active service, until in 1899 the entire force sent to South Africa was clothed in khaki. The greater range and accuracy of rifles imperatively dictated invisibility in clothing. The old staring reds and blues had once been useful to distinguish friend from foe; but, with the new deadly weapons, the risk of being killed by friends was on the whole less than the certainty of being killed by enemies.[1] Colours were never taken on active service after 1880.

The Soldier's Comforts

The last and most beneficial change in these years was the steady decrease of drunkenness in the Army, due, perhaps in part

---

[1] Sir Redvers Buller, who had seen much service in China, Ashanti, South Africa (1878-9), Egypt, the Sudan and South Africa (1899-1900) told me that he could hardly remember an action in which British troops had not fired on each other.

to the greater youth of the recruits, in part to other causes, but in any case most remarkable. Spirits had been banished from canteens in 1839, and replaced by beer; but up to about the year 1880 it was the rule for old soldiers to return to barracks three-parts drunk. Twenty years later such a thing would not have been tolerated by the men themselves. Canteen-profits suffered in England because few of the men drank beer. London clubs suffered because few of the officers drank wine. British officers have always been in nearer touch with their men than in any other army, and in these years they were drawn closer than ever. All the improvements in the condition of the soldier—schools, savings-banks, gardens, recreations, theatrical clubs, suppers, even medals—were first originated by regimental officers, though some of them were adopted later by the State. Indeed, it is hardly too much to say that the Army has been kept alive by the devotion of regimental officers to their men. In the period under review a little group of officers, none of them rich, being dissatisfied with the prices charged and the profits returned to their men in their canteens, put together £400 to found a Co-operative Canteen Society for the supply of canteens. Regiment after regiment supported it, with the best results to the comfort and nourishment of the men. In a few years its annual turnover was £240,000, and it has now found its final form as the Navy, Army and Air Force Institute, with an annual turnover of six millions. Games, and particularly football, also strengthened those bonds between officers and men,[1] which are a peculiar source of strength to the British Army.

In brief the status of the soldier, when once the nation had ceased to be afraid of reservists, was completely transformed. It needed a whole generation to work the change, but worked it was. It used to be said, too often with truth, that through fast living the long-service soldier was an old man at forty. Now the old soldier, having served his seven or eight years, was in the prime of life, bringing with him habits of discipline and cleanliness which made him a very acceptable worker, and a love of regiment and a pride in the army which rendered him a very valuable citizen.

Extension of the Empire in Africa

A word—there is no space for more—must be added as to extension of the Empire

[1] The Guards played football during the Waterloo campaign; but as a national pursuit, in which the Army takes a prominent part, football has grown up entirely within the writer's life-time.

THE SCRAMBLE FOR AFRICA

during the period 1870-1900. This, apart from conquests mentioned in their place, was effected chiefly in Africa. About the year 1883 there began a kind of scramble among the European powers for the unoccupied parts of Africa. In England there were formed Companies—the East African, the Niger and the South African being the most conspicuous of them—for turning sundry territories to British account. From the first the Imperial Government eventually took over Kenya, including Uganda; from the second Nigeria, and from the third Rhodesia. These territories were not secured without fighting; and the British officer, as always in the history of the Empire, has left his mark upon them for good.

With these few preliminary remarks let us now follow the Army through the campaigns of these thirty years of transition.

CHAPTER XII

THE SECOND ASHANTI WAR OF 1873

IN January, 1873, after long renewal of the old quarrels with the native tribes, the Ashantis invaded British territory with 50,000 men, but failed to capture the coast towns. In September, Sir Garnet Wolseley was sent to organize native levies, which drove the Ashantis back. Three battalions (old soldiers) were sent out from England, and Wolseley, invading Ashanti in January, 1874, defeated the Ashantis in two engagements of forest-fighting, and on 4th February entered Kumasi, the capital, and burned it. The Ashantis then submitted, agreeing to open their country to trade, to abolish human sacrifices and to pay an indemnity. The troops suffered greatly from fever in that deadly climate.

The Afghan War of 1878-1880

Five years later came trouble on the north-west frontier of India. It must be noticed first that in 1876 Bulgaria, Serbia and Montenegro, then Turkish provinces, rose in

ACQUISITION OF CYPRUS

armed insurrection against Turkey and were put down with a very rough hand. In November, Russia intervened and, after an abortive conference of the European powers at Constantinople, she declared war and invaded Turkey. For a time the Russian arms met with little success; but towards the end of the year they gained decisive superiority, and by January, 1878, were threatening Constantinople. Then England interposed. It had long been her policy to maintain Turkey as a menace to Russia's flank during Russia's continued progress eastward; and in these years Russia's advance towards the Indian frontier—itself as inevitable as the British advance from the Bay of Bengal to the Indus—had become strongly marked. To strengthen England's diplomacy, the reserves were called out in April, 1878, and Indian troops were brought to Malta. The Liberal Party, being then in Opposition in Parliament, brought forward a motion, condemning the employment of native Indian troops out of India. It was lost; and this same Liberal Party, when in office, did not hesitate to summon Indian troops to Egypt in 1882, thus wisely confirming the precedent of 1878. These measures caused the British intervention to prevail, and incidentally England gained the island of Cyprus.

But Russia, though constrained to complaisance in the west, was still active against the British in the east; and owing to the intrigues of Afghanistan with her agents, the British Government demanded that a British commission should be received at Kabul. The Amir of Afghanistan replied that, if such a commission were sent, it would be opposed by force. After due warning, the British, on 20th November, 1878, invaded Afghanistan in three columns: 10,000 men under Sir Samuel Browne advancing through the Khyber Pass, 5,500 men under General Roberts through the Kuram Pass, and General Donald Stewart with 10,000 men through the Bolan Pass. All three brushed away opposition with little difficulty or loss, Roberts mastering a strong position at Peiwar Kotal at a cost of fewer than 100 casualties; and in January, 1879, Stewart entered Kandahar. In May, the Amir of Afghanistan sued for peace, and under a treaty Afghanistan became a feudatory of the British Crown. Thereupon the troops began to return to India and a mission was sent to Kabul. On 3rd September, the members of the mission, with their small guard, were murdered by the Afghans, and the Amir fled to the protection of Roberts, who with 6,500 men advanced on Kabul which, after beating the Afghans at

SECOND AFGHAN WAR

Charasia, he entered on 9th October. In December the Afghans gathered round him and compelled him to retire within the fortified camp of Shirpur, where they held him besieged with 100,000 men. On 23rd December they attacked him; but, being repulsed with heavy loss, dispersed and enabled Roberts to reoccupy Kabul.

On 30th March, 1880, Sir Donald Stewart marched from Kandahar towards Kabul, repulsed an Afghan attack with heavy loss at Ahmed Khel on 19th April, and occupied Ghazni two days later, where he gained touch with Roberts, and took command of the combined force—some 18,000 men. The British, in July, installed Abdurrahman as Amir of Afghanistan; and once again the troops prepared to withdraw, when they were detained by the news that from 10,000 to 20,000 Afghans were advancing upon Kandahar. General Burrows with 2,500 men moved out to meet them, and at Maiwand was disastrously defeated, with a loss of 1,100 men, most of whom were killed. The survivors struggled back to Kandahar, which was at once besieged by the victorious Afghans; whereupon Roberts started from Kabul with 10,000 men and on the 31st August entered Kandahar, having marched 313 miles in 22 days. On the following day he attacked and dispersed the Afghans with great loss, his own casualties not exceeding 250. The British then evacuated Afghanistan, leaving Abdurrahman to rule independently, on condition that his foreign relations should be controlled by the British Government.

The few battalions of young soldiers, enlisted for short service, that were employed in this war succumbed so rapidly to hardship and sickness (for an Afghan campaign, owing to saline water and other causes, is always unhealthy) that Roberts on his arrival in England made a strong protest in favour of long service. The result was that the terms of enlistment were changed, as has been told, from 6 to 7 years with the colours and from 6 to 5 with the reserve.

The South African Wars. 1878-1881

Meanwhile the old centre of disturbance in Cape Colony became again active. The inevitable extension of British rule in South Africa brought about a rebellion of the tribes on the eastern frontier which had given trouble in former times. It was suppressed without great difficulty, and collapsed after the death, in action, of the chief, in 1878. The troops were then distracted towards Natal by the menacing attitude of the Zulus. The military power of the Zulus had been originally built

THE ZULU WAR

up by a chief who had fought against the British in 1799 and imitated their methods. They numbered some 40,000 warriors, and, though they used mainly shock-action, were the most formidable tribe in South Africa, owing to the perfection of their discipline and their military system. In January, 1879, 5,000 British troops, 1,200 mounted Colonists and 9,000 natives, under the command of Lord Chelmsford, invaded Zululand in three columns; and on the 22nd, Chelmsford moved out with the main body of his column, leaving his camp at Isandhlwana to the protection of 670 regulars, 110 Colonists and 900 native levies. Eluding Chelmsford, the Zulus came down upon the camp in great force and, after a desperate fight, which cost them 5,000 casualties, practically annihilated the defenders, which included 600 of the South Wales Borderers. The Zulus then pressed on to the invasion of Natal, but were stopped at Rorke's Drift, on the River Tugela, by a handful of the South Wales Borderers who had hastily entrenched themselves, and were beaten back with heavy loss. This proved that, with proper precautions, the Zulus should have been repulsed at Isandhlwana.

Chelmsford then fell back to await reinforcements, leaving, however, one of his columns isolated in an outlying fortified post. In March he advanced with 3,400 British and 2,300 natives, repelled an attack of the Zulus upon his camp on 2nd April, and next day brought off the beleaguered garrison. Colonel Evelyn Wood advanced simultaneously with another column, and after losing rather heavily in an offensive movement on 28th March, was attacked on the 29th by about 20,000 Zulus, whom he repulsed and dispersed with crushing loss. Meanwhile, reinforcements were pouring into Natal until they reached the number of 10,000; and Chelmsford, advancing with 5,000 of them upon the kraal of the Zulu Chief, Cetewayo, at Ulundi, was again attacked by 20,000 Zulus on 4th July. They were decisively defeated, and Cetewayo was hunted down and captured. The military system of the Zulus was abolished, and the various tribes settled down under British suzerainty. Sir Garnet Wolseley, who had arrived to supersede Chelmsford, by November concluded such petty operations as still remained necessary.

This Zulu War opened the eyes of the British public to the fact that they had for the present no striking force. Natal, in the middle of 1879, was swarming with troops, mostly boys, who sickened very rapidly, could stand no hard work and, to say the least of it, were unsteady in the field. The annihilation of the South Wales Borderers created something like a panic terror of the Zulus; and altogether the campaign was anything but creditable.

This was the last campaign in which soldiers were flogged on the field, the punishment being abolished in 1881.

The Boer War of 1880-1881

Then followed a quarrel with the Boers. In 1877 the Transvaal had been annexed by England. The Boers had never accepted this annexation kindly. The breaking of the Zulu power, which they dreaded, had something of the same effect upon them as the capture of Canada upon the Americans. The British mishaps in the Zulu War did not heighten their respect for their new masters. On 16th December, 1880, they declared their independence. Four days later 1,000 Boers attacked about 250 British infantry which were marching peacefully without any military precautions, and killed or captured every one of them; and then they beleaguered and isolated eight different British posts in the Transvaal. Sir George Colley thereupon collected a column in Natal to relieve these scattered garrisons. The Boers took up a position at Laing's Nek to bar his way. A British attack upon Laing's Nek on 28th January, 1881, was repulsed; and on 8th February a British patrolling column was likewise driven back. On 28th February, Colley, by a night march, seized Majuba Hill, which dominated the Boer camp. On the 29th the Boers attacked him and drove him out with heavy loss, Colley himself being killed. The three actions had cost about 600 casualties; and the Liberal Government, which had just taken office, decided to yield to the Boers and to grant them their independence, or, in other words, to defer the evil day to some uncertain future date, which proved to be 1899.

The Egyptian Campaign of 1882

Immediately afterwards the British troops were engaged in a country which they had not seen for eighty years. Egypt, as the short route to India, had long been an object of interest to England, and became so still more upon the opening of the Suez Canal in 1869. The purchase of a predominant number of Suez Canal shares from an impecunious Khedive in 1875 strengthened her interest in the country; and anxiety as to the European loans contracted by that Khedive impelled England and France to

EGYPTIAN CAMPAIGN, 1882

establish a dual control over Egyptian finance in 1878. In 1881, the Egyptians, under the leadership of Arabi Pasha, rose in revolt and compelled a new Khedive to dismiss his European employees. France and England protested, but France refused to join England in active intervention, and England decided to restore order alone.

The Egyptian Army was reckoned at 60,000 regular troops, besides an uncertain number of irregulars. It was therefore resolved to send 7,000 men from India, and 25,000 from England, though even that small number could not be produced without calling out a part of the reserves. Alexandria had already been taken by the fleet, but Sir Garnet Wolseley, who was in military command, after leaving a strong garrison there, shifted his base to Ismailia, in order to be sure of his water-supply. Here the main body disembarked and began their advance westward, driving back the Egyptians on 24th August and repelling an attack by them on the 28th. Arabi fell back with 25,000 men to an entrenched position at Tel-el-Kebir, which was stormed by Wolseley with 17,000 men before dawn of 13th September. The mounted troops pursued with such energy that they entered Cairo, some fifty miles distant, and received its surrender on the same day. All resistance then ceased. The Egyptian army was disbanded, and Egypt was garrisoned by a British force.

The Sudan War. 1881-1885

Meanwhile, before Arabi's rebellion, there had arisen in the Sudan a general revolt against Egyptian rule; and in August, 1881, a fanatic, named Mohammed Ali, proclaimed himself to be the Mahdi, the expected saviour of the Sudan. The tribes ranged themselves under his standard, and by 1883 it was reckoned that his following numbered 50,000 men. A force of Egyptians which attempted to face them was annihilated, hardly attempting resistance; and it was decided to withdraw the scattered garrisons from the Sudan and to reinstate Major-General Charles Gordon—who had already been Governor-General of the Sudan from 1874 to 1879—in his old place, that he might superintend the evacuation. Meanwhile, the tribes of the Eastern Sudan had also risen, and on 4th February, 1884, they likewise annihilated a force of some 3,500 Egyptians which attempted to oppose them. Since Egyptian fellaheen was evidently useless against the Mahdi's fierce and fearless warriors, the British Government determined, at any rate, to take over the defences of the port of

THE DESERT MARCH

Suakin, on the Red Sea; and on 28th February, 1884, a force of under 5,000 men was landed in the vicinity under General Graham. Graham had two successful encounters with the dervishes in February and March; but nothing decisive was attempted, and presently it was realized that Gordon was isolated and in imminent danger at Khartoum.

The March Across the Desert

Lord Wolseley was now sent out to take command; and it was resolved to send an expedition up the Nile to relieve Khartoum; but the peril of Gordon was so urgent that Wolseley decided to send a small column of 1,800 men, mounted on camels, straight across the desert from Korti. This column was made up of picked men from many regiments, cavalry, Guards, infantry of the line, marines and even blue-jackets, and was commanded by General Herbert Stewart. It left Korti on 30th December, to cross 176 miles of desert. The column on the 2nd January, 1885, reached the wells of Jakdul (98 miles distant) unopposed. Here 150 men were left to form a post, and on 14th January the march was resumed. On 17th January the force was attacked by some 5,000 dervishes, who were driven off with a loss of 800 killed; the casualties of the British being 168. On 19th January the column reached the Nile about 100 miles below Khartoum, when it was again attacked. The dervishes were again driven off, but Stewart was mortally wounded. An attempt was made on the 21st to capture the dervishes' position on the river, but in vain. A very small party then ascended the river in boats to Khartoum, only to find that the place had fallen on the 26th, and that Gordon and his garrison had been massacred. The desert column had suffered 125 more casualties between the 19th and the 21st, and was exhausted by hardship and fatigue. It therefore retreated; and the river-column which, after great exertion in ascending the cataracts of the Nile, had reached a point about 100 miles above Korti and had there stormed a dervish position, fell back likewise.

The Sudan Abandoned

The British Government then decided to abandon the expedition to Khartoum and to give up the Sudan; but meanwhile a new field force of some 11,000 men had been collected at Suakin; and it must be mentioned that even this small number could not be collected without the inclusion of three battalions of Guards. After more than one sharp fight in March and April, these troops were withdrawn upon receipt of the order to abandon the country. It is noteworthy that in this force of Graham's was a battalion of Australians which had volunteered for service. This was the first time, since the expedition to Carthagena in 1741, that British subjects in the Colonies had offered their help to the mother-country outside their own territory; and the fact should be gratefully remembered. In this campaign, also, captive balloons were for the first time used for purposes of observation by a British force in the field. The French had produced a captive balloon during the operations in the Low Countries in 1794, but the experiment had not been followed up.

A British force was left in Egypt, and frontier posts were established against a dervish invasion, while British officers quietly set to work to remake the Egyptian army.

The Third Burmese War. 1885-1891

Next, for the third time, British soldiers were summoned to the valley of the Irrawaddy. Burma had lapsed into anarchy under a bad king, with the result that there were constant outrages upon British traders and raids upon British territory. A commercial treaty between Burma and France had also been signed, which threatened British supremacy in Upper Burma; and the Indian Government, failing to obtain satisfaction from the king, dispatched a force of 9,000 men, one-third of them Europeans, to Rangoon under command of General Prendergast in November, 1885. Advancing up the Irrawaddy in boats, the expedition reached Mandalay on 28th November, after brushing away a feeble resistance, and took the king prisoner. The British then assumed the Government of Upper Burma. But gangs of dacoits, or banditti, at once sprang up, which overran the whole country and kept it in terror and confusion; and only after five years of hard work were these finally suppressed. The troops being broken up for this purpose into very small columns, frequently no more than a subaltern's command, this war was known as the "Subalterns' War." The casualties from hardship, fatigue and sickness in such a climate were considerable, malarial fever being, inevitably, very prevalent.

Ashanti Expedition of 1896

The next trouble arose on the Gold Coast; but this meant no more than a bloodless march to Kumasi, the result of which was the annexation of Ashanti.

THE SECOND SUDAN WAR

Second Sudan War. 1896-1898

Then the valley of the Nile again claimed attention. After the evacuation of the Sudan, the dervishes from time to time attempted invasion of Egypt, but were repulsed with heavy loss. In 1896 the Italians, who had quarrelled with the Abyssinians, sustained a disastrous defeat; and, to counteract the evil effect of this humiliation of Europeans in Africa, it was decided in the same year to reconquer the Sudan. General Kitchener accordingly, in June, with 9,000 Egyptian troops, stormed and captured a dervish frontier post, and pushed slowly but steadily up the Nile, consolidating his gains and building a railway. In February, 1898, about 12,000 dervishes moved down to meet them, and Kitchener, having now 3,000 British and 11,000 Egyptian soldiers, attacked and routed them on the 8th April at Atbara. The army was then further reinforced to a strength of 8,000 British and 18,000 Egyptians, and Kitchener, advancing upon Khartoum, encountered 50,000 dervishes at Omdurman (22nd September), and routed them with a loss of 30,000 killed and wounded, his own casualties being under 500. By the end of the year the last organized force of the dervishes had been broken up. The Mahdi's successor was killed in action in 1899, and the last of the formidable leaders was taken in January, 1900. England then assumed joint sovereignty with Egypt over the Sudan, the chief administrative posts being entrusted to British officers.

The Tirah Expedition. 1897-1898

Though it is quite impossible in a book of this kind to take note of the innumerable punitive expeditions against the tribes in the north-western and north-eastern frontiers of India, this expedition to Tirah, from its greater importance, cannot be omitted. The scene was the mountain tract to north of the Khyber Pass, which had never yet been entered by white man; and the cause was the attack and destruction by the Afridis of their own countrymen who, by agreement with the British Government, garrisoned the posts which guarded the Khyber Pass. It was reckoned that the tribesmen could put into the field 40,000 to 50,000 men, all armed with long-range breech-loading rifles—Sniders effective up to 900 yards, Martini-Henrys and Lee-Enfields effective up to 1,500 and 1,800 yards. The force employed was nearly 12,000 British and nearly 23,000 native troops, with 6 mountain batteries. The tribesmen only once faced an assault in force, and were then driven off at a cost of 200 casualties. They preferred to attack convoys, rear-guards and particularly the tail of any column, or any isolated body which was benighted and had to bivouac alone. Moreover, they kept every camp and bivouac under continual fire all night. The narrowness of the paths and tracks made transport and supply extremely difficult, and the long drawn out columns of march extremely vulnerable. Moreover, since the enemy had long-range rifles, it was necessary to clear the flanks to a much greater distance than heretofore, which was a new experience in an Indian mountain-campaign. The trial to the troops was therefore very severe. The rough climb over crag and ravine was always fatiguing, and their rest was perpetually broken. On the march they frequently had to cross icy mountain-streams waist-deep at every 200 yards; and on one occasion a column had to bivouac at an altitude of 8,000 feet, every man, including the Commander-in-Chief himself, wet through to the waist, in a temperature of 20 degrees of frost, without fire and without food. None the less, the untrodden land was traversed through and through by British columns, and the most recalcitrant of the tribesmen were brought to submission by a campaign which lasted from September, 1897, to April, 1898. The casualties in action numbered 1,150 of all ranks; but the exertion and hardship were such that more than one battalion was worn out before the end. Indeed, no troops could stand such work for very long.

The South African War. 1899-1902

Events in South Africa then strained England's military strength to the utmost, and gave her troops invaluable training for the great struggle that was to come in 1914. Discoveries of gold and diamond fields in the Dutch Republics had, since 1881, attracted great numbers of foreigners thither, who, though they outnumbered the whole Boer population and furnished most of the wealth on which the Republics flourished, were denied any voice in the government of the country. A foolish and abortive rebellion in 1895 gave the Transvaal Government a pretext for not departing from this policy. Negotiation produced no results. The situation became more and more serious. Reinforcements were sent out to the British garrisons; and in October, 1899, the Governments of the Transvaal and of the Orange Free State declared war.

It was reckoned that they could put into the field 60,000 men, all of them mounted and most of them good marksmen, though

THE SECOND BOER WAR

they were weak in artillery. This was far too low an estimate; and the area of the sphere of operations was so enormous that the reduction of so mobile and elusive an enemy —doubly elusive owing to the recent introduction of smokeless powder—promised to be a work of great difficulty. It was practically certain that the British must act from at least two bases—Capetown and Durban, which are 1,000 miles apart. For there were isolated British garrisons on the Cape Colony's side at Kimberley, 500 miles from Capetown, and at Mafeking, still further north, which would surely be (as in fact they were) at once besieged by the Boers; while on the side of Natal the British frontier ran up with a sharp salient into the enemy's country, offering every advantage to invaders.

The Initial Failures

The whole British force in South Africa in October, 1899, did not exceed 22,000 men, most of them on the side of Natal. In England the reserves were called out, and every preparation was made for speedy reinforcement of this small body; but meanwhile the Boers had their opportunity and seized it. In October they invaded Natal in detachments, which were at once attacked and checked at three different points by British forces (20th, 21st, 24th October); but a more solid counter-offensive by Sir George White with some 10,000 men was repulsed with a loss of 1,000 prisoners, and White within three days found himself beleaguered in his advanced base at Ladysmith.

Sir Redvers Buller, the appointed Commander-in-Chief, arriving in advance of his troops, soon decided that Natal was the quarter that demanded his presence; but, as the first reinforcements arrived in Cape Colony, 8,000 of them were led up by Lord Methuen to the relief of Kimberley. In three successive actions (23rd, 25th, 28th November) he attacked the Boers and drove them back, but in a fourth attack on 11th December was repulsed with heavy casualties. Meanwhile the Boers had invaded Cape Colony, and an offensive movement against them also failed (10th December) with appreciable loss. Lastly, Buller, attempting with 21,000 men to advance to the relief of Ladysmith, was also driven back (15th December). Thus the operations were brought to a standstill.

The Situation Restored

Troops of every possible kind—Yeomanry, Militia, Volunteers—were now appealed for

LADYSMITH AND PAARDEBERG

in England. Canada and the Australasian Colonies offered their help; and Lord Roberts, going out in supreme command, took charge of the operations on the side of Cape Colony. It was, however, long before reinforcements of sufficient strength could reach him, and meanwhile the Boer invaders of Cape Colony were only kept in check by incessant petty attacks. On 12th January Buller again advanced to the relief of Ladysmith, and after some days' fighting was again repulsed. On 5th February he made a third attempt which he soon abandoned. Then Lord Roberts began to move on the side of Cape Colony. Kimberley was relieved on 15th February, and on 17th February Buller, again advancing, succeeded, after several days' fighting, in relieving Ladysmith (28th February). On 27th February Roberts surrounded and captured 4,000 Boers at Paardeberg, and on 13th March he entered Bloemfontein, the capital of the Orange Free State.

Last Period of the War

Now came a pause, during which two small British columns were surprised and heavily punished by the Boers; and then Roberts resumed his advance northward, while Buller, after clearing Natal of Boers, also entered the enemy's territory. On 17th May Mafeking was relieved; and on 5th June Pretoria was occupied. Buller advanced still farther north; and President Kruger of the Transvaal Republic fled to Europe. Then the real trouble began, with the task of defending a line of communications 1,000 miles long against a highly mobile, skilful and cunning enemy which respected none of the conventions of war. The British gradually accumulated some 200,000 men of one kind or another (certain of them very queer material) in South Africa; and they were none too many, for there was much disloyalty even in Cape Colony.

The Boers had many little successes, which prolonged the struggle for another two years; and the British officers, copying their methods, retaliated in kind. Lord Kitchener was in command during this period, and it needed all his driving power to carry the operations to a successful issue. Indeed, victory was only achieved at last by cutting up the country with lines of blockhouses. The Boers made a very fine fight and had many successes which gained them much sympathy; but to the British the campaign was a weary business, where victory was, at the best, inglorious, and reverses humiliating. It may, however, be doubted whether any other European power, using the same numbers, would have fared much better, though it might certainly have spent less money. Lord Kitchener, unlike Wellington, was a bad horse-master, and the waste of horses was appalling. Moreover, neither he nor Lord Roberts, both having served all their time in the East, knew anything of the British Army, nor of the system of the Army Service Corps for transport and supply; and this led to some confusion. However, the war was at last brought to a successful conclusion in May, 1902. The Transvaal and the Orange Free State were annexed, and having, a few years later, had free institutions restored to them, were joined to Cape Colony and Natal in the South African Union. Two of the best Boer Generals, Botha and Smuts, accepted commands of British Armies in the German War, and rendered most valuable service.

The Period 1902-1914

The South African War concluded what may be called the century of consolidation of the Empire which had kept the Army fully employed, with hardly a year's respite, since the Mahratta War of 1803. The Empire had received other additions, notably (as has been told) on the East Coast of Africa and in Nigeria in the course of the 19th century, which, though

THE EMPIRE AND THE ARMY

they might require no express military expedition, demanded British officers and non-commissioned officers for the formation and training of local levies. We have seen how grievously the Army was overworked in the first half of the 19th century; and, though it had received considerable relief through the establishment of County police[1] as well as Metropolitan police at home, through the steady reduction of West Indian garrisons to a trifling minimum and through the withdrawal of all troops from the self-governing Colonies (excepting one or two naval stations) when self-government was granted to them,[2] yet the extension of the Empire in India alone, to say nothing of Egypt and the Sudan, was sufficient, on a balance, to leave the general burden upon it heavier than before. A few additional battalions were, indeed, raised between 1897 and 1900.[3] Meanwhile, Germany's steady resolution to increase her fleet and challenge our power at sea caused so formidable an increase

[1] In 1852.
[2] In 1856.
[3] Viz., a 3rd battalion each to the Coldstream and Scots Guards; a 2nd battalion to the Cameron Highlanders; 3rd and 4th battalions to the Warwicks, Royal Fusiliers, Lancashire Fusiliers, Northumberland Fusiliers, King's, Worcesters, Middlesex and Manchesters. The Irish Guards were also formed; and, with the 3rd Coldstream and 2nd Cameron Highlanders, still survive. The remainder were disbanded; the King's in 1901, and all except the Royal Fusiliers, Worcesters and Middlesex before the German War. The Welch Guards were not formed until after the beginning of the German War.

THE GERMAN DANGER

of naval expenditure, that it was impossible to afford much more money on the Army.

The whole situation was most difficult. The dangerous period of transition from long to short service had indeed passed away. The reserves, when called out for South Africa, had come up in greater strength than the War Office had looked for, which was so far satisfactory; but even so, the Army had been found too weak in numbers; and its force had been swelled only by shifts and improvisations of every description. No statesman dared to propose what the elder Pitt had designed in 1757, and Castlereagh had actually enforced in 1807—the compulsory training of the manhood of the nation in the ranks of the Militia. Yet many felt certain that before long England would have to fight, not only to keep her Empire, but to save herself.

CHAPTER XIII

MR. HALDANE'S REORGANIZATION

The "Old Contemptibles"

IT fell to Lord Haldane to make the best of the Army as it was, and herein he rendered transcendent service. He reorganized the regular troops at disposal into 6 or 7 divisions on the German model, turned the Militia into a special reserve for them, and the Volunteers into a territorial force, exacting from them better discipline and training. With four of these divisions—a mere handful compared with the vast hosts of Germany, Austria, France and Russia—we entered upon the war of August, 1914. Before a 5th division could join them the four were already seriously weakened, and before the war had lasted six weeks drafts from the Special Reserve—the old Militia—were already in the field. But what the Old Army lacked in quantity it made good in quality. Economy denied it sufficient machine-guns, but this defect was made good by incomparable rifle-fire. It began the campaign with the hardest trial of all, exhausting and precipitate retreat, but passed through the ordeal superbly. Then it turned eagerly to the attack, and finally it perished, annihilated but triumphant, in the supreme effort of repelling, with great numerical odds against them, the German onslaughts at the first battle of Ypres. With some knowledge of British military history the present writer unhesitatingly declares the work of the "Old Contemptibles" to have been the grandest ever done in every respect by any British Army. And their worth lay not only in their discipline, valour, endurance and devotion, but in the standard which they set for the rest of the Empire.

The Empire Springs to Arms

Their example was not thrown away. Special Reserve, Territorials and Yeomanry were already in action, and doing admirably on the Western front in 1914. Territorials and Yeomanry, originally designed for home-defence, offered themselves freely for service and did it right well, in all parts of the world. The young men of England offered themselves by their hundreds of thousands as recruits, though, as the provident had foreseen, it would have been better to resort at once to the compulsion which was bound to come and ultimately did come. However, whether for volunteers or for conscripts, the "Old Contemptibles"[1] had furnished the ideal that was to be striven for; and meanwhile the whole Empire, both temperate and tropical Colonies, sent the cream of its youth to join the Old Country in the fighting line. Magnificent soldiers they proved themselves to be. No one had dreamed what the British Empire could do when she put forth all her strength. Some little time was needed to develop it, but it is a plain fact that the Empire maintained in the field the largest and most efficient of all armies, those of the enemy included; that she supported also at sea the largest and most efficient Navy; and finally produced an Air Force, of which the very least that can be said is that it was also most efficient. Lastly, it must be emphasized that all parts of the Empire produced not only fine fighting men but fine leaders.

For the rest, it need only be added that all previous experiences of the British Army were repeated in this war. There was a disembarkation—the greatest known to military history—in face of a prepared enemy at Gallipoli; there was a river-campaign in Mesopotamia; there was a forest-campaign in East Africa; there were desert campaigns in South-West Africa and in Northern Africa—at least one of

[1] The German Kaiser has the credit of having alluded to the original British Expeditionary Force as "a contemptible little army."

them conducted by the novel instrument of motor-cars; there was a mountain-campaign on the familiar ground of Afghanistan, to say nothing of maritime exploits on the Caspian (unparalleled since the defence of Sicily by a military flotilla against Napoleon's armies), and of adventures in the 64th degree of north latitude, which is, I think, the nearest point to the North Pole[1] ever reached by British soldiers.

A Review of the Past

And so in this year 1928 the Empire still stands and, if mandated territories be included, spreads wider than ever. The forces which brought it into being are strangely complex. The failure to establish an Empire in France brought about a desolating civil war, from which England emerged, weak and enervated, to see Western Europe transformed by the discovery of the New World. Thereby new ways were opened to wealth; and wealth means, temporarily or permanently, power. The might of Spain made it a political and economic necessity for France and England also to seek resources in the New World. Spain had appropriated the precious metals; but tropical produce was second only to gold and silver, and new outlets for trade were potentially as

[1] The British have never fought nearer to the South Pole than lat. 42° S., though the Falkland Islands lie in lat. 52° S.

valuable. For two centuries the West Indies were the most treasured of British possessions. Even as early as 1680 a Jamaican planter with £12,000 a year (worth £120,000 now) was not esteemed an exceptionally rich man. The slave-trade, for supplying the British and Spanish West Indies and the tobacco-growing provinces of America with labour, brought in much incidental profit. Later the East Indian merchants—the Nabobs, as they were called— began to vie with the West Indian in riches. All alike bought seats in the House of Commons; and, in fact, until the Reform Bill of 1832,[1] some part of the British Empire was represented in the British Parliament; and the "West Indian interest" could not safely be ignored by any Ministry.

But the Empire thus represented was not the true Empire.

Theoretically and in outward semblance all Colonies originally stood upon the same footing. Every one, down to the tiniest West Indian island, had its constitution on the English model and enjoyed a large measure of self-government. Nevertheless, all alike were considered to exist mainly for the benefit of

---

[1] Joseph Hume proposed that the Colonies should send representatives to the House of Commons; but the framers of the Reform Bill of 1832 had not properly thought out the problem of representation even for the United Kingdom, much less for the Empire.

THE OLD COLONIAL SYSTEM

the mother-country, being bound by trade restrictions and expected to furnish convenient rubbish-heaps for the refuse of her population. All alike were, as has been told, supposed to provide mainly for their own defence, and on occasion to aid the mother-country in aggressive operations, as both the West Indies and some of the American provinces actually did in Cromwell's West Indian expedition of 1655 and in the Carthagena expedition of 1741. To the slave-employing Colonies these conditions were not really, on the whole, unfair. They were wealthy. Their ruling classes had crossed the sea to make fortunes, and had made them. White malefactors from England were not unwelcome to them as furnishing cheap labour. All Colonies very soon threw themselves upon the mother-country for defence, but the West Indian planters could, and did, afford to give extra pay to their British garrisons, fearing their own slaves as much as any external foe. The slave-owning Colonies of America had, until the French came to the Ohio in the middle of the 18th century, no serious enemy to dread on their borders. They, like the West Indian planters, were a rich aristocracy, and they remained so, distinct, until the American Civil War of 1861-1865.

But the true Colonists are those who traverse the ocean to make not a fortune but a home; and these were not represented in the British Parliament. They were found, as it chanced, in the Northern American Colonies which were nearest to the dangerous French neighbour at Quebec. It was chiefly for their deliverance that Canada was conquered. There was no question of greed on the part of the mother-country. She did not covet that vast territory for herself. She only wanted to rid the British settlements of a perpetual menace against which they were always crying out to her for help. The annexation of Canada was actually, at the time, a very serious embarrassment to England, so serious that it issued in the rupture with the American Colonies, and in a change in all ideas of Colonial policy. But the attitude, natural enough, of the American Colonies towards Canada, is typical of all British settlements all over the world. Few Englishmen realize the sensitiveness of, for example, the Australians concerning the Islands that are, or were, held by European nations in the Pacific. Yet a Colony's sense of insecurity is always construed by foreigners as the mother-country's instinct of rapacity.

Elsewhere the extension of the Empire has been due chiefly to the experience of all imperial nations from Rome onward, that order and chaos cannot live side by side. Clive sought earnestly to set fixed bounds to British territory in India, but failed abjectly; and no one of his successors has, despite of all efforts, redeemed his failure. The story has been the same in Africa. British statesmen of the 19th century, with the lesson of the American rebellion printed deep on their hearts, trembled before the very thought of Empire. Until Edward Gibbon Wakefield developed his plans, they could think of no better use for Australia than to continue it as a penal settlement. They groaned in spirit because Simonstown was not a Gibraltar, so that the rest of Cape Colony might be abandoned. They granted self-government to what we now call the Dominions and Commonwealths, with the unconcealed expectation—almost the hope —of parting with them presently on amicable terms. They even tried to avert extension of the Empire by keeping an army too small to look after it. But that army disappointed them by doing—few realize at what sacrifice—the work of two. Meanwhile the discoveries of gold in Australia and New Zealand and, later on, of gold and diamonds in South Africa, suddenly raised those countries to new importance. A "gold-rush" does not always bring the most desirable class of emigrant; but industrial progress had so enormously increased the population in England that new outlets were imperatively needed; and many who set out to make a fortune remained to make a home. Not the least valuable of these were discharged soldiers and retired officers, both from the British and the Indian Armies.

Not until the present writer had reached manhood did England suddenly awake to the existence of the Empire. She then felt rather proud, but a little frightened also. Trade was, of course, a principal link between mother-country and Colonies; but even stronger was their common taste for sport and their common love of a good horse. Outwardly there is now no link of union save the sentimental, which is embodied in the Crown; but since 1914 there is the far closer bond of tried brotherhood in arms.

Thus the British Empire still is; but without the British soldier it would never have been, Oliver Cromwell made the British soldier, and his work was taken over by a succession of great men. But for Marlborough, England might have sunk to a dependency of France; North America would be a French-speaking country; and there would be no United English-speaking States. But for the genius of Clive,

PAST AND PRESENT LEADERS

India, likewise, would be French; nor can it be doubted that France, predominant elsewhere, would, with her energy and great national gifts, have supplanted us in the Southern Hemisphere. But for Wellington, she might in spite of the British navy, have undone us after 1807. And, but for Haig, Germany might ten years ago have bent us to her will. Five men more widely different could hardly be found—Cromwell, the coarse and imperious; Marlborough, the invincibly patient and irresistibly charming; Clive, stricken by mysterious disease, the moody and melancholy; Wellington, the blunt, abrupt and bitter; Haig, a very fine example of the silent influence of a silent chief; yet all alike in transcendent common sense, firmness of resolution and devotion to patriotic duty. And if there be a grand roll of lesser men in Stringer Lawrence, Coote, Forde, Caillaud, Knox, Adams, Harris, Lake, Gillespie, Hastings, Gough and Outram; in Amherst, Wolfe and Seaton; in Ralph Abercromby, Charles Grey, John Moore, Charles Stuart and Harry Smith; in Roberts, Wolseley and Kitchener; we can match them with Allenby, Byng, Cavan, Horne, Marshall, Maude, Milne, Plumer and Rawlinson in the Old Country, while the Empire can add the honoured names of Jan Botha, Edward Chaytor, Henry

Chauvel, Arthur Currie, John Monash and Jan Smuts.

And be it remembered that it is not with the sword only that the British soldier has left his mark upon the Empire. India alone furnishes a long list of great soldier-administrators; and one of the greatest statesmen of the writer's own lifetime was Major Evelyn Baring of the artillery, first known as the author of a volume of *Staff College Essays*, but later honoured as the first Earl of Cromer. The Indian Army also produced many officers who did great work as antiquaries, at least one most learned historian in Colonel Mark Wilks, and a famous Assyriologist in Henry Rawlinson. The first great English authority on Greek antiquities was an artillery officer who was sent to teach gunnery to the Turks, Colonel William Leake. Lastly, there sprang from the ranks of the Army one of the greatest masters of English, William Cobbett, and from the commissioned officers one of the great military historians of all nations and all time, William Napier.

The Present Army

The British Army is now more than ever a little Army. Many pairs of cavalry regiments have been compressed into one, and two regiments have been converted into motor-units. Many batteries of artillery have been reduced; and the writer was himself a witness of the melancholy ceremony when twenty Irish battalions, three of them of great antiquity and with a glorious record of service, gave up their colours to the King on disbandment. But not yet is its work fully accomplished. Within the British Empire there is peace. It is (if the word have any meaning) an Empire of peace; but that peace has only been brought about and is only sustained by great and unremitting effort of the British officer and the British soldier. The status of both has undergone incredible change during the past sixty years. The qualifications for an officer, whether for entry into the service or advancement within it, depend on his stock of brains, rather than on his stock of cash. A commission means a post with a definite and, since very recent times, a sufficient salary. A general officer, to whom the country denied any pay as such until 1814, even then taking it grudgingly away for a time, has long since received a fixed stipend. The status of the soldier, already changed by short service, has been transformed by the conscription enforced during the late war. The stoppages from his pay have been steadily diminished, and the pay itself has been increased. He is no longer an outcast, an object for the vituperation of pamphleteers, of agitators, and of windbags in Parliament, but an honoured citizen who may rise high in his profession, and through whom the nation is beginning, perhaps, at last to understand the transcendent service rendered by his predecessors.

There is much talk in these days of making an end of war. No one has ever been able to define war or peace, and no one knows exactly what the words mean. We are supposed to live in peace here at home; but that is only through the existence of the Standing Army called the police. If there were no police, we could none of us go about our daily business unarmed. Peace, no less than war, rests upon armed force; and the model for the armed force of the British Empire has always been the British Army. The Metropolitan Police was formed out of old soldiers; the Australian Mounted Police of old days—long since disbanded but still remembered for its daring and devotion to duty—was made up of picked soldiers; the Canadian Mounted Police—an incomparable body of men—owes something at least to the old traditions. Every police force in the Empire, white or coloured, goes back to one model. What all of these are to

THE PRESENT ARMY

different portions of the Empire, that is the British Army to the whole.

And its achievements are not to be measured only in terms of valour and bloodshed. During the awful campaign in Burma of 1824-1826, any captured red-coat was sure of death by torture at the hands of the Burmese; at its close the population welcomed the presence and protection of the good-natured British soldier, and was loth to let him return to India. The old rough long-service warrior of a century ago was the same at heart as is his successor of to-day. The motto of all regular armies is duty and discipline. That of the British Army is duty, discipline and gentleness. It is not with lead and steel only that the British soldier has consolidated the Empire. He knows how to make war, when bidden, but he also knows how to make peace. Wherever he goes he has a strange power of making himself understood, for, though he has no special gift of tongues, he possesses that universal language which springs from simple good nature and kindness of heart. He has a great inheritance of glory, but he counts that as little beside his still greater inheritance of honour. He is less the conqueror than the missionary of Empire.

INDEX

A

ABERCROMBY, General John, 202
Abercromby, General Sir Ralph, 150, 156, 162–164
Abercromby, General Robert, 139
Abyssinian war, the, 271
Acts of Trade and Navigation, 38
Adams, Major Thomas, 109
Addington, Henry, Lord Sidmouth, 171
Aden (annexed, 1838), 2
Afghan war, the first, 244; the second, 286
Albuera, battle of, 200
Aldershot, purchase of, 258
Aliwal, battle of, 252
Alma, battle of the, 260
Almansa, battle of, 56
Almaraz, action of, 206
America, United States of, war with, 212–218
American Colonies, 26–27, 46; breach with, 112, 114; their alliance with France, 119; loss of, 132
Amherst, General Sir Jeffery, Lord, 96, 99–100
Amiens, peace of, 165
Antigua, 3, 27
Arabi Pasha, 295
Arass, action of, 111
Arcot, 89
Argaum, battle of, 167

ARMS, ARMOUR AND ACCOUTREMENTS
Cannon, 9
Defensive armour, 7, 8, 35
Epaulettes, 136
Equipment, 19, 135, 136
Grenade, 35
Long-bow, 8
Machine guns, 280
Pike, 8, 35
Rifle, m.l., 135, 161; Minie, 257; Enfield, 279; b.l., Snider, 280; Martini-Henry, 280: Magazine, 280
Small fire-arms, 9, 13, 35, 135
Wings, 136
Artillery, 10, 21 (*see also* Regiments, Royal Horse Artillery)
Artillery Company, the Honourable, 15
Ashanti war, the first, 238; second, 286; annexation of, 300
Auchmuty, General Sir Samuel, 203–204
Australia, 5, 231, 242, 299, 307

B

BADAJOZ, 198–199; storm of, 206
Badara, action of, 102
Bahamas, the, 3, 26
Baillie, Colonel, his defeat, 130, 159

INDEX

Baird, General Sir David, 159, 164, 174
Baksar, action of, 109
Balaclava, 260–262
Barbados, 3, 26, 97
Baring, Evelyn, Earl of Cromer, 322
Barrington, General, 97
Barrosa, battle of, 198
Baylen, action of, 183
Beaumont, action of, 148
Beckwith, General Sir George, 201–202
Belleisle, capture of, 106
Bentinck, Lord William, 218
Beresford, General Sir William, Lord, 191, 197, 199, 200
Bergen-op-Zoom, action of, 218
Berlin Decrees, 180
Bermuda, 3, 26
Berwick, Marshal, 56
Bhurtpore, first siege of, 169–170; second, 238
Bladensburg, action of, 216
Blakeney, General, 93
Blenheim, battle of, 53
Blücher, Field Marshal Prince, 219–220
Boer wars, 293, 304
Bonaparte, Joseph, King of Spain, 175, 193, 195
Bonaparte, Napoleon, Emperor of the French, 144, 151, 160, 170–171, 175, 180, 185, 219–221
Boscawen, Admiral, 96
Botha, General Jan, 309
Bouquet, Colonel, 113
Braddock, General Edward, 91–92
Brandywine, action of, 117
Brihuega, action of, 59
British Guiana, 4, 231
British Honduras, 4

Brock, General Isaac, 214–215
Browne, General Sir Samuel, 288
Buenos Ayres, expedition to, 174, 177
Bugle-calls, 138
Buller, General Sir Redvers, 279, 306–307
Bunker Hill, action of, 116
Burgos, siege of, 207
Burgoyne, General John, 117–118
Burmese war, the first, 235; the second, 254; the third, 299
Burrard, General Sir Harry, 185
Burrows, General, 289
Bushire, action of, 264
Bussaco, battle of, 196
Byng, Admiral, 94
Byng, Julian, Lord, 125

C

CAILLAUD, Captain John, 90
Camden, action of, 125
Campbell, General Sir Archibald, 235–237
Campbell, General Sir Colin, Lord Clyde, 267
Canada, 3, 96, 98–100, 242, 307
Canteens, 282
Canute, King, 6
Cape Colony (S. A. Union), 2, 151, 174, 231; first Kafir war, 240; second Kafir war, 255; third Kafir war, 290; Zulu war, 290; first Boer war, 293; second Boer war, 304
Carolina, 27, 122
Carthagena, expedition to, 71
Castalla, action of, 211
Castlereagh, Robert Stewart, Lord, 182

INDEX

Cathcart, Earl, 181
Cathcart, Lord, 72
Cavalry, early, 16-18
Cawnpore, 265-267
Cetewayo, Zulu Chief, 292
Ceylon, 2, 231 (*see also* Kandy)
Chamberlain, General Sir Neville, 270
Chaplains, 33, 228
Charles II, King, 25, 28
Charleston, 122, 125
Chatham, John, Earl of, 189
Chelmsford, General Frederick, Lord, 291-292
Chelsea hospital, 34
Chilianwala, battle of, 253
China war, first, 247-248; second, 264; third, 268
Chippewa, action of, 215
Churchill, John, Duke of Marlborough, 29, 41; his campaigns, 51-61; his services, 62-63
Cintra, Convention of, 185
Ciudad Rodrigo, storm of, 206
Clinton, General Sir Henry, 123, 128
Clive, Robert, Lord, 88, 89, 101-102, 108-109
Clothing, 13, 14, 32, 70, 135, 225-226, 263, 281
Cobbett, William, 322
Colborne, Sir John, Lord Seaton, 243
Colley, General Sir George, 293
Colonel, 12, 32
Combermere, Sydney, Lord, 238
Condore, action of, 102, 108
Coote, General Sir Eyre, 102, 108, 130-131
Copenhagen, expedition to, 181
Cornet, the, 10

Cornwallis, Charles, Marquis, 125-128, 138-139
Corporal, 11
Corsica, operations in, 145-146, 151
Coruña, battle of, 187
Cowpens, action of, 126
Craig, General Sir James, 173, 175
Crécy, battle of, 8
Crimean war, 258-263
Cromwell, Oliver, 16, 23-24
Cuesta, General, 192
Cyprus, 4, 287

D

Dabo, action of, 247
Dalrymple, General Sir Hew, 185
De Bussy, M., 131
D'Estaing, Count, 120, 123
De Grasse, Count, 128, 129
Deig, battle of, 169
Delhi, battle of, 168; siege of, 266
De Noailles, Marshal, 76
Dettingen, battle of, 76
Dominica, 106, 107, 172
Dost Mohamed, 244
Douro, passage of, 192
Dunbar, battle of, 22
Dunkirk Dunes, battle of, 24
Dunkirk, siege of, 143
Dupleix, Jean François, 88, 90
Dutch Guiana, 171

E

East India Company, 26, 37, 268
Egmont op Zee, action of, 157
Egypt, campaign of 1801, 162-164

INDEX

Egypt, campaign of 1807, 179; campaign of 1882, 294
Elphinstone, General, 246
Emsdorf, action of, 104
Enfield, Small Arms Factory at, 263
Enlistment, terms of, 13, 34, 223, 275
Eugene of Savoy, Prince, 53
Eutaw Springs, action of, 127
Eylau, battle of, 180

F

FALKLAND ISLANDS, 4
Ferdinand of Brunswick, Prince, 103
Ferguson, Major, 125, 135
Ferozeshah, battle of, 251
Florida, 107, 122, 132
Fontenoy, battle of, 78
Forbes, General, 96
Forde, Lieut.-Col., 102
Fraser, General, 169
Frederick, Duke of York, his campaigns, 143, 147-149, 156-157; his work at the Horse Guards, 158, 222
Frederick the Great, King, 74 75, 94, 103
Friedland, battle of, 181

G

GADALUR, action of, 132
Galway, Earl of, 56
Gambia, 2, 28
George I, King, 69
George II, King, 70, 74 78
Ghazni, storm of, 245

Gibraltar, 1, 62, 66; capture of 54; blockade of, 124, 129
Gillespie, General Robert, 181, 204
Gold Coast, the, 2
Gordon, General Charles, 296, 298
Goree, 132
Gough, General Hugh, Lord, 248-253
Graham, General Sir Gerald, 297
Graham, General Thomas, Lord Lynedoch, 198, 218
Granby, Marquis of, 105
Grant, General Sir Hope, 269
Grant, General William, 120
Greene, General Nathaniel, 126, 127
Grenada, 106, 107, 150
Grey, General Sir Charles, 145, 149
Grey, General Sir John, 249
Guadeloupe, 98, 145, 150, 201
Guilford, action of, 127
Gujarat, battle of, 253
Gurkha regiments, 267
Gwalior war, 248

H

HAITI, operations in, 145, 150
Haldane, Richard, Lord, 312
Halifax, 90-91
Hardinge, Henry, Lord, 200, 250
Harris, General, Lord, 158
Hastings, Marquess, 127, 234
Havana, capture of, 106
Havelock, General Henry, 266
Haydn, Joseph, 138
Heligoland, 230
Hill, Colonel, 59
Hill, Rowland, Lord, 206, 210

INDEX

Hislop, General, 234
Hobkirk's Hill, action of, 127
Holland and the Dutch, 15, 23, 28, 29, 51, 52, 54–56, 57, 142; expedition to north Holland, 156
Hong Kong, 248
Hood, Admiral Lord, 146
Hope, General John, 188
Howe, General Sir William, 116, 117
Hutchinson, General, 164
Hyder Ali, 110, 130–132

I

IMPERIAL DEFENCE, 37
India, 2, 87–90, 108–112, 130–132
Indian Mutiny, 265
Indian troops summoned to Europe, 287
Infantry, 8, 18–21
Inkerman, battle of, 261
Ireland, her help to American rebels, 133
Irish Constabulary, establishment of, 257
Isandhlwana, action of, 291

J

JAMAICA, 3, 23
James, Duke of York, later King James II, 29, 37, 39–41
Java, capture of, 203
Jena, battle of, 179
Jervis, Admiral Sir John, Lord St. Vincent, 145

K

KANDAHAR, 245, 289–290
Kandy, expeditions to, 170, 234
Katwa, action of, 109
Keane, Sir John (Lord), 245
Keating Colonel, 111
Kenya, 2, 285
Khartoum, 297–298, 301
Kitchener, Herbert, Field Marshal Earl, 301
Kloster Kampen, action of, 105
Knox, Captain, 108

L

LADYSMITH, 306–307
Lafayette, Marquis de, 128
Lake, General Gerard, Lord, 143, 167–170
Lance-corporals and Serjeants, 10
Landen, battle of, 45
Laswari, battle of, 168
Lauffeld, battle of, 81
Lawrence, John, Lord, 266
Lawrence, Major Stringer, 88–90
Leake, Colonel William, 322
Ligonier, General, 83
Linselles, action of, 143
Louis XIV, King of France, 41, 47, 49
Louisburg, 85–87 95–96
Lucknow, 265–267
Lundy's Lane, action of, 215
Luxemburg, Marshal, 45

M

MACARTHY, Sir Charles, 238–239
McGrigor, Dr., Sir James, 228

INDEX

Madras, 87
Maharajpur, battle of, 249
Mahrattas, 87, 110-111, 166-170, 234
Maida, battle of, 176
Maitland, General Sir Thomas, 150
Maiwand, action of, 289
Malacca, 3
Malplaquet, battle of, 57
Malta, 4, 155, 231
Manila, capture of, 106
Marengo, battle of, 160
Maria Theresa, Empress, 74-76
Marmont, Marshal, 200, 201, 206-209
Martinique, 97, 106, 145, 151, 201
Maryland, 27
Massena, Marshal, 196-200
Mauritius, 5; capture of, 202, 231
Medals, 246
Medical department, 227, 263
Mehidpur, battle of, 234
Mesopotamia, 2
Miani, action of, 247
Military terms, 10-12
Militia, 158, 258, 312
Militia Act of 1757, 95
Minden, battle of, 103
Minorca, 4, 57, 62, 66, 93, 107, 129, 132, 154
Miquelon, 132
Mir Kassim, 108-109
Mobile, 126
Monck, George, Duke of Albemarle, 22, 23-25
Monson, Colonel, 169
Montcalm, General Marquis, 99
Montserrat, 27
Moore, General Sir John, 135

Morgan, Colonel, 126
Mudki, battle of, 250
Multan, siege of, 253
Munro, Major Hector, 109, 130
Mutiny Act, 41

N

Namur, siege of, 46
Napier, General Sir Charles, 247
Napier, Colonel William, 322
Natal, annexation of, 255
Navy, the Royal, 36
Nelson, Admiral Horatio, Lord, 146, 152-154, 173
Nevis, 27
Newfoundland, 62, 67
New Guinea, 5
"New Model" Army, 15-24
New Orleans, action at, 217
New York, 27-29, 47, 85, 116
New Zealand, 5, 243; first war, 254; second war, 270
Nicholson, General John, 266
Nigeria, 2, 285
Nightingale, Florence, 263
Nile, battle of the, 153
Nipal, the war with, 233
Nive, battle of the, 210
Nivelle, battle of, 210
North Borneo, 5

O

Ochterlony, General David, 233
Ohio River, 91, 96
Omdurman, action of, 301
Ordnance, the Board of, 36, 263
Orthez, battle of, 211

INDEX

P

PAARDEBERG, action of, 307
Pakenham, General Sir Edward, 217
Palestine, 4
Palilur, action of, 131
Panniar, action of, 249
Patna, actions of, 108, 109
Pegu, annexation of, 255
Pennsylvania, 29, 117
Persian war, the, 264
Peterborough, Earl of, 55
Philadelphia, 117, 119
Pindari war, the, 233
Pitt, William, the elder, Earl of Chatham, 94-97, 115
Pitt, William, the younger, 141, 171
Plassey, battle of, 101
Plumer, Herbert, Lord, 125
Police, Metropolitan, established 257
Pollock, General, 246
Popham, Admiral Sir Home, 174, 177
Porto Novo, action of, 131
Portugal, French invasion of, 182
Prevost, General Augustine, 122-123
Punjab, annexation of the, 253

Q

QUATRE BRAS, battle of, 220
Quebec, 27, 47, 59, 98, 116

R

RAGLAN, Field Marshal Lord, 260-262

Ramillies, battle of, 55
Rawlinson, Sir Henry, 322

REGIMENTS

(The dates given are those when the unit was taken on to the establishment of the British or East India Company's service as a complete regiment or battalion.)

CAVALRY

Life Guards (raised as troops, 1660; as 1st and 2nd Regiments, 1788), 25, 46
The Blues (1661), 25
1st Dragoon Guards (1685), 40, 46
2nd Dragoon Guards (1685), 40
3rd Dragoon Guards (1685), 40, 46
4th Dragoon Guards (1685), 40, 46
5th Dragoon Guards (1685), 40
6th Dragoon Guards (1685), 40, 46
7th Dragoon Guards (1688), 40
1st Royal Dragoons (1661), 26, 137
2nd Dragoons (Scots Greys) (1681), 30, 83, 137
3rd Hussars (1685), 40, 77-78, 137, 251
4th Hussars (1685), 40, 83, 137
5th Lancers (old 5th Dragoons, raised 1689; disbanded, 1799; revived, 1858), 42
6th Dragoons (1689), 42, 83
7th Hussars (1689), 42, 65, 83, 138
8th Hussars (1693), 45, 65, 138
9th Lancers (1715), 65, 138

INDEX

REGIMENTS: Cavalry—*(continued)*
  10th Hussars (1715), 65, 138
  11th Hussars (1715), 65, 138
  12th Lancers (1715), 65, 138
  13th Hussars (1715), 65, 138
  14th Hussars (1715), 65
  15th Hussars (1759), 104, 146
  16th Lancers (1759), 104, 252
  17th Lancers (1759), 104
  18th Hussars (raised 1759; disbanded 1821; revived, 1858)
  19th Hussars (raised for India, 1781; disbanded, 1821; revived, 1860), 167
  20th Hussars (raised 1791; disbanded, 1819; revived, 1860)
  21st Hussars (raised 1794; disbanded, 1819; revived, 1860)
  Royal Horse Artillery (1793), 138, 158
  Royal Regiment of Artillery (1727), 68, 118
  Royal Engineers (1788), 95, 138

INFANTRY
  Grenadier Guards (1660), 25, 45, 53, 198, 221
  Coldstream Guards (1650), 22, 45, 58, 198
  Scots Guards (1685), 30, 59, 198
  Royals, 1st Foot (1661), 25–26, 41, 53, 221
  Queen's, 2nd Foot (1661), 26
  Buffs, 3rd Foot (1665), 28, 58, 200
  King's Own, 4th Foot (1680), 30
  Northumberland Fusiliers, 5th Foot (1685), 39
  Warwickshire, 6th Foot (1685), 39, 45, 56

REGIMENTS: Infantry—*(continued)*
  Royal Fusiliers, 7th Foot (1685), 39, 45, 200
  King's, 8th Foot (1685), 39
  Norfolk, 9th Foot (1685), 39, 56, 198, 251
  Lincolnshire, 10th Foot (1685), 39
  Devon, 11th Foot (1685), 39, 207
  Suffolk, 12th Foot (1685), 39, 80, 103, 104
  Somerset L.I., 13th Foot (1685), 39
  West Yorkshire, 14th Foot (1685), 39
  East Yorkshire, 15th Foot (1685), 39
  Bedfordshire, 16th Foot (1688), 40
  Leicestershire, 17th Foot (1688), 40
  Royal Irish, 18th Foot (1689) (disbanded), 42, 46
  Green Howards, 19th Foot (1689), 42, 235
  Lancashire Fusiliers, 20th Foot (1689), 42, 103, 104, 118, 156
  Royal Scots Fusiliers, 21st Foot (1689), 42, 77, 118
  Cheshire, 22nd Foot (1689), 42, 247
  Royal Welch 23rd Fusiliers, Foot (1689), 42, 53, 77 80, 103, 200
  South Wales Borderers, 24th Foot (1689), 42, 253, 291, 293
  K.O. Scottish Borderers, 25th Foot (1689), 42, 103
  Cameronians (Scottish Rifles), 1st Batt., 26th Foot (1689), 42; 2nd Batt., 90th Foot (1794), 147

INDEX

REGIMENTS: Infantry—*(continued)*
Royal Inniskilling Fusiliers, 1st Batt., 27th Foot (1690), 42, 221; 2nd Batt., 108th Foot
Gloucestershire, 1st Batt., 28th Foot (1694), 50, 164, 198, 221; 2nd Batt., 61st Foot (1756), 95, 129, 207
Worcestershire, 1st Batt., 29th Foot (1694), 50, 200; 2nd Batt., 36th Foot (1701), 50
East Lancashire, 1st Batt., 30th Foot (1694), 50; 2nd Batt., 59th Foot (1755), 93
East Surrey, 1st Batt., 31st Foot (1702), 50, 251, 252; 2nd Batt., 70th Foot (1756), 95
Duke of Cornwall's L.I., 1st Batt., 32nd Foot (1702), 50, 221; 2nd Batt., 46th Foot (1741), 74
Duke of Wellington's, 1st Batt., 33rd Foot (1702), 50; 2nd Batt., 76th Foot (1787), 138
Border, 1st Batt., 34th Foot (1702), 50; 2nd Batt., 55th Foot (1755), 93
Royal Sussex, 1st Batt., 35th Foot (1701-1702), 50; 2nd Batt., 107th Foot (1854)
Hampshire, 1st Batt., 37th Foot (1702), 50, 103; 2nd Batt., 67th Foot (1756), 95
South Staffordshire, 1st Batt., 38th Foot (1702), 50, 67; 2nd Batt., 80th Foot (1793), 146
Dorsetshire, 1st Batt., 39th Foot (1702), 50, 101, 249; 2nd Batt., 54th Foot (1755), 93

REGIMENTS: Infantry—*(continued)*
South Lancashire, 1st Batt., 40th Foot (1717), 67, 249; 2nd Batt., 82nd Foot (1793), 146, 198
Welch Regiment, 1st Batt., 41st Foot (1719), 67; 2nd Batt., 69th Foot (1756), 95, 152
Black Watch, 1st Batt., 42nd Highlanders (1739), 69, 113, 162, 164, 221; 2nd Batt., 73rd Highlanders (1780), 235
Oxfordshire L.I., 1st Batt., 43rd Foot (1741), 74, 173; 2nd Batt., 52nd Foot (1755), 74, 173
Essex, 1st Batt., 44th Foot (1741), 74, 91; 2nd Batt., 56th Foot (1757), 93
Sherwood Foresters, 1st Batt., 45th Foot (1741), 74; 2nd Batt., 95th Foot (1824, the fifth regiment to be numbered 95th)
Loyal North Lancs., 1st Batt., 47th Foot (1740), 74; 2nd Batt., 81st Foot (1793), 146
Northamptonshire, 1st Batt., 48th Foot (1740), 74, 91, 200; 2nd Batt., 58th Foot (1755), 93
Royal Berkshire, 1st Batt., 49th Foot (1744); 2nd Batt., 66th Foot (1755), 95
Q.O. Royal West Kent, 1st Batt., 50th Foot (1755), 93, 252; 2nd Batt., 97th Foot (1824, the fifth regiment so numbered)
K.O.Y.L.I., 1st Batt., 51st Foot (1755), 93, 103, 129; 2nd Batt., 105th Foot (1839, the fifth regiment so numbered)

INDEX

REGIMENTS: Infantry—*(continued)*
- K.O. Shropshire L.I., 1st Batt., 53rd Foot (1755), 93; 2nd Batt., 85th Foot (1794), 146, 207
- Middlesex, 1st Batt., 57th Foot (1755), 93, 200; 2nd Batt., 77th Foot (1787), 138
- King's Royal Rifle Corps, 60th Foot (1755), 93, 113, 161
- Wiltshire, 1st Batt., 62nd Foot (1756), 95, 118; 2nd Batt., 99th Foot (1824, the fifth regiment so numbered)
- Manchester, 1st Batt., 63rd Foot (1757), 95; 2nd Batt., 96th Foot (1824, the fifth regiment so numbered)
- North Staffordshire, 1st Batt. 64th Foot (1758), 95; 2nd Batt., 98th Foot (1824, the sixth regiment so numbered)
- York and Lancaster, 1st Batt., 65th Foot (1758), 95; 2nd Batt., 84th Foot (1793), 146
- Durham L.I., 1st Batt., 68th Foot (1758), 95; 2nd Batt., 106th Foot (1826)
- Highland L.I., 1st Batt., 71st (1777), 119, 174; 2nd Batt., 74th (1787), 138, 167, 199
- Seaforth Highlanders, 1st Batt. 72nd (1778), 119; 2nd Batt. 78th (1793), 146
- Gordon Highlanders, 1st Batt., 75th (1787), 138, 241; 2nd Batt., 92nd (1794), 147, 221
- Q.O. Cameron Highlanders, 79th Foot (1793), 146, 199, 221

REGIMENTS: Infantry—*(continued)*
- Royal Ulster Rifles, 1st Batt., 83rd Foot (1793), 146; 2nd Batt., 86th Foot (1794), 146, 253
- Royal Irish Fusiliers, (amalgamated), 1st Batt., 87th Foot (1793), 146, 199; 2nd Batt., 89th Foot (1793-1794), 146, 215
- [Connaught Rangers (disbanded), 1st Batt., 88th Foot (1793), 146; 2nd Batt., 94th Foot (1823, the second regiment so numbered)]
- Argyll and Sutherland Highlanders, 1st Batt., 91st (1794), 147; 2nd Batt., 93rd (1800)
- [Royal Munster Fusiliers (disbanded), 26, 101, 110; 1st Batt., 101st Foot (1756); 2nd Batt., 104th Foot 1839)]
- [Royal Dublin Fusiliers (disbanded), 26, 101, 110; 1st Batt., 102nd Foot (1748) 2nd Batt., 103rd Foot (1661)]
- Rifle Brigade (1800), 161, 199
- [West India Regiment (disbanded), first formed, 1795. There were 12 West India Regiments in 1800; 8 West India Regiments in 1800-1815; afterwards for some time two, which were made one]
- Army Service Corps, 114, 147, 157, 261, 279

Regimental system, 31
Rhodesia, 285
Roberts, Sir Frederick, Earl, 288-290, 307-309

INDEX

Rodney, Admiral Lord, 129
Rohillas campaign, 111
Roliça, action of, 184
Rorke's Drift, action of, 291
Rose, General Sir Hugh, Lord Strathnairn, 267
Roucoux, action of, 81
Royal Military College, 222

S

SACKVILLE, Lord George, 104
St. Kitts, 129
St. Lucia, 106, 120, 132, 145, 171, 231
St. Pierre (island), 132
St. Pierre, action of, 210
St. Vincent, Lord, *see* Jervis
St. Vincent (W.I.), 106, 107, 150
St. Vincent, Cape, naval battle of, 152
Ste. Foy, action of, 100
Salamanca, battle of, 207
San Sebastian, 209–210
Saratoga, disaster of, 118
Savannah, action at, 122–123
Saxe, Marshal, 79, 81, 82
Sebastopol, 259–263
Senegal, 132
Seringapatam, first capture of, 139; second, 158–159
Shah Shuja, 244
Sholinghur, action of, 131
Shrapnel, Colonel Henry, 226, 229
Sicily, occupation of, 155, 175
Sierra Leone, 2
Sikh war, first, 250–252; second, 252–254
Sikhs, the, 87
Simcoe, Colonel James, 125
Sind, conquest of, 247
Singapore, 3

Sirpur action of, 108
Smith, Admiral Sir Sidney, 176
Smith, General Sir Harry, 240–241, 251, 252, 256
Smith, Lady (Harry), 249 *n.*
Smuts, General Jan, 309
Sobraon, battle of, 252
Socotra, 2
Somaliland, 2
Sorauren, action of, 209
Soult, Marshal, 187, 195, 198–200, 206, 209–212
Spain, Napoleon's invasion of, 183
Spanish Succession, war of the, 49
Spencer, General Sir Brent, 183
Squadron, 11
Staff College, 222
Stair, General Lord, 75, 78
Stannope, General, 57, 59
Steenkirk, battle of, 45
Stewart, General Sir Donald, 288–289
Stewart, General Sir Herbert, 297–298
Strahan, Admiral Sir Richard, 189
Stuart, General Sir Charles, 154, 160, 173
Stuart, General James, 132
Stuart, General Sir John, 176
Sudan, 4; the campaigns in, 296, 298, 301
Suez Canal opened, 272
Suvorof, General, 159
Sweden, expedition to, 183–184

T

TALAVERA, battle of, 193
Tallard, Marshal, 53
Tangier, 26, 29–30
Tarleton, Colonel Banastre, 125, 126

INDEX

Tel-el-Kebir, action of, **295**
Territorial system, the, 276
Ticonderoga, 96
Tilsit, Treaty of, 181
Tipu Sahib, **132**, 138–139, 158–159
Tirah Expedition, 302–304
Tobago, 107, 132, 171, 231
Torres Vedras, lines of, 196
Toulon, operations at, 144
Toulouse, battle of, 212
Tourcoing, battle of, 148
Trafalgar, naval battle of, 173
Transport and Supply, 36, 227
Treasury, the, 36
Trichinopoly, 89–90
Trinidad, 150, 231
Turenne, Marshal, 23, 29
Turkey, 179, 259, 286–287

U

UGANDA **285**
Umbeyla Expedition, the, 269
Undwa Nala, action of, 109

V

VALENCIENNES, siege of, **143**
Vellinghausen, action of, 105
Vellore, the mutiny of, 181
Victor, Marshal, 192–193
Victoria Cross, the, 263
Villars, Marshal, 57, 58, 60, 61
Villers-en-Cauchies, action of, **148**
Vimeiro, battle of, 184
Virginia, 27
Vitoria, battle of, 209

W

WADE, General, 69, 78
Wagram, battle of, 194
Walcheren Expedition, **188**
Warburg, action of, 105
Washington, George, 92, 117, 118, 133
Waterloo, battle of, 220–221
Wellesley, Arthur, Duke of Wellington, 149, 159, 166–167; his first landing in Portugal, 184; his campaigns in the Peninsula, 190–201, 204–212; his tactics, 229
Wentworth, General, 72
White, General Sir George, 306
Whitelocke, General John, 178–179
William, Duke of Cumberland, 78, 79, 83
William III, King, 29; his campaigns, 43–46, 50
Wolfe, General James, 96, 98
Wolseley, Sir Garnet, Lord, 286 **295**, 297
Wood, Field Marshal Sir Evelyn, 292
Worcester, battle of, 22

Y

YEOMEN of the Guard, 14
Yorktown, disaster of, **128**

Z

ZANZIBAR, 2
Zulu War, the, 290

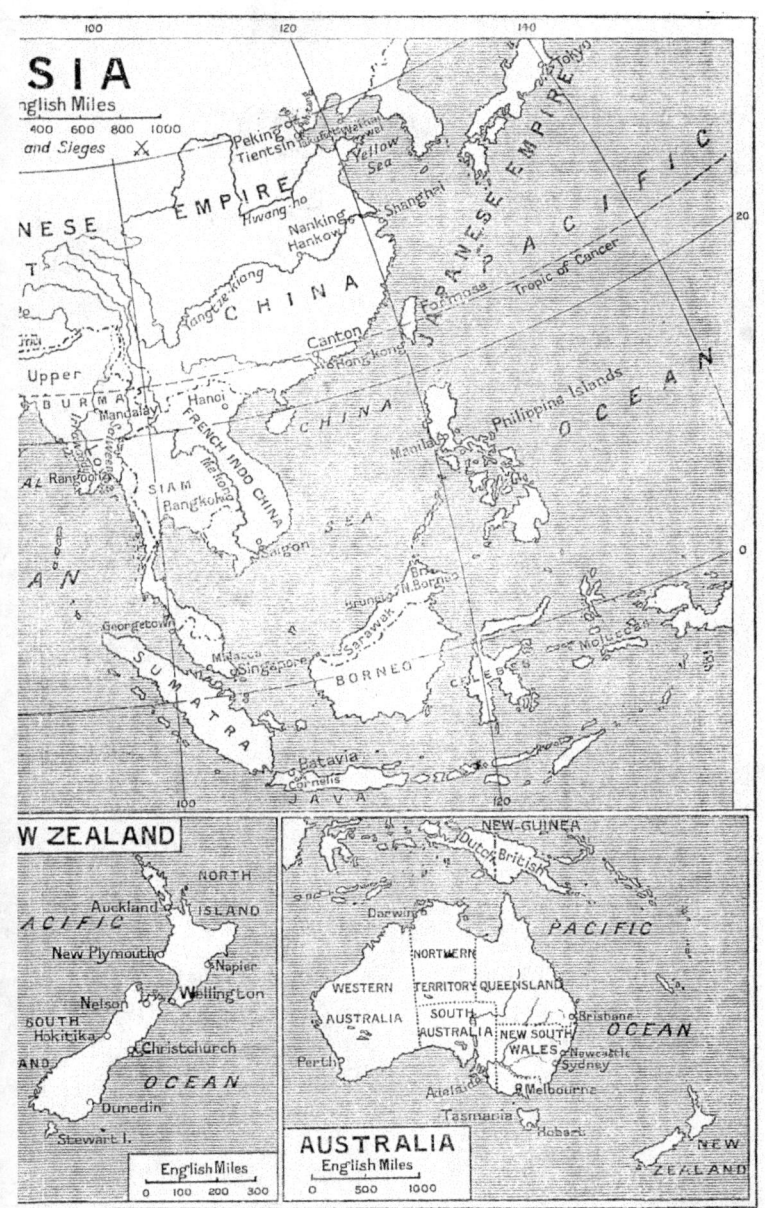

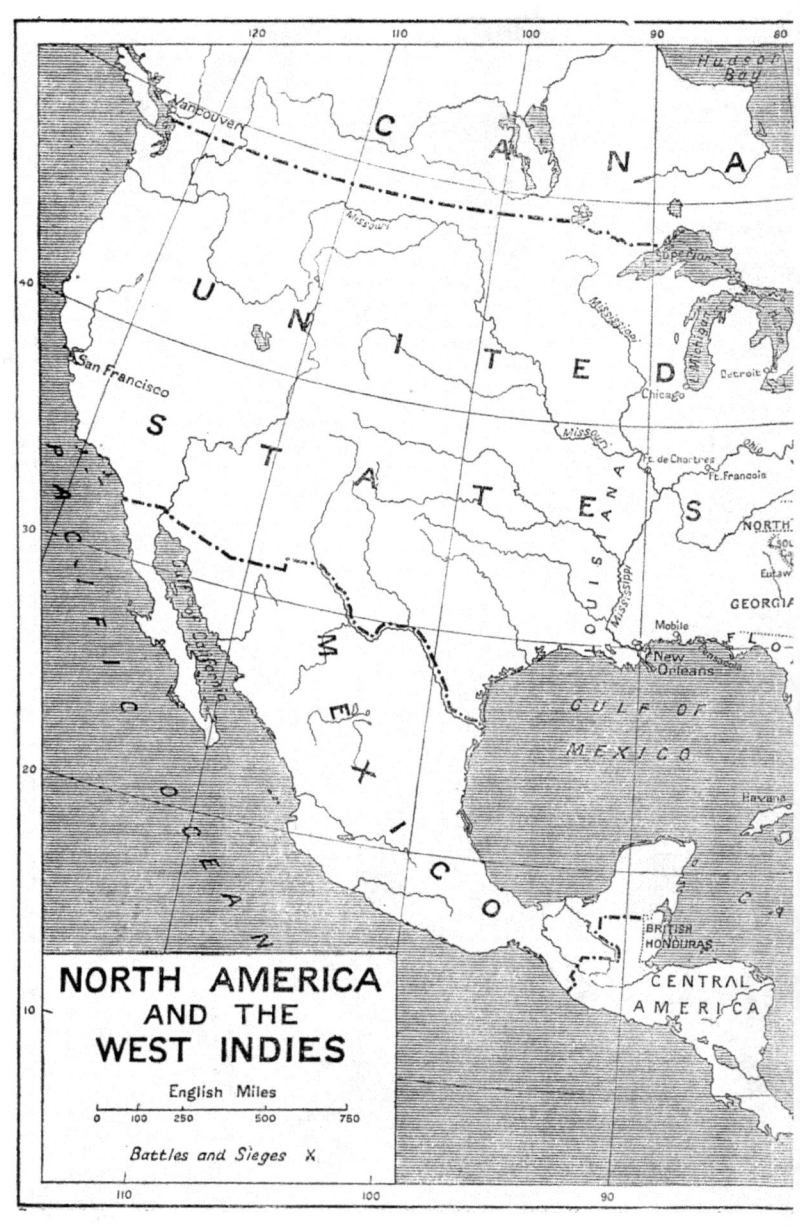

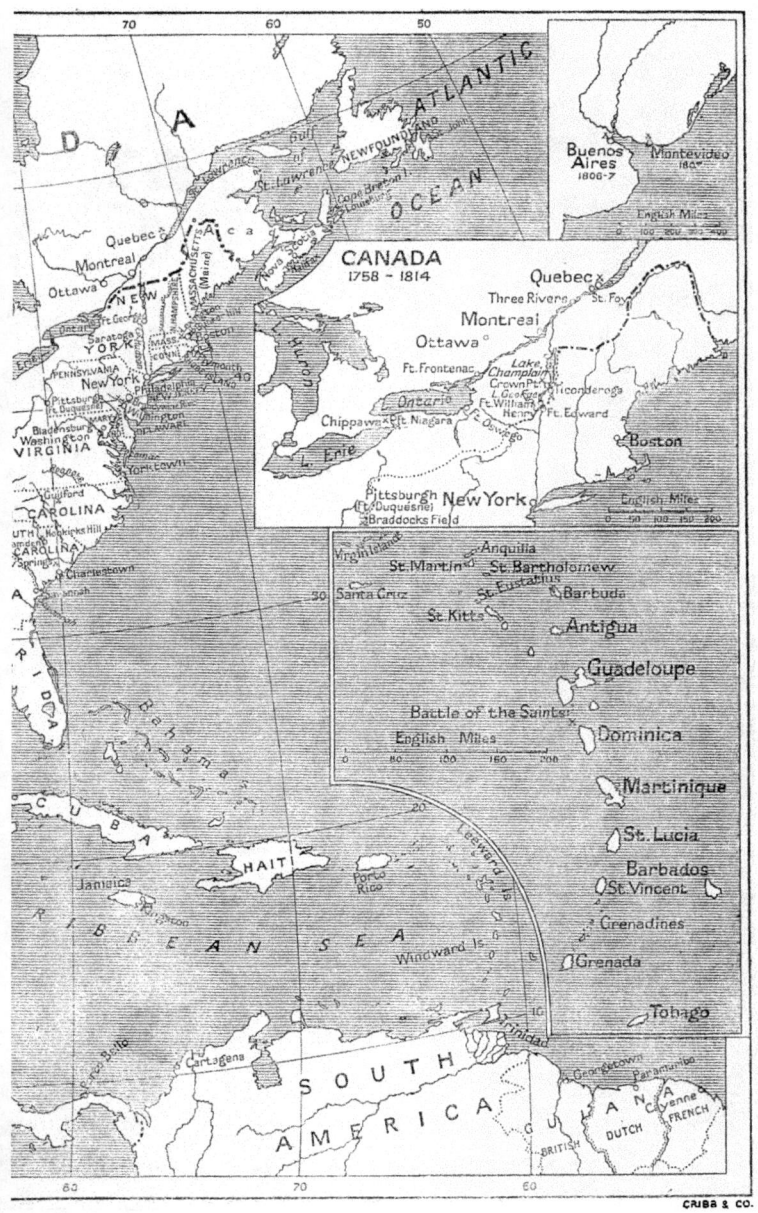

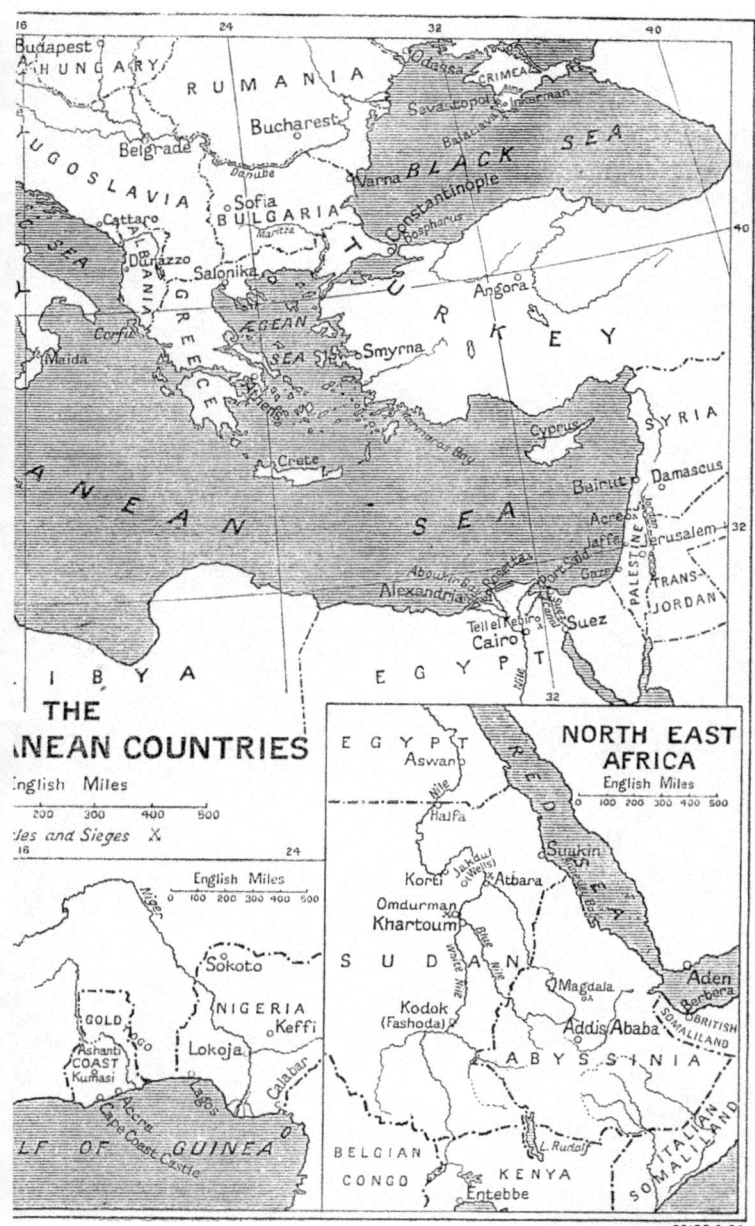